Theories of Violent Conflict

This textbook introduces students of violent conflict to a variety of prominent theoretical approaches, and examines the ontological stances and epistemological traditions underlying these approaches.

Theories of Violent Conflict takes the centrality of the group as an actor in contemporary conflict as a point of departure, leaving us with three main questions:

- What makes a group?
- Why and how does a group resort to violence?
- Why and how do or don't they stop?

The book examines and compares the ways by which these questions are addressed from a number of perspectives: constructivism, social identity theory, structuralism, political economy, human needs theory, relative deprivation theory, collective action theory and rational choice theory. The final chapter aims to synthesize structure and agency-based theories by proposing a critical discourse analysis of violent conflict.

This book will be essential reading for students of war and conflict studies, peace studies, conflict analysis and conflict resolution, and ethnic conflict, as well as security studies and IR in general.

Jolle Demmers obtained her PhD in 1999 at Utrecht University. In 1999, she co-founded the Centre for Conflict Studies (CCS), an interdisciplinary research and training centre at the Faculty of Humanities at Utrecht University, where she currently holds the position of Associate Professor.

Theories of Violent Conflict

An introduction

Jolle Demmers

Routledge
Taylor & Francis Group

LONDON AND NEW YORK

First published 2012
by Routledge
2 Park Square, Milton Park, Abingdon, Oxon, OX14 4RN

Simultaneously published in the USA and Canada
by Routledge
711 Third Avenue, New York, NY 10017

Routledge is an imprint of the Taylor & Francis Group, an informa business

British Library Cataloguing in Publication Data
A catalogue record for this book is available from the British Library

Library of Congress Cataloging in Publication Data
Demmers, Jolle, 1969-
Theories of violent conflict : an introduction / Jolle Demmers.
p. cm. – (Contemporary security studies)
Includes bibliographical references and index.
1. War (Philosophy) 2. Political violence –Social aspects. I. Title.
JZ6390.D46 2012
303.6–dc23
2011048394

ISBN13: 978-0-415-55533-3 (hbk)
ISBN13: 978-0-415-55534-0 (pbk)
ISBN13: 978-0-203-86951-2 (ebk)

Typeset in Times
by Taylor & Francis Books

MIX
Paper from
responsible sources
FSC
www.fsc.org FSC® C004839

Printed and bound in Great Britain by
TJ International Ltd, Padstow, Cornwall

In memory of Alex E. Fernández Jilberto

Contents

Figures, tables and boxes

Figures

Tables

Boxes

Acknowledgements

This book results from teaching the course Analysis of Contemporary Violent Conflict for over eight years to students in the MA Conflict Studies and Human Rights at Utrecht University, The Netherlands. Invaluable support came from my colleagues at the Centre for Conflict Studies: Chris van der Borgh, Mario Fumerton and Georg Frerks, Luuk Slooter, Lauren Gould, Theo Hollander and Rens Willems. I am grateful to the Dutch Science Foundation (NWO) for providing me with a writing grant, which enabled me to write the first draft of the book. In addition, I am indebted to Andrew Humphrys and Annabelle Harris from Routledge for their patience and professional support and to Routledge's anonymous reviewers for their valuable suggestions. This book comes out of the discussions in class, the fresh criticism and new ideas brought forward by my students. In many ways, their thinking shaped this book.

I thank Sameer and Manu for being a home and a family and for tolerating my solitary confinement in The Egg. I dedicate this book in loving memory to my academic mentor Alex E. Fernández Jilberto.

Introduction
Conflict analysis in context

Of the many accounts of the tragedy of the war in former Yugoslavia, and particularly of the belated and reluctant international response to this catastrophe, one story is often told. In 1993 the US considered invading Bosnia. It had become increasingly clear that Serb militias were stepping up systematic attacks on the Bosnian Muslim population. But then President Clinton allegedly got Robert Kaplan's widely acclaimed bestseller *Balkan Ghosts* for Christmas. Kaplan's is a typically primordial explanation of war. It portrays the region as plagued by ancient hatreds and eternal violence between ethnic groups. According to numerous accounts, the book had a profound impact on Clinton and other members of the administration shortly after they came into office.[1] In his 1997 book on the war, Sarajevo-based editor Kemal Kurspahic wrote: 'At a time of crucial decisions [President Clinton] simply read the wrong book, or more precisely drew the wrong conclusions from *Balkan Ghosts* by Robert Kaplan, which led to the comforting thought that nothing much could be done in Bosnia "until those folks got tired of killing each other"' (1997: 32).

Behind every analysis of violent conflict is a set of assumptions. Assumptions about what moves human action and how to study it, and about the interests, needs, instincts, structures or choices that explain why and how people resort to violence. These assumptions are usually very basic, and fundamentally subjective. Assumptions form the base of academic theories of conflict. Indirectly, they also inform the ways policy-makers and politicians 'read' a conflict. Their interpretation of a conflict determines – to a certain extent – what sort of intervention politicians and policy-makers design. If a conflict is understood as stemming from 'ancient hatreds' between ethnic groups there is little outsiders can do: for as soon as 'third parties' pull out old animosities will flare up again and violence will be resumed ('they'll be at each other's throats again'). With the benefit of hindsight, it can be safely concluded that the Clinton administration's interpretation of the conflict in Bosnia was not, or insufficiently, based on solid case analysis. And it does not stand alone. Lack of grounded and critical analysis of violence and war results in misreading and inaccurate strategies and interventions, with at times dramatic consequences. This calls for a defined specialist field of study which provides analytical frames, research methodologies and skills to explain and understand contemporary violent conflict. Why and how do wars happen? Why are people prepared to kill and die in the name of an ethnic or religious group? How are people mobilized to join in? How can 'neighbours turn into enemies'? And, more fundamentally: what is the role of identity, deprivation, structural change, rationality and discourse? What is the impact of social media and the Internet on repertoires of contention, and what are the connections between the global spread of neoliberalism and local forms of violence? There has been sustained debate in academic disciplines on the causes, dynamics and consequences of violent conflict. However, despite the wealth of material on violence and war there remains much to understand and there remains much to learn from earlier insights and theories of conflict.

This book has a threefold aim. First and foremost, it brings together a diverse range of theoretical frameworks that try to explain and understand how and why (groups of) people resort to violent action against other (groups of) combatants, civilians, organizations or the state. Second, it addresses the idea of multidisciplinarity. Conflict Studies is a field of study, not a discipline. As such, the view is widely held that violent conflict is a complex social phenomenon that can only be understood and explained from a multidisciplinary approach. In practice, however, scholars largely remain within their disciplinary boundaries. The various approaches to conflict and violence that the academic field seeks to combine under the heading of 'multidisciplinarity' are not simply heterogeneous, but in fact often depart from fundamentally different ontological and epistemological stances. Certainly, there are affinities between some of them, but there are strong tensions as well. The field of Conflict Studies bears a multivalent, and at times even contradictory theoretical burden. This book explores the ways in which a selection of theoretical traditions relate to each other. It aims to review these theories by tracing their underlying assumptions, their ontological and epistemological stances, so as to identify the affinities and contradictions between them. We will see how each of the selected approaches revolves around a different puzzle, and is very capable of explaining certain components, dynamics, processes, mechanisms and/or relations but not others. This book aims to further your capacity to analyse violent conflict in a theoretically knowledgeable way. It also hopes to improve your capacity to recognize and assess axioms and paradigms underpinning explanations of contemporary violent conflict in, for instance, the media, policy reports and academic research.

Had Clinton received another, 'right' book on the Balkan wars for Christmas, one which stressed that there was nothing ancient or innate about the 'ethnic' violence in Bosnia, a book that showed how violence was carefully orchestrated by political elites and local strongmen looking for ways to gain power, would he have opted for another strategy? Possibly. Probably not. We all know that political strategies and military interventions are shaped by other elements than case-analysis alone (domestic and international politics, economic interest, public opinion, routine, belief, doctrine and ideology, even fashions) and that indeed, politicians tend to select the interpretation of a conflict that best supports their interests.

It is this insight that brings us to the third aim of this book, that is, to carry out conflict analysis in a reflexive and critical way. The selection of a form and level of explanation of violent conflict is not only a difficult but also a delicate act, for by categorizing and labelling a conflict, the analyst, intentionally or not, becomes engaged in discussions on legitimacy, blame and responsibility. As a field of knowledge, Conflict Studies is situated in and shaped by highly political and messy practices of categorizing and coding. It is therefore not only important to engage in systematic research on individual cases of violent conflict, but also to study the ways conflicts are labelled and coded (by policy-makers, in public debate and in the media) and to think through the consequences of these representations. This book thus not only aims to review the explanatory power of theories of violent conflict, it also aims to gain insight into how theories of conflict themselves are produced, shaped and applied in contexts of power.

It suggests placing 'conflict analysis in context' and trying to understand how and why certain interpretations of conflict have come to dominate others.

The interpretation of conflict: shifting frames

Contemporary research on violent conflict has typically focused on causes of conflict, with war and conflict differently defined in various datasets. The Uppsala Conflict Data Program (UCDP), for instance, defines armed conflict as:

> a contested incompatibility that concerns government or territory or both, where the use of force between two parties results in at least 25 battle-related deaths in a year. Of these two parties, at least one has to be the government of a state.
>
> (Harbom and Wallensteen 2010: 508)

The difference between 'conflict' and 'war' is determined by the casualty threshold: as soon as the number of annual battle-related deaths reaches the threshold of a 1000 the conflict is defined as 'war'. Data sets such as UCDP show a global shift from *inter-state* conflict to *intra-state* conflict in the post WWII era, with a big peak in the early 1990s, when over 50 of these conflicts were recorded (see figure 0.1). Of the 118 conflicts that have taken place between 1989 and 2004, only seven have been inter-state wars (Harbom and Wallensteen 2005). For 2004–9, all 36 registered armed conflicts were fought within states, with the exception of the inter-state conflict between Djibouti and Eritrea in 2008. However, seven of these intra-state conflicts were internationalized, in the sense that they 'involved troops sent from external states in aid of one of the warring parties'. These conflicts were in Afghanistan, Algeria, Iraq, Rwanda, Somalia, Uganda and USA (Harborn and Wallenteen 2010: 503). This category of armed conflict is defined as 'internationalized internal armed conflict'.

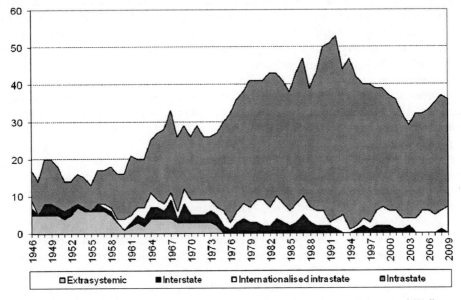

Figure 0.1 Number of armed conflicts by type, 1946–2009. Taken from Harbom and Wallensteen 2010: 503

The boundaries between classifications of violent conflict are contested. On the one hand, academics cannot do without categorizations. As Cramer (2006: 57) puts it: 'Classifying is a compulsion of the curious'. Without categorical distinctions and groupings the things we try to understand are too diverse and complex to deal with. On the other hand, categorizations often hide more than they reveal. The Uppsala Program, for example, neglects several types of violence. Our understanding of civil strife suffers from reducing the focus on violence to direct clashes between the government and rebel groups (see: Raleigh et al. 2010). Reports on complex conflicts such as in the Democratic Republic of the Congo and Somalia show more activity of rebel organizations fighting each other or killing civilians than engaging with government troops. A conflict zone such as Mexico, with a reported death toll of 15,000 in 2010, is missing from the Uppsala Program. Also, the classification of the wars in Afghanistan and Iraq as primarily internal (but internationalized) downplays the role of the US. We will return to the question of the categorization of violence later in this chapter. For now, it suffices to state that – despite the many controversies – the view of the post WWII conflict landscape as dominated by largely internal forms of violence and 'small wars' is widely held.

The past decades have seen a growing preoccupation with this type of 'internal' violent conflict. The end of the Cold War nuclear stand-off opened new possibilities for direct political and military intervention in local zones of conflict. Western governments, in collaboration with international bodies such as the UN, NATO, the Council of Europe and the OSCE, formulated policies to prevent, mitigate and settle violent conflict, often combined with military interventions and peace-enforcing operations. It also enabled the UN to establish supranational juridical institutions such as the international war tribunals for the former Yugoslavia and Rwanda and the International Criminal Court. In addition, aid organizations and development NGOs adopted 'peace-building' as their core business and set up projects on social justice, reconciliation, war time rape, child soldiers, human security and post-war trauma healing. The heightened policy attention for intra-state violent conflict, and the desire to contain this type of conflict intertwined with a boom in academic research and training centres (including new undergraduate and graduate teaching programmes), but also think tanks and conflict monitoring websites mushroomed. The steadily inflating 'conflict field' consists of a transnational, networked congregation of people working for donor governments, aid coordinating bodies, international NGOs, UN agencies, the World Bank, local NGOs, community groups, private military corporations, as well as private contractors and commercial companies, who – in collaboration and competition – seek to provide solutions.

Although the field shows a lot of heterogeneity, it is possible to detect certain trends. Over the past decades, mainstream views on violent conflict have shifted substantially. During the Cold War, local conflicts were mostly seen as 'proxy wars' and explained in terms of ideological divides (communism/capitalism) and super power strategy, connected to processes of post-independence state-building. After the Cold War, violent conflicts were coded as 'ethnic' or 'ethno nationalist': ancient hatreds and primordialist identities were seen as root causes. Since the late 1990s, conflicts are framed as driven by greed, 'terror' and evil. Particularly after 9/11, terror became the dominant policy framework through which local wars were understood and dealt with. Organized violence in the Democratic Republic of the Congo, Nigeria, Liberia, Somalia, Sierra Leone, Colombia, Chechnya and Afghanistan is depicted as greed-motivated and potentially threatening regional and global security. This new understanding of local war was supported by the World Bank report 'Breaking the Conflict Trap' of 2003. The latest fashion is the framing of violent conflict in terms of human (in)security and state fragility. Generally, the mainstream view on intra-state violent conflict in the post Cold War era is that it can be characterized as a-political, excessively cruel, with an emphasis on breakdown, insecurity and criminality.

For the study of contemporary violent conflict it is important not to take these trends for granted, but to situate them in (geo)political contexts of power. One way of doing this is to point at their functionality. Authors such as Helen Dexter (2007) and Mark Duffield (2007) are critical about the characterization of post Cold War violent conflicts (the 'new wars') as unusually cruel and largely directed against civilians. They argue that what has changed, apart from the undeniable shift from inter-state to internal war, is not so much the nature of violence, but the international denial of any legitimacy to warring parties, particularly within developing countries (often referred to as 'Fragile States'). During the Cold War era, supporting conflicts waged by irregular armies was an accepted feature of international conflict. Largely, these wars were seen as legitimate and were supported with funding, arms and political patronage. With the end of the Cold War, internal wars continued but lost their international, geopolitical function and hence legitimacy. The functionality of labels such as terror and barbarity is that they provided a moral justification for the increased interventionism of the late 1990s.

Seen in this light, the academic field of Conflict Studies (or 'new wars' studies) is itself intractably related to, and shaped by changing views on 'necessary' versus 'senseless' wars, on representations of 'victim' and 'perpetrator' and 'just' and 'unjust' military interventions.

Defining the field

How to begin studying such a politicized, theoretically heterogeneous and contested field? A first step is to give an overview of a number of key definitions. Definitions are necessary tools to make sense of the immense complexity of social life. This section first introduces the reader to a general definition of conflict, into which most examples and categories of conflict can be placed. It then looks at the relation between conflict and violence, and discusses a number of prominent classifications.

Conflict

In 1981, Chris Mitchell presented a general model of conflict that has become something of a standard in the field. His triangular typology of conflict is inspired by one of the 'founding fathers' of Peace Studies, Johan Galtung (whose work will be discussed in chapter three). For Mitchell a conflict is 'any situation in which two or more "parties" (however defined or structured) perceive that they possess mutually incompatible goals' (1981: 17). Any conflict consists of three component parts: goal incompatibility, attitudes and behaviour. The first and crucial component of a conflict situation is *incompatibility*: actors or parties think that the realization of one or more of their objectives is blocked by the other party's attempt to reach its own respective goal. Mitchell's conflict triangle model takes the occurrence of goal incompatibility as the starting point from which a conflict becomes manifest and each of the three elements begins to interact. Goals are defined as consciously desired future outcomes, conditions or end states, which often have intrinsic (but different) values for members of particular parties. The second component consists of *conflict attitudes*: those psychological states (both common attitudes, emotions and evaluations, as well as patterns of perception and misperception) that accompany and arise from involvement in a situation of conflict (1981: 27). There is a difference between emotional orientations (feelings of anger, distrust, resentment, scorn, fear, envy or suspicion of the intention of others) and cognitive processes (such as stereotyping or tunnel vision). The third component of conflict is behaviour. *Conflict behaviour* consists of actions undertaken by one party in any situation of conflict aimed at the opposing party with the intention of making that opponent abandon or modify its goals (1981: 29).

The triangle model highlights conflict as a dynamic process in which incompatibilities, attitudes and behaviour are constantly changing and influencing each other. Conflict formations may widen and transform, drawing in new issues and actors, or generating secondary conflicts within the main parties or among outsiders. Conflict situations, emotions and actions are deeply intertwined and dialectic. As Mitchell claims: 'For one thing, conflicts are not static phenomena, and hence the dynamic aspects of conflict which alter both structure and inter-party relationships over time, are essential aspects of any satisfactory analysis' (1981: 33).

Different research traditions emphasize different components of conflict. Although generally recognizing the transformative capacity of conflict, analysts place the source of conflict at different corners of the triangle. Some approaches are primarily concerned with the underlying *conditions* which produce conflict situations, such as scarcity of valued goods (both material and non-material) or the unequal distribution of resources. These perspectives are interested in how structural incompatibilities in the organization of society can lead to actual conflict behaviour. Marxian approaches, for instance, point at the inherently exploitative nature of capitalism as the 'master' incompatibility. Authors working from a Durkheimian perspective emphasize how conflict occurs when social change ruptures the collective belief system that 'keeps people in their places'. The sources of conflict are thus those conditions in a party's environment leading to situations of goal incompatibility, and ensuing attitudes and behaviour (Mitchell 1981: 26). We will discuss these structure-based traditions in chapter three. There is also a substantial body of literature which places emphasis on *attitudes*. Here human conflict is primarily seen as an 'internally' generated phenomenon, its root causes lying not in the party's environment but in his or her individual make-up. These motive-orientated approaches include social identity theory and human needs theory, which emphasize how people's engagement in conflict stem from a series of deep-seated needs and cognitive imperatives. Rational choice approaches, departing from the idea of the individual as utility maximizer, argue that the large majority of contemporary conflict is greed-motivated. Both structure-based and individual-based approaches, as well as perspectives that aim to combine or look beyond structure-agency orientations will be discussed in this book.

Although intrigued by the same questions, the theories under review work from divergent positions and use different vocabularies. Where some use terms such as 'behaviour' and 'habit', others say 'action' and 'practice'. The same goes for 'agent'/ 'subject', 'structural'/'systemic' and 'manifest'/'subjective'. Given that there is no unambiguous vocabulary for the analysis of violent conflict, this book will simply shift about these terms undogmatically, clarifying terms as we go.

Violence in conflict

We have defined conflict as any situation in which parties perceive they have incompatible goals (Mitchell 1981: 17). This broad definition sees conflict as a *situation* and thus includes the possibility for inaction. People do not always act upon situations of conflict. And certainly, violence does not automatically result from perceived goal incompatibility. In chapter six, Schröder and Schmidt (2001), for instance, argue that for violence to break out parties first have to come to look upon the incompatibility as relevant, and second (and more important) violence needs to be sanctioned as the legitimate course of action. Other theoretical frames explain inaction as resulting from a lack of 'awareness' (chapter three); a lack of 'mobilizing capacity' (chapter four), or, simply as 'cost-beneficial' (chapter five). Another implication of Mitchell's working definition is the unimportance of violence as a criterion for conflict behaviour. In his view, conflict behaviour can take on a wide variety of forms in addition to 'physical damage to people and property'. Conflict behaviour includes all actions undertaken by one conflict party aimed at the opposing party with the intention of making that adversary abandon or modify its goals. Repertoires of conflict range from demonstrations and strikes, to self-destructive strategies such as hunger-strikes or suicide, but can also include more subtle forms of 'everyday resistance' (Scott 1990) such as sabotage, disobedience or non-cooperation. This book, however, is explicitly interested in violence as a form of conflict.

In everyday representations violence is often conceptualized as a *degree* of conflict: as something that occurs automatically when conflict reaches a certain 'temperature'. In contrast, most authors in this book argue that we lack evidence showing that higher levels of conflict lead to higher levels of violence. Rather, violence is a *form* of conflict: 'Violence is not a quantitative degree of conflict but a qualitative form of conflict, with its own dynamics' (Brubaker and Laitin 1998: 426). The turn to violence during conflict is a 'phase shift' that requires particular theoretical attention. This is illustrated, for instance, by the work of Della Porta and Tarrow (1986) on the tendency of political violence in Italy in the early 1970s to occur not at the peak of protest mobilization but toward the end of a mobilization cycle. At the moment that mobilization was waning, splinter groups in Italy resorted to violence as the only way left to cause disruption. Rather than seeing violence as a natural, self-evident outgrowth of conflict, this book distinguishes violence from conflict. To be exact, this book aims to address how different research traditions explain and understand the occurrence of violence in situations of conflict. Our focus is on violence in conflict, not on conflict as such.

It is important to make this distinction between the larger scholarly field of conflict (including e.g. inter-personal or corporate conflict) and that concerned only with violent conflict, or, more precisely, violence in conflict. Not because general theories of conflict have nothing to offer to the analysis of violent conflict, but because the subfield of violent conflict involves specific puzzles, and revolves around a particular set of questions, which require particular theoretical attention. The following chapters discuss the multiple forms and functions of violence in conflict: its relation to identity and rationality; the connection between 'structural' and 'manifest' violence; the mobilization of collective violent action; and the ways violence is imagined and legitimized.

We have already briefly addressed the contested nature of classifications of violent conflict. The term may include a multitude of situations ranging from wars between states, revolutions, insurgencies, genocides, civil wars, lethal ethnic or religious conflicts, to riots and pogroms, and as such is notoriously difficult to define. Scholars have identified a number of rules and thresholds for deciding what (not) to include into their analysis. We will here consider a number of prominent definitional boundaries between inter-state and intra-state violent conflict, civil war and communal violence.

Definitional boundaries

Up until the 1990s, violent conflict and war was predominantly studied from the perspective of international relations and strategic studies. Systemic, global or world wars such as the Cold War, WWI and WWII attracted the lion's share of scholarly attention. Analytical perspectives such as systems theory, realist theory and game theory prevailed (Dougherty and Pfaltzgraff 1981). Smaller wars, or 'low intensity conflicts' were largely seen as by-products of the Cold War bipolarity. The study of violent conflict was fragmented between disciplinary boundaries, and there was no or very little integration of, for instance, anthropological 'ethnographies of violence' and the knowledge produced in the field of international relations on world systems, nuclear deterrence, arms races, balances of power and inter-state wars.

Ironically, while the overwhelming majority of scholarly attention was directed to the 'big wars' the conflict landscape around the world was gradually assuming a different profile (Gomes Porto 2002). As indicated by Harbom and Wallensteen (2010), from the 1960s to the 1990s there was a sharp increase in the total incidence of violent conflict *within* states. It was particularly during the 1990s, when the number of intra-state wars peaked, that many scholars began to realize the limited explanatory power of the 'proxy war paradigm'. Evidently, the end of the Cold War and the 'triumph' of the neoliberal democratic model did not bring the 'end of history'. War and violent conflict prevailed, but now predominantly on a local scale. Small wars turned out to have a dynamics of their own.

The realization that local conflicts had in fact become the rule caused an important shift in the study of violent conflict and war. Traditional theories of international relations and strategic studies proved incapable of grasping the dynamics and complexities of the 'new wars'. Turning away from the inter-state level, analysis began to focus on local actors and local contexts: on identity formation, group dynamics, ethnicity, resource abundance, collective grievances and collective action. A new, but fragmented field of study emerged, and with this a plethora of definitions and classifications. Roughly, the 'new wars' are seen to differ from inter-state or conventional conflict in a number of ways. First, they do not have precise beginnings and endings. They do not start with a declaration or war, and lack 'definitive battles, decisive campaigns and formal endings' (Gomes Porto 2002: 5). Second, the 'new wars' are protracted: they typically last for decades, during which episodes of fierce fighting alternate with times of relative peace. Often the war/peace boundary is blurry: both in time and across space. While rebel groups may rule a certain territory by night, army forces can be in control during day time. War is fought in certain specific contested areas (border zones, mines, urban centres) without necessarily affecting outlying territories. Third, there are differences in modes of warfare. The new type of war is fought by loosely knit groups of 'regulars' and 'irregulars': soldiers, rebels and civilians, local warlords, cadres and paramilitaries, and not by two (or more) conventional clear-cut national armies. Fourth, external support for local wars typically comes from overseas diaspora, lobby groups or foreign mercenaries. Importantly, local war economies are not funded by taxation by the state, but sustained by global networks of trade, outside emergency assistance and the parallel economy, including drugs trafficking, oil bunkering, trade of diamonds, timber or coltan. Fifth, due to the revolution in communication technology, new wars are deterritorialized: involving globally dispersed networks of actors and organizations (or 'cells'). Strategic decisions can be made and instantly communicated across the globe. Finally, it is identity groups (ethnic, religious, cultural or other) and organizations claiming to represent groups that are at the core of contemporary violent conflicts (see: Azar 1990; Van Creveld 1991; Holsti 1996; Kaldor 1999).

In relation to this Miall et al. (1999: 66) raised a number of definitional questions:

> What are we to call these conflicts? Current terminology includes 'internal conflicts' (Brown 1996); 'new wars' (Kaldor and Vashee 1997), 'small wars' (Harding 1994), 'civil wars' (King 1997), 'ethnic conflicts' (Stavenhagen 1996), 'conflict in post-colonial states' (van de Goor et al. 1996) and so on, as well as varying expressions used by humanitarian and development NGOs and international agencies, such as 'complex human emergencies' and 'complex political emergencies'.

All these labels underline the necessity to theoretically distinguish inter-state war from intra-state war. From the above list, two definitions are broadly applied: *internal violent conflict* and *civil war*. Of the two, internal violent conflict is the more general. The term is not only applied to distinguish internal violent conflict from inter-state war but also from other types of large-scale social and political violence. Definitions emphasize the internality of the conflict to the *territory of a sovereign state* and the participation of the *government as combatant* and often include a requirement that the conflict exceeds a certain threshold of deaths (as in Harbom and Wallensteen 2010). Classic definitions of civil war often strongly resemble those of internal conflict. In their seminal study *Resort to Arms*, Small and Singer define civil war as 'any armed conflict that involves (a) military action internal to the metropole, (b) the active participation of the national government, and (c) effective resistance by both sides' (1982: 210). More recently, however, scholars have argued for the necessity to specify the term, and to indicate rules and thresholds to analytically distinguish civil war from other forms of large-scale violence such as homicide, riots or communal violence. We will briefly look into this here.

Civil war

Definitions of civil war generally include criteria such as state involvement and level of political organization of the group or party opposing the state. Nicholas Sambanis (2004: 829–30) uses no less than 11 criteria to define civil wars. His description of civil war location and parties is stated as follows:

> (1) The war takes place within the territory of an internationally recognised state with a population of more than 500,000 (the smallest population size allowed by most coding rules); (2) The parties to the conflict are politically and militarily organised, and they have publicly stated political objectives – this distinguishes insurgent groups and political parties from criminal gangs and riotous mobs; (3) The government must be a principal combatant – or, at least, the party

representing the government internationally and claiming the state domestically must be involved as a combatant; (4) The main insurgent organisation(s) must be locally represented and must recruit locally. Additional external involvement and recruitment need not imply that the war is not intra-state. Insurgent groups may operate from neighbouring countries, but they must also have some territorial control (bases) in the civil war country and/or the rebels must reside in the civil war country.

Sambanis is equally precise when it comes to defining the beginning and ending of civil war, which he ties to the level of war-related deaths:

> (5) The start of the war is the first year that the conflict causes at least 500 to 1,000 deaths. If the conflict has not caused 500 deaths or more in the first year, the war is coded as having started in that year only if cumulative deaths in the next three years reach 1,000; (6) Throughout its duration, the conflict must be characterized by sustained violence, at least at the minor or intermediate level. There should be no 3-year period during which the conflict causes fewer than 500 deaths; (7) Throughout the war, the weaker party must be able to mount effective resistance. Effective resistance is measured by at least 100 deaths inflicted on the stronger party. A substantial number of these deaths must occur in the first year of the war. But if the violence becomes effectively one-sided, even if the aggregate effective-resistance threshold of 100 deaths has already been met, civil war must be coded as having ended and a politicide or other form of one-sided violence must be coded as having started; (8) A peace treaty that produces at least 6 months of peace marks an end to the war; (9) A decisive military victory by the rebels that produces a new regime should mark the end of the war. Because civil war is understood as an armed conflict against the government, continuing armed conflict against a new government implies a new civil war (allowing researchers to study the stability of military victories). If the government wins the war, a period of peace longer than 6 months must persist before we code a new war; (10) A cease-fire, or truce, or simply an end to fighting can also mark the end of a civil war if they result in at least two years of peace; (11) If new parties enter the war over new issues, a new war onset should be coded. If the same parties return to war over the same issues, this is coded as a continuation of the old war, unless any of the above criteria for coding a war's end apply for the period before the resurgence of fighting.

This extremely fine-tuned definition is an attempt to bring consensus into the divergent, and often fuzzy, coding rules used in the analysis of civil wars. Particularly, scholars aiming to measure the onset and termination of civil war through large-N statistical analysis claim that such a precise definition of what is and what is not a civil war is necessary. For Sambanis (2004), without a clear operational definition research-ers run the risk of making inferences from unstable empirical results. This will make it difficult, if not impossible, to measure and predict civil war.

No definition comes without its hazards, and the categorization of contemporary violent conflict as civil war, or 'internal' is criticized for a number of reasons. First of all, both terms tend to obscure the international element in conflict. For Cramer (2006: 65), it is questionable whether 'it makes sense to think in terms of civil war if many, if not most of these conflicts are characterized to a large extent by the interdependence of the countries where they occur with other parts of the world?' The Spanish Civil War of the 1930s, the wars in El Salvador and Nicaragua of the 1980s, and the more recent conflicts in Sierra Leone, Liberia, Nigeria, Colombia, Sudan, the DRC, Iraq and Afghanistan are all heavily internationalized (and regionalized) in their origins and conduct. Many of the origins of conflict stem from the conditions of dramatic social change related to post-colonialism, Cold War military involvement, spill-over effects from neighbouring wars, the War on Terror, and their integration into the global neo-liberal market. Hardt and Negri (2004: 4) coined the term 'global civil war' to express the necessity to understand local war as part of a 'grand constellation'. Keen (2008) too, argues against the term, when pointing at the classic case of the 1994 Rwandan genocide. Key members of the UN Security Council used the classification of 'civil war' during the early stages of the Rwandan genocide and this allowed the UK, the US and France to argue that a major peace-keeping operation was inappropriate in such a context – effectively giving Rwandan extremists free rein for mass killing. For Mary Kaldor, 'the new wars have to be understood in the context of the process known as globalisation' (1999: 3). Edward Azar (1990) argued that we should dismiss the term and use 'international social conflict' instead.

Another critique pertains to the criterion of 'government involvement'. Large-scale violence not directly involving the state is set apart as analytically different from civil wars. But the distinction between civil war and communal violence may fade in some zones of conflict. Government involvement can be cryptic, such as when governments indirectly support militias. In other cases, it may not be possible to identify 'who represents the government' because all warring parties may be claiming the state (e.g. Somalia after 1991).[2] State–society relations are often characterized by complex networks of political patronage, with blurry distinctions between private/public and political/personal, state/non-state. Ethnographic research on inter-communal pogroms in Gujarat, for example, revealed the role of political middlemen in instigating what was coded as 'communal violence'. The dependence of the poor on political middlemen in their dealings with the state, permitted these 'brokers' to mobilize their 'clients' for politically motivated violence (Berenschot 2011). Micro-analyses of communal violence, riots and pogroms show that state officials and agencies are often implicated (e.g. Horowitz 2001). There is more political organization in this type of violence than meets the eye. A form of conflict that is also excluded from the civil war category is what Duffield (2002) describes as 'network wars'. Here warring parties find it no longer necessary to project power through the bureaucratic control of a fixed territory. The state is replaced by multiple centres of authority, controlled by warlords and business networks, who no longer consider the state the main 'trophy' in war.

A final sense in which the category of civil war is analytically fragile concerns the distinction between criminal and political violence. Violent conflict in Colombia (after 1993) and Mexico (after 2006), for example, shows the deep entanglement of political and criminal agendas of state and non-state parties. The FARC (Fuerzas Armadas Revolucionarias de Colombia), once a traditional peasant guerrilla movement, is sustained by coca production and drugs trafficking. La Familia Michoacana, one of the most powerful drug cartels of Mexico, presents itself as an insurgency movement rather than a criminal enterprise. La Familia solidifies its power base through the selective and symbolic use of extreme violence, but also allegedly provides charity and services, propagating a public image of defender of the poor (using Facebook, Twitter, but also bill-boards and newspaper advertisements) and directly challenges the Mexican state.

By most definitions, Mexico is excluded from any set of civil war. Yet the duration and scale of violence (with an alleged death toll of over 34,000 for the period between 2006 and 2010), the conflict over territory between cartels and the government, as well as the capacity of the cartels to mount effective resistance (with at least 500 deaths inflicted on the side of the state), and the way they publicly voice their objectives, suggest that this type of large-scale violence is in many ways relevant to the study of civil war and internal violent conflict.

In sum, the boundaries between global/local, inter/intra, state/non-state, political/criminal are blurry. Definitions and classifications of violence are tools to advance our thinking, but can also have the opposite effect, and muddle analysis. Furthermore, the act of categorizing always has a political dimension, for one aspect is singled out, often for a reason. Cramer (2006: 84) emphasizes this as follows:

> [S]tandard labels or categories used to classify violence and violent conflict are unwieldy. A category involves a definition (and criteria by which events are judged to 'fit' that definition). On the one hand these definitions are extremely useful. The definitions, and classification systems they support, have as their purpose the clarification of a complex and divers world. On the other hand the process of clarifying through classification systems and categorical distinctions necessarily involves simplifying the world. Again, this is not necessarily a bad thing. However, the simplification can be misleading. It arises because the definitions involved work like borders separating artificially or at least crudely phenomena that might be closely related.

The point is to accept the complexity and multifacetedness of violent conflict and its transformative capacity: various forms of violence overlap and mutate into each other. This does not mean we should refrain from categorizing altogether. As can be learned from the above discussion, there are convincing arguments to analytically distinguish violent conflict as a sub-field of study.

Approach: group formation and violent action

In reviewing theories of 'violence in conflict' this book takes the centrality of the group as actor in contemporary conflict as a point of departure. The key role of the group and the organization claiming to represent the group – insurgents, rebels, guerrillas or others – is widely acknowledged. Any meaningful study of violent conflict should thus consist of a systematic analysis of (identity) group formation, dynamics of interaction and collective action. This is *not* to say that 'identity' or 'identity differences' are causing violent conflict. Rather, *identity boundary drawing* is a central aspect of the mobilization of support for armed conflict in the world today. Clearly, group identity labels should be handled with caution: collective actors in violent conflict cannot be treated as if they were unitary, bounded entities. Often the relationship between organizations in conflict and the groups they claim to represent is deeply ambiguous (see: Brubaker 2004). Violent conflicts are complex phenomena that foster interaction among actors with distinct identities, needs and interests. It is this complex interconnectedness between different actors and levels (local, global, state, region) that endows contemporary violent conflict with its particular character and leads to joint violence that 'straddles the divide between the political and the private, the collective and the individual' (Kalyvas 2003: 487). The study of contemporary conflict involves the analysis of relations and interactions at different levels and between a variety of actors: insiders and outsiders, individuals and organizations, civilians and armies.

By taking the process of group formation and violent action as point of departure we are left with three rather straightforward questions:

1. What makes a group?
2. Why and how does a group resort to violence?
3. Why and how do they (not) stop?

In the following chapters, we examine and compare the ways by which these questions are addressed (and at times *critiqued*) from a number of prominent theoretical traditions.

Conflict analysis

The task of conflict analysis is to unravel the complex dynamics of interactive processes in order to explain and/or understand how and why people resort to violence. The making of such an analysis is part of doing social research. We will here briefly discuss a number of guidelines on how to do theoretically informed analysis with the help of Charles Ragin's *Constructing Social Research* (1994) and Martin Hollis' *The Philosophy of Social Science* (1994).

In essence, Ragin argues, social research involves a dialogue between theory (ideas) and evidence (data). Theories help to make sense of evidence, and researchers use evidence to extend, revise and test theories. The end result is a representation of social life that has been shaped and reshaped by ideas. An important part of doing social research is dedicated to the analysis of the phenomena the researcher is studying. Analysis means 'breaking phenomena into their constituent parts and viewing them in relation to the whole they form' (Ragin 1994: 55). In analysing a violent conflict, a researcher aims to break the conflict up into its component parts, dissecting the different key elements and conditions that combine to 'make' the conflict. A first possible step in making such an analysis is conflict mapping.

Mapping a conflict

By 'mapping' a conflict, you visually (on a flip chart, blackboard) break a conflict into its key component parts. These parts can then be studied in isolation from one another, in relation to one another, or in relation to the larger conflict. Basic questions that will help you to map a conflict are:

1. Who are the main parties?
2. What is happening between them?
3. What is happening within them? (distinguish positions, interests, needs, fears)
4. Who are the secondary parties (or other stakeholders)?
5. What is happening between them all?
6. What is happening between the parties and the external environment?
7. Where are you on the map?[3]

Conflict mapping is used in many different ways. It is used by analysts to get a good snapshot overview of a conflict situation. It is also used as a method in conflict resolution workshops: to bring out the different perceptions of conflict. In Wehr's words, conflict mapping is 'a first step in intervening to manage a particular conflict. It gives both the intervener and the conflict parties a clearer understanding of the origins, nature, dynamics and possibilities for resolution of the conflict' (Wehr 1979: 18 quoted in Miall et al. 1999: 91). Above all, mapping is a playful way to organize evidence. Drawing a conflict map allows you to think through relationships between parties, their alliances and split-off movements and their relation to their 'constituency'. It is a way to trigger questions on not just the more obvious core parties (e.g. the Tamil Tigers fighting the Government of Sri Lanka army), but also on the wider network of stakeholders (e.g. Tamil diaspora groups lobbying in Brussels). It also shows how (1) a conflict mostly consists of a cluster of conflicts and (2) conflicts involve different 'levels-of-analysis'. Apart from individuals (leaders, elites), organizations (the Tamil Tigers, Lord's Resistance Army, the FARC) and groups ('Tamils', 'Acholi', 'peasant population'), conflicts involve state and international sources. It is exactly these complexities that can be visualized on a conflict map and serve as a starting point for further research (e.g. by zooming in on a specific relationship, or sub-conflict). Conflict mapping is also an exercise in 'mind mapping': for by drawing 'your' map you bring out your own perceptions and 'reading' of a particular conflict.

Conflict analysis is not just an exercise in the organization of evidence, it is also about 'explaining' or 'making sense of' particular phenomena. It is here that the dialogue with theory becomes apparent. What defines a group? What is ethnicity? When is a Tamil not a Tamil? Can individuals cross group boundaries? How do organizations in conflict sustain themselves? How are people mobilized for violent action? Why do people follow? How is power organized? What is the role of fear, poverty or inequality in explaining people's readiness to wage war? These are just a few questions that will automatically pop up when mapping a conflict, and which require a more abstract level of thinking. Abstract knowledge about social life is called *social theory*. In Ragin's words, social theory is 'an attempt to specify as clearly as possible a set of ideas that pertain to a particular phenomenon or set of phenomena' (1994: 25). As it turns out, most people know at least something about conflict theory without studying it. They are, after all, confronted with imagery and news reports on violence and war on a daily basis. They know, for instance, that 'violence begets violence' and that populist leaders try and scapegoat certain groups in society. They do not need to study elite theories of conflict – a branch of conflict theory discussed in chapter 1 – to know this. Most people have heard about stereotyping and exploitation without reading social identity theory (chapter 2) or Galtung's work on structural violence (chapter 3). They know that grievances and propaganda play a role in conflict, also without Edward Azar (chapter 4) or studying discourse analysis (chapter 6). They may acknowledge that people have a tendency to act in self-interested ways and do not need a theory of rational choice (chapter 5) to understand that this may also be the case in war. Still, theory is valuable because this body of thinking explores these ideas in depth, learning from, and building on earlier insights. How and why are people resistant or receptive to populist rhetoric? Why do groups end up in an escalatory dynamics of identity competition? Is violence always a visible and concrete act of physical hurt, or can it also be indirect and hidden, such as when people die of poverty, or a lack of medicine? When is violence rendered a normal and legitimate course of action? And how do we distinguish rational from irrational behaviour in war? Everyday understandings of war are often seriously flawed as well. Many commonsense ideas on the role of ethnicity, poverty and utility are contradicted by the body of knowledge gathered here in this book.

Theories of conflict form an important resource and guidance in grasping the complexities of war. Roughly, theories are informed by different underlying claims on 'what there is'˙(ontology) and 'how to know' (epistemology). As a way to bring out the affinities and contradictions between the theories reviewed in the following chapters I propose to try and situate them in what is here coined the 'Hollis matrix'.

Ontological and epistemological stances

In the end, the many different theoretical traditions of violent conflict are all simply variations on two sets of ontological and epistemological themes: structure and agents as ontological stances, and explanation or understanding as epistemological stances. Martin Hollis scrutinizes these positions in great depth in his book on *The Philosophy of Social Science* (1994). We will here – in a simplified way – lay out the very core positions. The matrix will be discussed in greater detail at the end of each chapter.

The first divide is that of ontology: theories are informed by two different claims on what primarily moves people. There is a fundamental ontological divide in the social sciences between approaches that attempt to account for human action by reference to movement in an encompassing social structure (structuralism); and approaches that take the actions of individuals to be the stuff of history and that regard structures as the outcome of previous actions (individualism). So, does structure primarily determine action or does action determine structure? Do we take the individual's agency, that is, his or her capacity to initiate change, as the starting point of our analysis, or do we choose to emphasize the structures that tell him or her how 'to do' social life? Do violent conflicts begin because of structural pressures or do they result from individuals acting in concert? And are these positions in radical conflict or can they also complement each other? We will deal with this 'chicken-or-egg' question later in the book. For now, we state that agency-based approaches locate the source of violent conflict at the level of the individual. Structure-based approaches, by contrast locate the causes of violent conflict in the organization of society. Ontological individualism maintains that 'the elementary unit of social life is the individual human action. To explain social institutions and social change is to show how they arise as the result of the action and interaction of individuals' (Elster 1989: 13 in Hollis 1994: 109). Ontological structuralism, in contrast, holds out for a focus on the power of structures. Power resides in institutions and as such is beyond the control of the individual. People's actions are constrained by the rules that tell them how 'to do' social life. It is the constitutive and regulative rules supporting, for instance, the system of capitalism, the modern state or global governance, that primarily explain human action and hence need to be placed at the core of analysis. There is, however, more to the structure–agency debate. Ontological claims are merely dogmatic unless connected to epistemological stances (Hollis 1994: 107). Before we turn to this connection we first outline the two different epistemological stances.

Epistemology is the theory of knowledge. There is a basic epistemological divide in the social sciences between scholars who argue that the social world can best be examined from *without* (explanation) and scholars who claim that the social world must be studied from *within* (understanding). The former position departs from the idea that human action is subject to a combination of causal laws and regulations.

Through the testing of a series of hypotheses it is possible to produce general explanations of human behaviour. Human action is taken as essentially determined and predictable. Theory is seen as a set of propositions that link cause and consequence. In contrast, scholars arguing from an 'interpretive epistemology' (understanding) claim that instead of looking for causes of behaviour, we are to seek the meaning of action. Actions derive their meaning from shared ideas and rules of social life. The construction of meaning is historically and culturally specific, and as such can only be studied 'in context' and by integrating the self-conscious perspectives of informants themselves. Scholars emphasize the creative (and unpredictable) way in which people construct meaning. Theory building is first and foremost about sense making. Researchers in this tradition are confronted with what is called the 'double hermeneutic': they aim to acquire knowledge by making an (academic) interpretation of how actors understand their social world.

Hollis connects these two views on epistemology to the earlier views on ontology by means of a basic matrix. His way of mapping the core assumptions underlying social theory in a matrix allows us to position the various conflict theories in their proper ontological and epistemological 'boxes'. Surely, the matrix is schematic. The idea is to use it as an organizational device, and to quiz, play with and if necessary critique the 'boxing' of theoretical traditions.

Let us walk through the four quadrants of the matrix, beginning with the upper row, 'Structuralism' (see table 0.1). By implication, there are two basic and different understandings of what structure is and does. The first, explanatory (or positivist) epistemological view, sees structures from without. Social structures are systems which are external and prior to actions and determine them fully. This view on society as functioning as an objective whole, such as a clock, beehive or body, external and independent of the actors involved, is little in use in academia today. Some scholars have ascribed this kind of objectivism to aspects of the work of Marx, where capitalism is presented as an objective system determining the lives of people. However, it is Marx's famous statement on social being in his Preface to *A Contribution to the Critique of Political Economy* (1859), which may incline us to rather fit him in the box next door, where structure is seen from within, from an (understanding), interpretative epistemology:

> It is not the consciousness of men that determines their being, but on the contrary, their social being, that determines their consciousness.
>
> (Marx 1963 [1859]: 51)

Table 0.1 The Hollis matrix (based on Hollis 1994, *The Philosophy of Social Science*)

Ontology/ Epistemology	Explaining (positivist)	Understanding (interpretative)
Structuralism	Social structures are systems (like clocks, planets, bodies, beehives) external and prior to actions and determining them fully.	Social structures are sets of meaning rules ('games') telling people how 'to do' social life (language, religion, economy). Actors are role/rule followers.
Individualism	Actors are self-contained units and the source of action (act upon individual laws of utility maximization, natural preferences, psychological laws).	Actors are embedded in society but have agency, they can act, initiate change, they have room for reflexive self-direction.

What this quotation in any case seems to imply, is that human beings are actors in a larger whole, and that it is their position in this larger whole that makes them who they are, not their individual agency, or 'consciousness'. Hollis suggests that we see this larger whole, the structure, as a game.[4] Games are sets of meaning rules, external to each of their players. Yet, in contrast to external structures or systems envisaged in the top left quadrant under the heading of 'explaining', games are internal to the players collectively. They are external to each, but internal to all: inter-subjective, rather than objective, one might say (Hollis 1994: chapter 7). So, structures are sets of meaning rules telling people how 'to do' social life. Examples of sets of rules are language, religion or the market economy. Although these rules are formed collectively, they hold great power over the individual. Actors are largely seen as rule followers, or as puppets on strings.

In a similar way can we discuss the two distinct views on the individual. Again, we see how from an explanatory epistemology the individual is studied from without. Here the main idea is not to study what people say (for they may say anything), but the way they behave (hence the term behaviourism). The idea is of the individual as self-contained unit, acting upon his or her 'internal computer', one might say. In rational choice theory, for instance, the individual is seen as acting upon individual laws of utility maximization. In Social Identity theories human behaviour is seen as primarily driven by a set of psychological laws or imperatives. In both cases, the individual is seen as the source of all collective action, and hence explanation. If we move to the bottom right quadrant, we will see that scholars working from an interpretative epistemology support this idea of the individual as initiator. By contrast, however, they aim to understand the individual from within. The actor here is not seen as self-contained unit, but as firmly embedded in society. He or she is seen to have agency and as capable of reflexive self-direction with room for moral and normative engagement but at the same time as firmly 'situated', and motivated by historical and cultural specific forms of meaning. The four core positions on structures and individuals are outlined in table 0.1.

This all may seem very abstract. 'Why bother?' you may ask. Or like the impatient gryphon in Alice in Wonderland you may demand: 'No, no! The adventures first! Explanations take such a dreadful time!' As described here, the matrix is merely a skeleton: a rough guide. Its usefulness will become apparent as we move through the chapters. What lies ahead is a range of theories on violence in conflict organized in six chapters. Clearly, justice cannot be done to the full writings of each of the theorists considered here and I hope this book will inspire you to read the original texts as given in the list of further readings at the end of each chapter. The approach is to inform you about this selection of ideas on violence and conflict, to try and unpeel layers of theoretical complexity and (with the help of the Hollis matrix) locate the ontological and epistemological assumptions underlying the approaches. So let's move to the 'adventures' now, and see how the different research traditions relate to the question, both unnerving and intriguing, of how and why (groups of) people resort to violent action.

1 Identity, boundaries and violence

Since this book takes the prominence of the identity group in conflict as its point of departure this first chapter aims to cover the discussion on identity, social identity and its relation to violence and conflict. It discusses approaches that focus on *processes of group formation and group attachment as possible sources of violent conflict*. First, we will look into ideas surrounding the definition of identity, and in particular social identity, and into critiques on the representation of identity groups as bounded and unitary. We then focus the discussion on the connection between identity groups and violent conflict by zooming in on *ethnic* groups, explaining and contrasting primordial and constructivist understandings of ethnic conflict. After highlighting the argumentation supporting the claim that ethnicity is socially constructed, this chapter then aims to specify *how* it is constructed, pointing at the role of violence as 'group-maker'. Consequently, we look into theoretical traditions that emphasize the political functionality of ethnic war and theories that primarily understand it as the outcome of historically conditioned cultural meanings. The chapter concludes by answering the book's leading questions and by looking at the assumptions underlying the various constructivist approaches to violent conflict.

Identity

Identity is one of the most popular buzzwords of our times. It is one of those container concepts that everyone refers to. People use it to categorize the self and the other; companies and organizations profile their 'corporate identity'; and in marketing and advertising products, businesses and services are increasingly branded as containing identity. The term is considered so obvious that it needs no further explanation. Identity is used in a plethora of ways: to describe, label and categorize, but also as 'doing things', that is, as driving individual and group behaviour. Mostly, identity is used in a normative sense: it is good and desirable to 'have identity': without it one is considered lost and weak. In the field of social and political analysis, the term gained prominence in the 1960s and since then has increasingly replaced class-based explanatory models. It is inescapable in any work on gender, migration, mobilization, culture, religion, ethnicity and nationalism. Also within the field of Conflict Studies 'identity talk' has proliferated. Mary Kaldor (1999) introduced identity, together with globalization as key concepts for understanding the 'new wars' of the post Cold War era. She contrasts the old 'politics of ideas' that had characterized conflict throughout most of the twentieth century, with what she signals as the rise of a new 'politics of identity', emerging out of the erosion of the modern state. One year earlier, Arjun Appadurai (1998) emphasized the need to grapple with the link between globalization and ethnic violence. He argues that the growing multiplicity of the identities available to individuals in the contemporary world feeds into a growing sense of radical social uncertainty, which can – at times – lead to anxiety and violence.

In the following section I will try to bring some conceptual clarity into the discussion on identity and violent conflict by defining the social identity concept. I will certainly not present an overview of the scholarly debate on social identity, but will focus on those components that help us to theorize ethnicity as a specific kind of collective or social identity, to then look into the relation between ethnic identity and violent conflict.

Identity, broadly defined, is the answer to the question 'who or what are you?'. That seems rather straightforward. But the enormity of the range of answers to this question calls for more precision. Are we free to define who we are? How do context and structure, roles and norms, discourses and symbolic orders impact our self-understanding? Why is it that some identities come to dominate others? Roughly, the vast field of identity studies stretches between traditions that locate the source of identity at the level of the individual and those who place it at the level of society. Erik H. Erikson, one of the first scholars to investigate the role of identity processes in social reality (and allegedly the father of the term 'identity crisis'), illustrates the multiplicity of identity by locating it in both the core of the individual and the core of the group, or, in his words, communal culture. In an article from 1966, Erikson introduces the identity concept with quotations from the two 'bearded and patriarchal founding fathers' of the kind of psychology on which he himself based his thinking on identity: William James and Sigmund Freud. The first quotation is taken from a letter of James to his wife in which he describes a man's 'sense of identity' as:

> discernable in the mental or moral attitude in which, when it came upon him, he felt himself most deeply and intensely active and alive. At such moments there is a voice inside which speaks and says: 'This is the real me!'.

Such experience includes: 'a mere mood or emotion to which I can give no form in words', and which 'authenticates itself to me as the deepest principle of all active and theoretic determination which I possess' (James 1920: 199 in Erikson 1966: 147). James here poetically describes identity as a rare and *unique sense of self.* Identity thus as utterly private and solitary experience. Subsequently, Erikson turns to Freud to highlight the other, *communal* dimension of identity. In an address to the Society of B'nai B'rith in Vienna in 1928 Freud said the following (Freud 1959: 273 in Erikson 1966: 148):

> What bound me to Jewry was (I am ashamed to admit) neither faith nor national pride, for I have always been an unbeliever and was brought up without any religion though not without a respect for what are called the 'ethical' standards of human civilization.
>
> Whenever I felt an inclination to national enthusiasm I strove to suppress it as being harmful and wrong, alarmed by the warning examples of the peoples among whom we Jews live. But plenty of other things remained over to make the attraction of Jewry and Jews irresistible – many obscure emotional forces (*dunkle Gefuehlsmaechte*), which were the more powerful the less they could be expressed

in words, as well as a clear consciousness of inner identity, the safe privacy of a common mental construction (*die Heimlichkeit der inneren Konstruktion*). And beyond this there was a perception that it was to my Jewish nature alone that I owed two characteristics that had become indispensable to me in the difficult course of my life. Because I was a Jew I found myself free from many prejudices which restricted others in the use of their intellect; and as a Jew I was prepared to join the opposition and to do without agreement with the 'compact majority'.

Identity, again difficult to 'express in words' here is experienced as sameness, as essentially sharing a 'common mental construction'. By means of these two examples, Erikson shows us the two faces of the identity concept. The two statements (and the life-histories behind them) help us to understand why identity is so 'tenacious and yet so hard to grasp'. For here we deal with 'something which can be experienced as "identical" *in the core of the individual* and yet also identical *in the core of a communal culture*, and which is, in fact, the identity of those two identities' (1966: 149). In the one case, it is the most individual sensation of a person's unique sense of self; that is, being utterly unlike anyone or anything else. In the other case, the essence of personal self is held to be one's membership of a social category or group, that is, being like a number of other people (Verkuyten 2005). Identity thus implies both *sameness* and *uniqueness*.[1] These two dimensions of identity, in less poetic terms, have become integrated in the way the term is defined in the social sciences. In social psychology, this is expressed in the distinction between the self-concept, or individual identity, and social identity. The self-concept is the total set of cognitions an individual has regarding who (s)he is. The self-concept thus subsumes the answers a person gives to the question 'Who am I?'. In turn, social identity is described by means of Henri Tajfel's canonical definition of the term as 'that *part* of an individual's self-concept which derives from his knowledge of his membership in a social group (or groups) together with the value and emotional significance attached to that membership' (Tajfel 1981: 63). A social identity, then, is one kind of answer to the question 'Who am I?' that is based on group membership. Tajfel – whose work we will discuss in the following chapter – defines the social identity group cognitively, in terms of people's self-conception as group members. He sees social identity as emerging from individual cognitive processes, and, as we will see in chapter two, as underpinned by a drive for order and simplicity. In social psychology, scholars are mainly interested in the individual's subjective experiences of identity, not in its social construction and political functions. For Verkuyten (2005: 62), using the term like this is misleading:

> If social identity coincided with self-understanding this would imply that an identity can change only when one's self-understanding changes. But of course it is not that simple. People can start to understand themselves differently, while from a social point of view they are still categorized and treated as if no change has occurred.

Someone born and raised in Amsterdam, for instance, who considers herself Dutch, may still be largely treated and categorized by her Moroccan heritage. Sociological approaches, therefore, place the origins of social identities in the social and the political, not the individual. Social identities are seen as socially constructed, as largely externally ascribed and as serving social and political functions. Evidently, these opposing views need not be mutually exclusive. Taking a middle ground position, Verkuyten argues that identity is not about individuals as such, nor about society as such, but the relation between the two. 'It is about the intricacies, paradoxes, dilemmas, contradictions, imperatives, superficialities, and profundities of the way individuals relate to and are related to the world in which they live' (Verkuyten 2005: 42).

Social identity

From the above we can learn that social identity is about the relationship between the individual and the social environment. It is about categories and relationships. The social identity concept tells us about the categorical characteristics – such as nationality, gender, religion, ethnicity – that locate people in social space. A person has a certain social identity if (s)he shares certain characteristics with others. Social identities are relational in the sense that they are limited: we are what we are *not*: Catholic not Protestant; female not male; Serb not Albanian. Hence, social identities are by definition divisive although not necessarily antagonistic or conflicting.

We have multiple identities: we form part of many different social categories. One can be an academic, mother, political activist, Muslim and French-Moroccan at the same time. However, these social identities mean different things in different contexts: they are contextual in the sense that depending of context one identity can become prominent whereas others recede into the background. In the setting of a university classroom persons are addressed by their social identity as students and professors, not as mothers, or believers. In turn, the university lecturer's professional identity plays a less prominent role in her interaction with small children at home. Social identities are dynamic and changeable. We may strongly identify with a religious group, a subculture or a profession in a certain period of our life, but we can also change faith, step out of certain communities, transform ourselves. Some social identities are more enduring than others: whereas one's membership of the category of university students is an – often intensive – temporal phase of three or four years, one's gender identity, national identity or ethnic identity tends to be much more permanent (the so-called primary identities). As we will discuss in more detail later in the book, there is scholarly debate about the extent to which actors have the freedom to construct their identity: whether their social identities are largely determined by societal rules, regulations and institutions, or whether in fact there is room for agency and initiative. The 'light' version of this discussion speaks of the difference between externally and internally ascribed social identities: some categorizations are forced upon us, that is to say, whereas others we can adopt ourselves. An 'identity conflict' arises when these two prove incompatible. For instance, in the case of homosexuality and Catholicism: someone can on a personal level ascribe to Roman Catholicism and be homosexual at the same time. However, from the outside this combination may be condemned and 'forbidden'. Likewise, second-generation migrants may see themselves as normal citizens of the country in which they are born and raised, but may be treated and categorized as disloyal outsiders on the local job market.

This automatically leads us into the realm of power. Each society is characterized by explicit and implicit rules and narratives about right and wrong, normal and abnormal. Some of these rules are firmly established and institutionalized, others are more subtle and negotiable. Nevertheless, they are all formed in historical contexts of power: some groups in society have more 'power to define' than others. Social identities are shaped and transformed, constrained and facilitated by these social and political environments and their definitional powers. In this context, the modern state has been one of the most important agents of categorization, classification and identification. As pointed out by the work of for instance Foucault, Bourdieu and Wacquant, the state monopolizes, or seeks to monopolize, not only legitimate physical force but also legitimate symbolic force. Including the power to name, to identify, to categorize, to state what is what and who is who. The state aims to classify people in relation to citizenship, ethnicity, gender, literacy, criminality, property-ownership or sanity, supported by symbolic and material resources ranging from schools to prisons and asylums (see: Brubaker and Cooper 2000; Ferguson and Gupta 2002).

As will happen more often in this book, we run into definitional boundaries. If we indeed define social identity as the answer to the question of what someone is taken to be socially, this would also allow for answers – such as my students like to give – including 'human', 'lazy' or 'funny'. Clearly, not all categorizations (moods, tastes, preferences, roles or labels) and possible group memberships are recognized as social identities.

Scholars agree that for the membership of a collective of some sort to form a social identity, individual members should view them as more-or-less unchangeable and socially consequential. Fearon and Laitin (2000: 848) propose to define social categories as:

> sets of people given a label (or labels) and distinguished by two main features:
> 1. rules of membership that decide who is and is not a member of the category; and 2. content, that is, sets of characteristics (such as beliefs, desires, moral commitments, and physical attributes) thought to be typical of members of the category, or behaviours expected or obliged of members in certain situations (roles).

Together, 'boundary rules' and 'content' thus form the necessary, and highly interrelated components of social identities.

Social identity and group conflict: the unitary trap

It is not hard to see the salience of social identity in violent conflict. Very often social identities such as ethnicity, religion, clan or nation are seen as the primary fault line between groups in conflict. People seem to be willing and able to kill and die in the name of the group. Indeed, the social identity concept is crucial to the understanding of violent conflict, but it should be handled with caution. It is easy to fall into what I call the 'unitary trap' for at least two reasons. First, by making use of the term 'identity group conflict' we seem to imply, often unintentionally, a causal link between 'identity' or 'identity differences' and violent conflict. As will be outlined below, a way to deal with this problem is to contrast primordial and constructivist approaches to social identity, and to introduce the term 'everyday primordialism'. Second, we need to rethink the 'group' in applying the social identity concept to violent conflicts. Contemporary wars are not binary conflicts between unitary and bounded groups or blocks A and B. The levels of 'groupness' of parties in conflict is not constant, they vary, from very loose and socially almost insignificant ascriptions (category) to high and intense forms of interaction and organization (group or community). Handelman (1977) and more recently Brubaker (2004) explain that by distinguishing between categories and groups we can problematize – rather than presume – the relation between them.[2] We can ask ourselves how categories are transformed into groups, and study the political, social and psychological processes involved. This is significant, for often the crystallization of identity and groupness takes place during the course of a conflict: as we will see, high levels of groupness are often the *result* and not the cause of violent conflict. Another way to 'break' the unitary trap as proposed by Brubaker is to make an explicit distinction between groups and organizations. Again, many conflicts are portrayed as 'identity groups in conflict'. However, it is much more often not groups but various kinds of organization that are the protagonists of violent conflict (states, paramilitary organizations, political parties, churches, gangs, newspapers, radio and television stations) which cannot be equated with ethnic groups. Often the relationship between organizations in conflict and the groups they claim to represent is deeply ambiguous. In his comparative study of nationalist movements in the Israeli-occupied territories and Former Yugoslavia Bowman (2007) shows the multiplicity of identity, and the important role of organizations in both identity formation and group-making. For instance, the fundamental reason the Palestine Liberation Organization (PLO) was able to serve as an icon of Palestine identity was that it presented itself as representative of all of the diverse 'Palestinian' constituencies which had been disinherited by the creation of the Israeli state. 'Palestinians' were able to recognize themselves as addressed by the oppositional rhetoric of the PLO insofar as that rhetoric did not specify any particular identity to its addressees other than the recognition of themselves as somehow stripped of their rights by the antagonism of the 'Zionist entity'. In a very similar way, the Liberation Tigers of Tamil Eelam (LTTE) managed to present itself as the 'sole representative' of all of the diverse 'Tamils' deprived by the Government of Sri Lanka.

Although scholars recognize this, it is nevertheless not easy to integrate this knowledge into the ways we talk and write about conflict. However, by continuing to speak about 'Tamils and Singhalese' or 'Serbs and Albanians' we unwillingly, and unintentionally reproduce inaccurate typologies. By problematizing the connection between identity and violent conflict, and by making a clear distinction between groups and categories, and between groups and organizations, we can escape both everyday primordialism and the 'unitary trap', and the simplistic portrayal of identity group conflict as an identity-driven war of all against all.

Ethnicity: telling each other apart

Groups in conflict are often portrayed as sharing a unitary identity, and as fighting over this unitary identity. One such is the ethnic group. Indeed, ethnicity is often seen as the main divide between warring parties. Now, what is this? What 'makes' the ethnic group? And what is the connection between ethnic groups and violent conflict? How and why does the ethnic group resort to violence? First of all, as the conflict researchers' mantra goes: things are much more complex than they seem. The average media report on ethnic violence and conflict speaks of relatively clearly defined categories of people who wage war against each other, based on easily identifiable ethnic differences. On the ground, however, ethnic violence is a messy and confusing affair. In many cases, protagonists of violence during ethnic conflict deal with very practical problems of miscategorization. In his book *The Deadly Ethnic Riot* Donald Horowitz (2001: 130) relates the following story:

In Sri Lanka (1983), Sinhalese rioters suspected a man in a car of being a Tamil. Having stopped the car, they inquired about his peculiar accent in Sinhala, which he explained by his lengthy stay in England and his marriage to an English woman. Uncertain, but able to prevent his escape, the rioters went off to kill other Tamils, returning later to question the prospective victim further. Eventually, he was allowed to proceed on his way, even though the mob knew it risked making a mistake, which in fact it had: the man was a Tamil.

Members of groups may attempt to 'place' each other by using a variety of tests, ranging from physical checks (e.g. for circumcision), to behavioural checks (e.g. language or accent), to knowledge checks (in the above case, the would-be Tamil victim was asked to recite Sinhalese nursery rhymes). However, many empirical cases suggest that mistakes are made, as is illustrated by this account of a priest eye-witnessing a massacre by Hutu rebels in Buta (Burundi) in 1997:

> There were 250 children, ages 11 to 19. On April 30, around 5:30, we heard shots. In several minutes, the assailing rebels had become masters of the seminary. The soldiers charged with protecting us fled. A troop of rebels had taken over the dormitories ... The assailants gathered us in the middle of the room and demanded that we separate into Hutu and Tutsi. The students refused. They were united. Then the leader of the group, an enraged woman, ordered their killing. There were 70 students. The assailants fired their grenades.[3]

Ethnic war is often waged between groups of people who cannot tell each other apart. Although the outcomes of the two examples were different, the lesson of both accounts is identical: ethnic identity differences are not as readily apparent as most commonsensical explanations of ethnic violence assume.

To further our understanding of the connection between ethnicity and violence we have to begin by making a clear distinction between the *primordial* (or 'everyday') and the *constructivist* (or 'analytical') understanding of both ethnicity and, by implication, ethnic violence. Basically, both approaches see the ethnic group as a communal group or community, and they also see ethnic groups as larger than social formations such as the family, clan or face-to-face groups such as neighbourhoods. Ethnicity is related to a sense of belonging based on the belief in shared culture and common ancestry. However, where primordialists see the ethnic group as a *natural* community, the constructivist approach claims it is *socially* constructed.

Everyday primordialism

In academia the primordial view of identity is only discussed as a fallacy. It is mainly used to explain what constructivism is arguing *against*. Why it is still of such importance, however, is because 'on the ground' primordialist assumptions underlie many accounts of ethnic identity. It is an important narrative through which both insiders and outsiders understand, and act upon ethnic violent conflict. People often believe that their ethnicity is a natural, inevitable fact of life. Ethnicity is seen as a communal bond given by nature, as something that is in your blood, and therefore unchangeable. Beliefs in the naturalness of social identities such as gender, race or religion are often rooted in socio biology or for instance theology, and standardized in histories of state and nation building. Fearon and Laitin (2000) have termed these beliefs regarding social identity *everyday primordialism*. 'People often believe, mistakenly, that certain social categories are natural, inevitable and unchanging facts about the social world. They believe that particular social categories are fixed by human nature rather than by social convention and practice' (2000: 848). Examples of everyday primordialism are not hard to find: in many situations of conflict people refer to themselves and the other as essentially and biologically different. Many contemporary conflicts revolve around narratives of origin and blood, where the territorial claims of forebears on ancient soil are relived and used to legitimize contemporary and future violence. 'This is my land. You do not belong here. We were here first.' What is implied, is both simple and (hence) attractive: conflict results from difference. It is because of their natural and essential ethnic difference that groups such as Tamils and Singhalese, Kikuyu and Luos, Serbs and Albanians clash and fight. The primordialist approach to ethnic conflict rests on the premise that since groups are essentially different, these differences (in temperament, in ways of life, in being) will, perhaps not always, but time and again, provoke inter-ethnic clashes and violence. This means that although there may be ways to contain violence, there is no real solution other than segregation and avoidance. In some cases, this approach argues, ethnicity simply breeds violence. This is inevitable and unchanging, it is innate to human groups.

Although long banned from the academic textbook, primordialist assumptions, because of their commonsensical simplicity, and also because they are 'out there' in the mouths of bystanders and protagonists of war, regularly creep into journalistic reports seeking to make sense of war. Since people – politicians, NGOs, the public – act upon these understandings of the self and other, they form an important component of contemporary war, and hence deserve our attention.

Constructivism

The constructivist approach to ethnicity is often traced back to the work of the German sociologist Max Weber (1864–1920), who conceived ethnicity as a mode of drawing boundaries between individuals and hence group-making.[4] Another important scholar in this tradition is Fredrik Barth, in particular his work on *Ethnic Groups and Boundaries* (1969). Barth was one of the first scholars, together with for instance the anthropologist Micheal Moerman, who carried out ethnographic research on processes of ethnic group formation.[5] Like Moerman, he came to the conclusion that the 'trib-alist' preoccupation of classical social anthropology with defining the ethnic group with reference to objective features was a dead end. Barth and his collaborators found convincing evidence of how ethnic group boundaries were actually permeable and changeable. They documented how, for instance, in Pakistan, a Pathan could assume the ethnic identity of a Baluch, in Sudan a Fur could become recognized as a Baggara, and in Rwanda it (once) was possible to cross Hutu–Tutsi boundaries. They also showed that two groups may seem culturally similar, yet they can distinguish themselves as ethnically very different. Barth and Moerman produced evidence of how, in terms of listed features, ethnic groups showed as much overlap with neighbouring groups as they showed variety within their boundaries. In a study of ethnic relations in Thailand, Moerman (1965) asked himself the question 'Who are the Lue?'. However, after listing all the characteristics to demarcate the Lue, such as religion, language, livelihood, customs and political organization, he came to the conclusion that the Lue both shared many features with other groups with whom they lived in close interaction and showed substantial variety within the Lue group. In the end, Moerman was forced to conclude that someone is Lue 'by virtue of believing and calling himself Lue and of acting in ways that validate his Lueness' (Moerman 1965: 1219, in Eriksen 1993: 11). Hence, 'Lueness' resulted from social processes of ascription and identification, not from sharing objective properties. In a very similar way, Barth argued for the rejection of preoccupations with the 'cultural stuff' that ethnic groups may share and focusing instead on the boundaries that separate ethnic groups. 'The critical focus of investigation ... becomes the ethnic *boundary* that defines the group, not the cultural stuff that it encloses' (Barth 1969: 15). According to his findings, what makes an ethnic identity 'ethnic', is to be sought in the 'social processes of maintaining boundaries that the people themselves recognized as ethnic' (Baumann 1999: 59). The ethnic group thus is an imagined, constructed community, created through social interaction. This means that ethnicity is not a thing in itself, but contextual. And therefore dynamic and changeable. This way of understanding ethnic groups has become very influential in the social sciences (see: Eriksen 1993; Baumann 1999).

The constructivist understanding of ethnic identity runs into what Baumann (1999) has called 'intuitive scepticism'. Are these examples of ethnic crossing not the exception? If ethnicity is nothing but a social construct, can a blue-eyed German then become a Kurd, or a Tamil, or a Hutu just by identifying with that group? Perhaps it is good to include another example. Let us take the Tamils of Sri Lanka. Now, what 'makes' Tamil ethnicity? We run into the same problems as Moerman did earlier. Certainly, Tamils share certain features (Tamil language, Hindu religion, cultural characteristics such as caste system, appearance). However, most of these features they share with other ethnic groups in the region (e.g. the Tamils of Tamil Nadu, Sri Lankan Singhalese), and some features such as religion they do not share with their fellow ethnics (there are Christian, Buddhist and Muslim Tamils). Still, one could argue, there is a set of criteria that more-or-less makes the 'Tamil profile'. The question then is, if outsider X takes on these characteristics, if (s)he converts to Hinduism, and speaks Tamil, does this then make him or her a Tamil? Let us return to Fearon and Laitin's definition of social category. Whether or not X can become a Tamil relies on the *rules of membership* (Barth's social processes of boundary maintenance). These rules of membership, or 'boundary rules', differ per ethnic group and change over time. In some cases, outsiders are accepted into the group largely based on economic status, as once was the case in Rwanda. In other cases, it is enough to marry an insider. Often, it takes two or more generations before the offspring of a newcomer is accepted as part of the ethnic group. Some groups and boundaries are tenacious and change only slowly, while in other cases substantial shifts occur over the course of a lifespan. Generally, it is a combination of requirements, covered by what Fearon and Laitin call *boundary rules* and *content*.[6]

Still, sceptics may ask: why does it matter? Does it make a difference whether a Hutu militia kills in the name of primordial or social group belongings? Is it not the killing that needs to be explained, instead of the nature of the group bond?

Constructivism forces us to not take ethnicity for granted as innate and unchangeable, as 'simply there'. This has implications, not least for the field of conflict analysis. For if indeed we find convincing evidence that ethnic groups are constructed, or more precisely, that they result from social processes of boundary drawing and maintaining, this implies asking questions about how and why group boundaries are drawn, maintained and contested. Who decides who is in and out? In whose interests are the 'boundary rules' of a group? How are ethnic boundaries materialized, institutionalized and policed? How and when do which actors pursue what strategies of boundary making? For what reason?[7] It also implies asking questions that may touch upon reconciliation: whether it is possible to deconstruct or reconstruct ethnic divides. This is not a new thought. Brubaker and Cooper (2000), Fearon and Laitin (2000) and Brubaker (2004) called for taking the constructivist approach to ethnicity a step further by arguing that after we have established *that* ethnicity is constructed we have to specify *how* it is constructed. Here the idea of everyday primordialism comes back in. Analysts not only should seek to *disprove* primordialism, they should also try and *account for* primordialism: how is it that we have come to understand ethnicity as natural? 'We should seek to explain the processes and mechanisms through which what has been called the "political fiction of the nation" – or of the "ethnic group", "race", or other putative "identity" – can crystallize, at certain moments, as a powerful, compelling reality' (Brubaker and Cooper 2000: 5). Perhaps it is useful to briefly address the notion of reification.

Reification

In her book *Balkan Express* Slavenka Drakulic (1993) meticulously analyses the effect the war in former Yugoslavia has on herself and the people around her. What she notices, is that when in the early 1990s the battlefront is nearing her town, Zagreb, and stories about atrocities are creeping in, a certain transformation begins to take shape. Whereas before, she felt Yugoslavian, and her putative 'Croatianess' meant nothing to her, she now feels this identity is closing in on her. She compares her national identity with wearing an ill-fitting shirt. 'You may feel the sleeves are too short, the collar too tight. You might not like the colour, and the cloth might itch. But there is no escape; there is nothing else to wear' (1993: 52). It becomes very hard to continue to shrug off this 'Croatianess', when at the same time people are killed and massacred only because they are Croats.

> So right now, in the new state of Croatia, no one is allowed not to be a Croat. And even if this is not what one would really call freedom, perhaps it would be morally unjust to tear off the shirt of the suffering nation – with tens of thousands of people being shot, slaughtered and burned just because of their nationality. It wouldn't be right because of Vukovar, the town that was erased from the face of the earth. Because of the attacks on Dubrovnik.
>
> (1993: 52)

This process, during which a putative identity is turned into something hard, unchangeable and absolute, is called *reification*. According to Baumann (1999) to know this term is probably the most important step in turning a person into a social scientist. Reification means thingification, or turning concepts into things. Berger and Luckmann (the 'founding fathers' of social constructivism) defined the term in 1967 as 'the apprehension of human phenomena as if they were things, that is ... the apprehension of the products of human activity as if they were something other than human products – such as facts of nature' (1967: 10). Reification is a social process and as such it is central to the politics of ethnicity. In trying to understand the role of identity in conflict, analysts should carefully study the way in which social products such as ethnicity become cemented and 'thingified' during the course of war. In doing this, Brubaker and Cooper (2000: 5) warn us, analysts should carefully 'avoid unintentionally *reproducing* or reinforcing such reification by uncritically adopting categories of practice (everyday use) as categories of analysis'.

With this in mind, let us explore the explanatory power of the constructivist approach to ethnicity for the study of violent conflict. The primordialist view on ethnic violent conflict was easy to understand: ethnicity simply breeds violence. But how to understand ethnic violent conflict from the constructivist stance? How do scholars account for the salience of ethnicity in contemporary conflict: how and why is ethnic identity turned into a powerful and compelling divide? And what are the connections with violence and conflict?

By asking these questions we enter a controversy in the field of contemporary Conflict Studies that can be defined – in a simplified way – as the 'elite-versus-mass' view of violent conflict. It can also be framed as the rational action, or instrumentalist approach versus the culturalist or ethno-symbolic approach to conflict. Both views support the constructivist understanding of ethnicity, but whereas the former emphasizes the *political functions* of ethnic boundaries, the latter is more concerned with their *social meaning*.

Ethnic war: function and meaning

Function: elite theories of conflict

At the core of elite theories of conflict is the assumption that ethnic war is functional. Ethnic violence does not result from irrational and spontaneous eruptions of mass anger or frustration, but is deliberately orchestrated and planned by elites and organizations to increase group cohesion and build a loyal support base. Although elite analyses of conflict are quite heterogeneous, they generally place emphasis on the role of violence: on how violence is strategically instigated to create or affirm boundaries between groups of people. As Fearon and Laitin explain: 'Elites foment ethnic violence to build support; this process has the effect of constructing more antagonistic identities, which favours more violence' (2000: 853). This instrumentalist strand within constructivism has proliferated since the 1990s.[8] Evidence supporting this approach can be found in a diversity of case-studies on violence in ethnic conflict, ranging from Rwanda (e.g. Gourevitch 1998; Prunier 2008), Central Africa (Lemarchand 2009), Sudan (Deng 1995; Mamdani 2009), India (Brass 1997), the Former Yugoslavia (Woodward 1995; Mueller 2001); Sri Lanka (Tambiah 1996); and visually documented in for example *The Death of Yugoslavia* (Norma Percy, BBC 1995). In all these studies, violence, and fear of violence proves to be an effective key to group-making. As soon as people are targeted because of their putative identity, they start to act and feel collectively. In war, it becomes very hard to distance oneself from this process of social closure. This is vividly described by Drakulic, but Gourevitch also refers to just this when he notices, in the case of inter-ethnic violence in Rwanda, that 'genocide, after all, is an exercise in community building' (1998: 95).

Typically, elite theories of violence emphasize the ways in which leaders who fear losing power, or new leaders trying to create their own constituency may gamble for resurrection or rise to power by provoking ethnic conflict. A classic example is that of elites who, when confronted with systemic transformations beyond their control – such as market liberalization or economic recession – try to divert political debate away from the root of the problem toward other issues, defined in terms of culture or identity, that appeal to the public in non-economic terms. Elite factions opt to play the 'ethnic card' by mobilizing their 'own' ethnic followings and by scapegoating and name-calling others. By actively provoking and creating violent incidents (instigated by militias, or private thugs) leaderships construct an image of overwhelming threat to the group from the outside and of themselves as saviours of the ethnic nation. As Gagnon points out, such an image of overwhelming threat to the 'ethnic collective' is particularly helpful in silencing dissent, especially if dissenters can be portrayed as selfish and uninterested in the well-being of the group, and can therefore be branded as traitors (Gagnon 1997: 138). In answering the question 'why do people follow?', elite theorists emphasize the control or ownership of mass media, especially television, and increasingly also the Internet, as a key element. Collective fear of violence and the mechanism of social closure induced by this 'fear for the other' is also seen to explain people's submissiveness. Evidently, the role of direct coercion, and its material and spatial dimensions (gates, fences, checkpoints, identity cards) is of key importance. Underlying elite theory is the assumption that largely people consent to the orders imposed on them by elites, including categories of ethnic belonging. The picture that emerges is that of masses who passively receive and internalize dominant discourses and orders, with little room for autonomous agency.

In sum, constructivist elite theories of conflict argue that ethnic violence is a political strategy to create, increase or maintain group boundaries and political support. In this sense, they stand in direct opposition to commonsensical primordialism, in arguing that ethnic 'groupness' is the *result* of violence, not the *cause*. Ethnic wars are understood as top-down and elite-driven struggles for power. Essentially, ethnic violence is a political strategy: it is used as a means to acquire power.

Function: dynamics of interaction theory

As will be discussed later, ontologically, elite theories of conflict take an individualist, rational actor approach. The source of ethnic conflict is placed at the level of the individual agent rationally pursuing his or her interest. However, according to some of its critics, the problem with the elite approach is that it is too narrow and top-down. Agency is only placed at the level of (often ill defined) predatory elites. They are the ones who, through careful calculation, manipulation and intimidation, aim at acquiring as much power as possible. In this picture, the 'masses' are generally seen as followers, as passively subjected to the propaganda and manipulations of elites and rulers. Scholars such as Brass (1997) Kalyvas (2003, 2006) and Keen (2008) reject this understanding of ethnic war as too simplistic. In an article on the ontology of political violence Kalyvas argues that the locus of agency is as likely to be at the bottom as at the top of society. 'Civilians cannot be treated as passive, manipulated, or invisible actors; indeed, they often manipulate central actors to settle their own conflicts' (2003: 481). Kalyvas explains that violence in civil war is multifunctional and only possible through alliances between groups and factions at different levels of society. He argues for an understanding of intra-state war informed by the dynamics of local cleavages and intra-community dynamics. It is misleading to see the actions, motivations and identities of local actors as mere replicas of central (national) actors. Local actors, at times under the heading of a 'master cleavage' (such as ethnic war) pursue their own agendas, both private and political. Hence, 'violence in an ethnic or class war may not be ethnic or class violence' (2003: 481). Often, the larger context of war allows for the use of different types of violence: private, domestic, criminal, sexual. Although central 'master cleavages' certainly inform and motivate local dynamics, Kalyvas notices a disjunction between central and local allegiances. Facilitated by the larger war context people set out to settle local feuds and rivalries. In return, these local forms of violence feed back into the general war dynamics. This calls for a fine-grained and systematic analysis of the *dynamics of interaction* and the logic of violence in contemporary war. Kalyvas holds that civil war fosters interaction among a range of rational actors: local and central, insiders and outsiders, individuals and organizations, civilians and armies. These actors have different identities and pursue different interests. 'It is the convergence of local motives and supralocal imperatives that endows civil war with its particular character and leads to joint violence that straddles the divide between the political and the private, the collective and the individual' (2003: 487).

In a similar way, Keen (2008) aims to show the multiple functions served by violence in settings of war and disaster. Rather than conceptualizing war as a contest or a collapse, Keen suggests investigating war and disaster as alternative systems of profit, power and protection. For Keen, 'events, however, horrible and catastrophic, are actually *produced*, they are made to happen by a diverse and complicated set of actors who may well be achieving their objectives in the midst of what looks like failure and breakdown' (2008: 15). Both authors support an approach to power not as negotiated and carried out from the central level but as constructed and contested locally. Power and politics are shaped and mediated at the intersection of various levels (national, regional, local, private) (see Demmers 1999).

The above critique of elite theories of conflict, however, remains within the boundaries of the rational action framework. It shows a more complex picture of war, and the logic of violence in war. Elite theory is extended, not rejected. Ethnic identity is largely seen as instrumental: as a means to mobilize a support base, or as a cover up for the violent pursuit of local and private interests. The question 'why do people follow ethnic entrepreneurs?' is answered quite bluntly: they do not follow! In contrast, 'people' are rational actors who pursue their own interests. That is, all within the limits of what is strategically possible.

Meaning: culturalism and ethno-symbolism

The instrumentalist notion of ethnicity as a means to an end, and of ethnic groups as interests groups, is often criticized as limited and a-historic. Although this critique is rather heterogeneous, stemming from socio-psychology (e.g. Kaufmann 2006) and anthropology (e.g. Smith 1996 on ethno-symbolism), it generally emphasizes ethnic identities as socially meaningful. There is more to ethnicity than interests and instrumentality. Ethnicity is important for its own sake. People can feel deeply attached to their ethnic group, they love their ethno-nation and culture. The emotional power of ethnicity, that is to say, is too easily neglected. Although the power of predatory elites is widely recognized, the success of such ethnic entrepreneurs is seen as dependent upon the historically conditioned cultural meanings of their politics of fear.

Although scholars acknowledge that ethnic attachments are ultimately socially constructed and malleable, they at the same time emphasize the persistence and emotional power of these attachments. The ethno-symbolist approach, for instance, stresses the importance of deep ethno-symbolic resources that ethnic groups can draw on. Anthony Smith (1996) discerns three sets of ethno-symbolic components that can explain the variety and persistence of ethnic groups. The more groups can rely on a glorious, well documented past (of heroism and sacrifice, wealth, and military victory); on sharing a sacred mission as a Chosen People with a special contract to God; and as related to an ancestral homeland, the greater their capacity to sustain themselves. Building on this, Stuart Kaufmann (2006) grounds his theory of extreme ethnic violence on the relation between an ethnic group's myth-symbol complex and violent conflict. According to his model of symbolic politics, the critical causes of extreme ethnic violence are group myths that justify hostility, fears of group extinction and a symbolic politics of chauvinist mobilization. In fact, Kaufmann's model reverses the causality implied by elite theories of conflict: it is not predatory elites that instigate collective fears and hostile mass attitudes, it is the other way around. It is ethnic mythologies, producing emotion-laden symbols and hostile mass attitudes which create a context for leaders in which predatory policy is more popular than moderate policy. In a way, these approaches are primarily concerned with analysing the cultural contextualization of ethnic violence. They aim to show that even excessive ethnic or ethno-religious violence 'makes sense' in historically and culturally defined contexts. In other words, the question 'why do people follow ethnic entrepreneurs?' needs to be reversed: it is the elites who follow the masses, and not the other way around. The source of ethnic violence is to be sought in the cultural constructions of fear and hostility which render violence necessary and meaningful.[9]

The problem with culturalist views, critics argue, is that what one may call the 'predatory myths' are seen as a given, as almost naturally grown out of societies, and, more importantly, as 'doing things'. The myth itself is given great explanatory power and is therefore essentialized and reified. Ethnic groups and nations share a great diversity of legends and myths: tales of war, animosity and hatred as well as peace and brotherhood. They themselves cannot explain why violence occurs at a particular time. In the end, critics of the culturalist approach argue, it is the active selection and framing of certain ethnic mythologies as powerful and meaningful to the present, by certain individual or collective agents, which explains why ethnic violence comes to be seen as necessary and legitimate. Again, this directs us back to the role of the protagonist and crafter of war, and his or her mobilizing capacity.

This does not mean, however, that the emotional value of ethnicity, its historical grounding and cultural meaning is irrelevant to the study of violent conflict. On the contrary, it is important to acknowledge that it is exactly because ethnic attachments can be emotionally powerful that they have such high mobilization levels.

Meaning: the emotional value of ethnicity

There are a number of reasons why ethnic attachments are emotionally powerful. First of all, as is the case with national identity and statehood, 'ethnicity is something we are socialized into' (Verkuyten 2005: 86). We are born into societies where the notion of ethnic affiliation, strong or weak, is apparent. From a very early age onwards children learn about ethnic categorization through their interaction with parents and significant others and internalize related cultural meanings, such as language, religion, history and beliefs. Through their early identifications with family and relatives children generate an affective sense of ethnic belonging. Verkuyten describes this process of enculturation as follows:

> Cultural meanings that are related to ethnicity – such as language, history, and values – develop into durable tendencies and an emotional and self-evident frame of reference. Social positions become dispositions, and cultural meanings become personal beliefs. That is how a sense of ethnic identity develops, and people cannot simply do away with the initial attachments and 'habitus' (Bourdieu 1987) which they have developed at a tender age.
>
> (2005: 86–7)

Similarly, Horowitz argues that 'the ethnic group is family writ large'. Often, the emotional attachments to actual family and relatives are transferred to the larger ethnic category or community. Narratives and mythologies of blood and belonging importantly fortify these identifications. Symbolic references to kinship, ancestry and a common history create a 'moral community' characterized by reciprocity, trust and a sense of solidarity. As we will see in the following chapter, social psychologists working with social identity theory (SIT) are particularly interested in how these processes of in-group solidarity at the same time create out-group exclusion, and how, in certain cases, this leads to hostility and violence.

A second reason why anthropologists argue that ethnic attachments are appealing and powerful is that ethnicity can provide an answer to fundamental problems of human existence. As Benedict Anderson explained for the case of the nation, ethnic attachments answer to people's need to belong, to have a place in the world, a sense of destiny, immortality and continuity:

> If nation-states are widely conceded as to be 'new' and 'historical' the nations to which they give political expression always loom out of an immemorial past, and, still more important, as gliding into a limitless future. It is the magic of nationalism to turn chance into destiny. With Debray we might say, 'Yes, it is quite accidental that I am born French; but after all, France is eternal'.
>
> (Anderson 1991: 11–12)

A powerful component of ethnic belonging is the way it is expressed and celebrated collectively. Marches, parades and memorial ceremonies allow people to 'join in' and symbolically and visually mark themselves as part of a larger, but limited, whole. For the case of Northern Ireland, a young loyalist, referring to the annual Orange march on 12 July, expressed the 'magic of nationalism' as follows:

> Whenever my father, God forbid, everybody has to die, whenever my father leaves and dies … If I am walking the 12th [July] march … I can say: I can remember 40 years ago, my father and me walking down here together, at a march here.[10]

It is the emotional power of ethnic attachments and the depth of their historical meanings which is at the core of culture-orientated approaches to ethnicity and ethnic conflict. Without taking these into account, any analysis of ethnic war is unlikely to be convincing.

Here it is necessary to position the notion of ethnic belonging into the larger context of state and nation building.

Ethnicity and nationhood

Many groups in contemporary conflict appeal to ancient nations and states, to traditions and territorial claims of ancestors, in whose name war is fought and legitimated. On a pro-Sinhalese website a Sri Lankan nationalist claims that 'the sovereign country of Heladiva (Sri Lanka) is the motherland of the Sinhela. The Sinhela nation possess a written history of 2,500 years and an unwritten history of 30,000 years on the island.' We are so used to having a national identity, and belonging to a nation, that the division of humanity into a world of separate nation-states seems to be the natural order of things. The idea of the nation, and hence the idea of nationalism, is soaked in the obvious, in casualness and naturalness. There is a rich body of literature, however, which contests the commonsensical view of the nation as an ancient and natural way of classifying men. Authors such as Ernest Gellner (1983), Benedict Anderson (1991) and Eric Hobsbawm (1990) but also historians such as Patrick Geary (2002) confront us with quite the opposite. They point out that, in fact, nationalism, defined by Gellner (1983: 1) as 'primarily a political principle which holds that the national and political unity should be congruent' is actually a recent phenomenon, and can be traced back to political and socio-economic transformations in eighteenth- and nineteenth-century Europe. Due to complex, but contingent, transformations such as the rise of capitalism, technological innovation, Reformism, bureaucracy and the standardization of certain languages, important changes took place in the organization of power. These changes allowed for the rise of the modern state system, where the nation became a suitable replacement for the dynastic realm and religious community. This is not the place to discuss the origins of state and nation building and nationalism. Suffice it to say that claims made by contemporary groups in conflict are rooted in this larger political repertoire of national self-determination, which itself finds its origin in modernity, in particular the 1919 Declaration of Self-determination of Versailles. Since that time, the belief that every nation, generally understood as a 'people', deserves to have its own state is widely seen as legitimate. The nationalist adagio 'let all nations have their own roofs, and let all of them refrain from including non-nationals under it' finds resonance in many parts of the world (see box 1.1 on nationalist nightmares).[11] In this discussion the difference between nation and ethnic group is not always clear. Some authors make a distinction between a 'civic nation' and an 'ethno-nation'. Whereas the civic nation is defined as a group of people with a 'shared culture', open to all who are willing to assimilate into this shared culture, the ethno-nation is open only to those who are defined as sharing the same (primordially defined) ethnic ties. Others point at territorial claims in distinguishing the ethnic group from the nation. Nations, as opposed to ethnic groups, in this definition, are people who exercise, or hope one day to exercise, sovereignty over a given territory (Danforth 1995: 14). This would imply that, strictly speaking, an ethnic group turns into a nation as soon as members of the group seek a degree of sovereignty. Whereas the helpfulness of such a divide is contested, it is clear that part of the distinctive emotional and political attractiveness of ethnicity is that it can serve as a vehicle to claim group rights and self-rule. Ethnicity matters because the modern nation-state is built on ethno-national principals of political legitimacy.[12]

Box 1.1: Nationalist nightmares

In *Nations and Nationalism* (1983) Ernest Gellner defines nationalism as 'primarily a political principle which holds that the national and the political unit should be congruent' (1983: 1). The nationalist thus dreams of having the boundaries of the nation ('the people') coincide with the boundaries of the state. There is a variety of ways in which the nationalist principle can be violated:

1. The political boundaries of a state can fail to include all members of the nation. This is the case with Serbs living in Kosovo or Croatia. The nationalist reaction to this can be either to bring nationals back into the territorial boundaries of the state, or to change the territorial boundaries in such a way that nationals are included (irredentism).
2. The political boundaries of the state include all members but also include some 'non-nationals' (migrants, minorities). History has seen many different 'solutions' to this violation of the nationalist principle: forced assimilation (non-nationals are forced to become part of the 'shared culture' of the nation, this is also called 'civic nationalism'), but also expulsion, ethnic cleansing and genocide.
3. The rulers of the political unit belong to a nation other than that of the majority of the ruled. This is often called the 'nationalist worst nightmare'. Examples are the Hutu majority ruled by the Tutsi minority in Rwanda, or the Singhalese majority placed in an inferior position vis-à-vis the Tamil minority under British colonial rule.
4. A combination or complication of (parts of the) above scenarios. For, instance, the case of a nation living in a multiplicity of states (as in the case of Kurdistan, the Yugoslavia wars of the 1990s).

The above categorizations may appear clear and orderly. The social constructivist approaches discussed in this chapter, evidently, contest this. They aim to explain and understand the complex and messy processes and mechanisms defining 'units' and 'boundaries'. How and why do people imagine themselves as part of a nation, or are categorized as such by others? How and why do groups engage in a struggle for their own state? Who is drawing the boundaries between nationals and non-nationals? Who decides who is in and out? When does a minority become part of the majority? When does an outsider become an insider, and the other way around? These are some of the core questions this field aims to address.

Conclusions

We have looked at a selection of theoretical approaches that aim to understand the connection between ethnic identity and violence through an emphasis on processes of identity group formation and group attachment. The debate between different approaches to ethnic violent conflict is often conducted in an either/or fashion. The first main controversy is that between primordialism and constructivism. Whereas scholars recognize the importance to grapple with primordialism as 'category of practice', it is nevertheless dismissed as a 'category of analysis' (Brubaker and Cooper 2000). By claiming that identities are perennial, objective and timeless, and as such inherently conflictual, primordialism 'simply assumes, rather than explains, the link between who one is and what one does' (King 2004: 435). It is because of this emphasis on human action as predetermined and set that I suggest putting primordialism in the upper left quadrant of the Hollis matrix. Inasmuch as primordialism is rejected, constructivist understandings of ethnic war have proliferated. There is convincing evidence that social identities are made, not begotten, and that violence itself can play an important role in the cementing of social identities. Epistemologically, this way of thinking finds its roots in social constructivism and phenomenology (see, for instance, Berger and Luckmann 1967). It clearly sits at the 'interpretative' side of the Hollis matrix in arguing that we construct reality through social interaction. Our everyday realities are socially constructed systems of knowledge and meaning that 'thingify' over time, and that are often taken for granted by group members. It is hence through this system of 'thingification' or 'institutionalization' that meaning is embedded in society. In phenomenology, the role of the academic is to 'de-construct', and to question our way of looking at and our way of being in the world. An important aspect of the constructivist approach to ethnic war is that the group animosities legitimating war are seen as socially constructed, implying that, at least theoretically, there is room for deconstruction and reconstruction. Hence, ethnic war is by no means inevitable, or 'natural'. Wars are produced, they are made to happen, and because of that, they can also be unmade.

It is on the matter of 'how wars are made' that constructivist approaches diverge. We see scholars who understand ethnic violence as *elite* driven and those who emphasize ethnic violence as *mass* driven. This is the second main controversy that runs through this chapter. This elite–mass divide can also be framed as the difference between *instrumentalism* and *culturalism:* between those explanations that see ethnic violent conflict as primarily politically *functional* and those that emphasize conflicts as socially *meaningful.* Let us turn to the three 'book questions' as a way to outline the differences between instrumentalism and culturalism.

What makes a group? How and why does a group resort to violence? How and why do they (not) stop?

Instrumentalist views understand both ethnicity and 'ethnic violence' as functional: as a political strategy and a tool to acquire power. Scholars applying this perspective are likely to answer the first book question by stating that the (ethnic) group results from social and political processes of boundary drawing and maintenance. The answer to the second question on how and why a group resorts to violence is more ambiguous. There is agreement that violence is seen as deliberate and orchestrated and the key to group boundary drawing. Views differ, however, on whether violence is instigated by predatory elites seeking power, or whether it is an outcome of complex and multi-levelled dynamics of interaction. When it comes to the third question, the instrumentalist approach, by implication, holds that (ethnic) war continues as long as the main actors continue to reach their objectives, indeed, as long as war is functional. Instrumentalist approaches aim to explore the determinants of what ethnic violence is 'really' about. By carefully tracking strategic action and identity politics they aim to demonstrate how power is acquired and reproduced. As we have seen, it is the portrayal of elite–mass relations that has given rise to criticism. In particular, elite theory is critiqued for attributing too much power to the machinations of predatory elites and for portraying the masses as pawns in a propagandistic conspiracy (see: King 2004).

Ontologically, elite theory takes an individualist stance by placing its 'elites' in Hollis' lower right box: as shrewd and purposeful agents, with the capacity to initiate change. Conversely, its 'masses', are seen as passive and slavishly obedient rule followers (and hence as living upstairs: in the upper right quadrant of our matrix). As we stated earlier, authors such as Brass, Kalyvas and Keen reject this dichotomy and see wars as produced by a more diverse and complicated set of actors, all trying to achieve their objectives.

Approaches focusing on meaning take a more culturalist or ethno-symbolic stance. Although these approaches largely embrace the constructivist approach to ethnicity, they tend to address more importance to *content* than to boundaries. Ethnicity and ethnic violence are seen as primarily emerging from ethnic group content, such as hostile mass attitudes and ethnic mythologies. Ethnic attachments are seen as primary socializations and as having a high emotional value. Individuals are portrayed as strongly embedded within cultural contexts. Much less focus is put on how ethnic categories are formed, contested and policed. The answer to what makes a group is hence less straightforward and, as has been said, rather content-driven. It is common myths of origins and shared memories of collective experiences of successive generations that hold the ethnic collective together. Certain groups are prone to violence because they have cultures of hostility and predatory myths vis-à-vis others. Because of the emphasis on culture as 'doing things', this way of thinking is at times accused of essentialism. Ontologically, culturalism and ethno-symbolism position the actor as the sum of his roles in the normative structure of society, and hence most comfortable in Hollis' upper right box.

Evidently, in their specific ways both instrumentalist and culturalist approaches to ethnicity and violence help us unravel the complex dynamics of interaction that characterizes violent conflict. Smaje (1997: 310) argues that 'approaches to ethnicity which do not address both its depth of historical meaning and its contemporary functionality are unlikely to be convincing'. The question is hence not whether or not these approaches should be combined, but rather how to go about this. Considering that instrumentalism and culturalism start from such different ontological positions on the critical causes of ethnic violence, can we synthesize these approaches and escape 'theoretical stacking'? Simply put, can we fix the elite–mass and structure–agency divide that runs through this chapter or should we simply accept it? We will revisit, and deal with, this question later in the book. For now, the best we can do is conclude that from a social constructivist position violence is a political strategy to create and maintain group boundaries that are politically functional and socially meaningful.

In the next chapter we remain focused on group processes, but will move from anthropological foci on boundaries and content to socio-psychological ideas on in-group love and out-group hate.

Table A

Ontology/Epistemology	**Explaining (positivist)**	**Understanding (interpretative)**
Structuralism	Primordialism	Ethno-symbolism Culturalism
Individualism		Elite theory

Further reading

Barth, Fredrik (1998) [1969] *Ethnic Groups and Boundaries: The Social Organisation of Cultural Difference*, Long Grove, IL: Waveland Press.

Baumann, Gerd (1999) *The Multicultural Riddle: Rethinking National, Ethnic and Religious Identities*, London and New York: Routledge.

Berger, Peter and Thomas Luckmann (1967) *The Social Construction of Reality: A Treatise in the Sociology of Knowledge*, Harmondsworth: Penguin Books.

Brubaker, Rogers (2004) *Ethnicity without Groups*, Cambridge, MA: Harvard University Press.

Drakulic, Slavenka (1993) *The Balkan Express*, New York: W.W. Norton & Co.

Eriksen, Thomas Hylland (1993) *Ethnicity and Nationalism: Anthropological Perspectives*, London: Pluto Press.

Horowitz, Donald (1985) *Ethnic Groups in Conflict*, Berkeley: University of California Press.

Wimmer, Andreas (2008) 'The Making and Unmaking of Ethnic Boundaries: A Multilevel Process Theory', *American Journal of Sociology* 113 (4): 970–1022.

Recommended documentaries

We Are All Neighbours (Tone Bringa, Granada TV, 1993).
Blood and Belonging: Journeys into the New Nationalism (Michael Ignatieff, BBC, 1993).
The Death of Yugoslavia (Norma Percy, BBC, 1995).

2   On love and hate

Social identity approaches to inter-group violence

The field of violent conflict studies revolves around a set of rather unnerving questions about what ordinary human beings are capable of in settings of war. Why are people prepared to die for the notion of a 'mother country', a nation or an ethnic group? What moves people to fight their neighbours, city members or acquaintances in the name of ethnic or religious identity? What is it that has to happen to ordinary people to make them support or even commit atrocities against people they have lived with peacefully for decades? Both from an analytical and commonsensical point of view, understanding the social psychology aspect of this problem seems crucial. In the previous chapter we looked at group formation and attachment as possible sources of violent action. We have seen instrumentalist explanations focusing on the seemingly cold blooded and calculated crafters of group violence, who are in it for gain and power. And we addressed the emotional force of group belonging as at the base of violent conflict. In this chapter we remain focused on the emotional power of group attachments, on 'in-group love' and 'out-group hate' as propelling violent conflict, but now through the lens of social identity approaches. These hold that although analyses of elite machinations, power interests and resource deprivation are undoubtedly important to understand conflict, they do not represent the whole story. What is argued for is that violent conflict is not likely to occur in the absence of an escalatory process of *identity group dynamics*. This chapter discusses a selection of social identity approaches that examine the connection between in-group formation and out-group hate, hostility and violence. The assumption underlying social identity approaches is that group violence is inherently related to a set of rather fundamental human needs, implying that violence between groups may result from almost inevitable social automata. This position stands in stark contrast to the earlier discussed constructivist view on group conflict as actively produced and politically constructed.

Us and them: social categorization and its consequences

At the base of many socio-psychological theories of group conflict lies a number of commonsensical assumptions: people have a universal and fundamental need to *categorize*, they have a need to *belong* and they have a basic need to a *secure sense of self*: this is often referred to as the 'identity impulse'.

We all have a need to form descriptions of the world as a way to try and figure out what is going on. This is our 'cognitive imperative': the human need to impose order on the world by mental processes. As such, we form categories of description: both physically and socially. We can make distinctions between tables and chairs, apples and pears, rivers and oceans, but we also classify people by means of certain prototypes: 'child', 'adult', 'male', 'female'. Often, the categorizations we stick to cannot be articulated easily, since they are typically non-conscious. In social psychology, this tendency to classify the social world is seen as a cognitive process that is underpinned by a natural need for order and simplification. According to Tajfel (1981: 132):

> Stereotypes arise from processes of categorization: they introduce simplicity and order where there is complexity and nearly random variation. They can help us to cope only if fuzzy differences between groups are transmitted into clear ones, or new differences created where none exist.

Social categories, however, are not merely cognitive concepts that help individuals to make sense of their social world. They are also evaluative and emotional (Tajfel 1981: 229).[1] As soon as people identify with a group, that group becomes the basis for thinking, feeling and acting (Verkuyten 2007: 350). 'Categorizing of the self as an in-group member implies assimilation of the self to the in-group category prototype and enhanced similarity to other in-group members' (Brewer 2001: 20). This process of self-categorization lays the groundwork for further social differentiation (Turner et al. 1987). Social psychologists working in the tradition of social identity are interested in the *consequences of social categorization*. Since the 1980s, social identity approaches have developed into an influential theoretical perspective on the collective self and inter-group processes (e.g. Robinson 1996; Abrams and Hogg 1998). Research experiments, mostly laboratory-based, have focused on issues such as stereotyping, prejudice and discrimination, self-conception, uncertainty reduction, multiple categorization and diversity (for an overview see Hogg 2006). In this chapter, we will only discuss a specific selection of social identity approaches that deal with inter-group violent conflict. These hold that our human need for social categorization, together with the value and emotional significance attached to group membership, is crucial to explain inter-group violence. The first approach, which finds its base in social identity theory (SIT), argues that people identify with groups as a way to feel good about themselves (the 'in-group positivity principle'). Group violence becomes likely if the members of a group feel they can only achieve this positivity by degrading an out-group. The second approach, Brewer's theory of optimal distinctiveness, argues it is rather our need for a secure identity that, if endangered, may cause hatred of and disgust towards 'the other', and a readiness to use violence. We will discuss the two theories here.

Social identity theory

Although social identity theory is largely known for its dependence upon laboratory based evidence, it was the horrors of WWII that inspired its 'founding father' Henri Tajfel (1919–82) to develop his social psychological approach to inter-group conflict. Tajfel's experiences as a Polish Jew in Europe during the rise of the Nazis, WWII, the Holocaust and the post-war relocation of displaced Europeans shaped his interest in prejudice, discrimination and inter-group conflict. Tajfel rejected what he called the 'blood-and-guts model' of inter-group relations that dominated social psychology in the post World War era with its focus on human instinct (biology) and the unconscious (psychoanalysis) as important drivers of social group relations. His principal argument was that collective phenomena such as inter-group violence cannot be reduced to the individual's drives, instincts or personality traits, but must be understood as resulting from the individual's membership in social groups. Inter-group relations cannot be properly understood without the help of their cognitive aspects. Tajfel, like Sherif (1961), believed that social forces configure individual action. The challenge for social psychology is to theorize how this happens (Hogg 2006: 112). At the core of social identity theory is the idea that individuals seek to reduce uncertainty and achieve a secure and positive sense of self through their participation in groups. This human tendency results in the formation of in-groups and out-groups. Of relevance for the study of inter-group violence is the way social identity theory highlights how social categorization sets in motion an escalatory dynamics of group *comparison*, group *competition* and ultimately, group *hostility*. The idea that there is a connection between group formation and inter-group violence is certainly not new. In his classic book *Folkways* (1906) the social Darwinist William Graham Sumner introduced the term 'ethnocentrism' as a syndrome whereby:

> a differentiation arises between ourselves, the we-group, or in-group, and every-body else, or the others-group, out-groups. The insiders in a we-group are in rela-tion of peace, order, law, government, and industry, to each other. Their relation to all outsiders, or other-groups, is one of war and plunder, except so far as agree-ments have modified it ... The relation of comradeship and peace in the we-group and that of hostility and war towards others-groups are correlative to each other ... Ethnocentrism is the technical name for this view of things in which one's own group is the center of everything, and all others are scaled and rated with reference to it. ... Each group nourishes its own pride and vanity, boasts itself superior, exalts its own divinities, and looks with contempt on outsiders.
>
> (1906: 12–13)

This view of the human tendency to 'cleave and compare', as proposed by Sumner, gave impetus to a series of experiments carried out in the 1950s by Leon Festinger and later by Tajfel and his collaborators at Bristol university, and formed the base for social identity theory. Sumner's four progressive elements of ethnocentrism, although contested, are still considered the backbone of many theories of inter-group violent conflict. From Sumner's text the following four principles can be discerned (Brewer 2001: 19):

1. The *social categorization principle*. Human beings have a fundamental universal need to categorize their social world: human social groups are organized into discrete in-group–out-group categories.
2. The *in-group positivity principle*. Individuals value their in-groups positively and maintain positive, cooperative relationships with members of the in-group.
3. The *inter-group comparison principle*. In-group positivity is enhanced by social comparison with out-groups in which in-group attributes and outcomes are evaluated as better than or superior to those of out-groups.
4. The *out-group hostility principle*. Relationships between in-group and out-groups are characterized by antagonism, conflict and mutual contempt.

Sumner claimed that these four elements cohere into a pattern that is universally characteristic of inter-group relations. Indeed, the assumption that human beings have a natural and universal need for identity and belonging, expressed in group attachments (step one), and that humans have a need for positive self-esteem (step two), underlies many contemporary socio-psychological theories of inter-group relations. But whereas the first two principles are generally seen as fundamental and universal, there is considerable debate on the shift from step three to four, that is, from group comparison to group hostility, as either inherent to a universal process of group formation, or requiring specific and additional conditions. Tajfel and Turner, for instance, insisted on bringing in 'competition' as an additional element to explain the shift to group violence. We will here discuss the steps one by one: comparison, competition, hostility.

Comparison and the narcissism of minor difference

As stated, one of the central findings of SIT is that humans seek a secure sense of self by striving to achieve or to maintain a positive social identity. People have a deep-seated cognitive imperative to perceive their in-groups as favourable, even if the in-group categorization is imposed on them quite randomly in the setting of a laboratory experiment (see box 2.1. on the minimal group paradigm). What is implied, is that the roots of prejudice and stereotyping lie in rather ordinary processes of thinking, and in particular in processes of categorizing. In Sumner's words, we all want to 'boast ourselves superior'. But how is this positivity established, particularly in 'real life' settings?

Box 2.1: The minimal group paradigm

Based on laboratory experiments Tajfel and his associates found out that individuals try to achieve in-group positivity by favouring their in-group members and disfavouring out-group members, even if they have been assigned to a group based on trivial differences, no differences and even at random. Simply put, their 'minimal group paradigm' experiments pointed out that what produces group feeling and discrimination is a simple division into categories. It takes a boundary to make a group. A second, and perhaps even more remarkable finding relates to the nature of the discrimination practised by the groups under study. The research design was such that it permitted participants to give out rewards in any of three ways. Participants could (1) maximize the joint profit of both in-group and out-group; (2) maximize the total profit of the in-group; or (3) maximize the difference between the profit of the in-group and that of the out-group. Clearly, the act of apportionment did not involve any necessary conflict of interests, for positive-sum outcomes were possible. Nevertheless, participants were not interested in the option of joint (both in-group and out-group) profit. The outcome that appealed most was that of maximal differentiation between groups, even when this implied less profit for the in-group than they otherwise could have obtained. In other words, participants were willing to sacrifice greater profit in absolute terms in order to achieve a relatively higher profit for the in-group as compared to the out-group. Building upon these findings, Tajfel and his colleagues (1981) argued that not only does in-group loyalty take hold quickly, it also produces a desire for relative group advantage, even if this implies sacrificing economic gain. These findings importantly cast doubt on materialist, resource-based theories of conflict (see Tajfel 1981; and Horowitz 2001).

An important component of SIT is Sumner's comparison principle: we assess our status by comparing ourselves with others. However, standards of evaluation are not absolute or clear-cut, and positivity is mostly relative: we can only be 'rich' if others are 'poor', 'industrious' if others are 'lazy', 'progressive' if others are 'traditional', and 'advanced' if others are 'backward'. 'Whether one regards one's social identity positively depends, to a significant extent, upon how favourably the group(s) with which one identifies compare to other groups' (Seul 1999: 557). This process of intergroup comparison produces a competitive dynamic in which groups try to enhance their status relative to other groups. 'The attempt to achieve a comparatively superior position for the in-group, on the basis of valued dimensions, is the key factor leading to discriminatory intergroup behaviour' (Tajfel and Turner 1986: 83). For conflict analysts, this step from comparison to competition is significant, for it implies a shift to overt conflict. But let us first take a closer look at the comparison principle. As mentioned before, group members try to achieve a positive collective identity through a comparison with outsiders. Knowledge of the status of outsiders becomes important to assessing the status of the in-group. This is particularly the case when there is uncertainty about the group's social standing (Festinger 1954). This seems rather obvious. However, not just any comparison will produce the same outcome. Just as I will only boost my self-esteem as a well-trained swimmer by overtaking an equally strong (or rather: a superior) swimmer and not by beating a group of five-year olds, so do group-members have a tendency to compare themselves to *relevant* others. The relevance required is particularly interesting because it implies that the self (in-group) and other (out-group) must be perceived as similar in some sense. If indeed comparison for the purpose of enhancing (collective or individual) self-worth is only meaningful when the other is perceived as relevant for comparison, and hence in a sense similar, as social identity theory seems to imply, this importantly helps to answer the question posed at the beginning of this chapter, 'Why do neighbours turn into enemies?' It is exactly neighbours, if we mean by neighbours those people who have a lot in common, who turn against each other. The more alike people are, the more relevant they will perceive the other for the purpose of identity comparison and the more acute their possible inter-group competition. In a very different time and context, this is what Freud called the 'narcissism of minor difference'. In an article he wrote toward the end of WWI, 'The Taboo of Virginity' (1918), he noticed that 'it is precisely the minor differences in people who are otherwise alike that form the basis of feelings of strangeness and hostility between them'. Whereas originally Freud's analysis was focused on sexual differences, he later applied the idea of narcissism of minor differences to groups. Here he explains how narcissism lies at the core of antagonistic self-definitions:

> In the undisguised antipathies and aversion which people feel towards strangers with whom they have to do we may recognize the expression of self-love – of narcissism. This self-love works for the preservation of the individual, and behaves as though the occurrence of any divergence from his own particular lines of development involved a criticism of them and a demand for their alteration.
>
> (1918: 199)

In his book *The Warrior's Honor* (1999), Michael Ignatieff, extrapolating from Freud's idea of minor differences, proposes to think of ethnic nationalism as a kind of narcissism. Importantly, he points out how Freud's analysis focuses our attention on the paradoxical relation between narcissism and aggression. 'It is precisely because the differences between groups are minor that they must be expressed aggressively. The less substantial the differences between two groups the more they both struggle to portray those differences as absolute' (1999: 51). A nationalist, Ignatieff argues, takes 'minor differences' – unimportant in themselves – and transforms them into major differences: the systematic overvaluation of the self results in a systematic devaluation of the other. Often, this is a schizophrenic endeavour. As Freud pointed out, individuals pay a psychic price for group belonging: they must turn the aggressive desire to conform to the group against their own individuality. Ignatieff uses the example of villagers turning against each other during the Serb–Croat war of the early 1990s. The men on either side of the front line once were neighbours: they went to the same school, worked in the same garage, played in the same soccer team. Now they have to repress their memories of common ties and former friendships with those on the other side, and exclusively relate to each other as 'Serb' versus 'Croat'. As Ignatieff noted: 'they must do a certain violence to themselves to make the mask of hatred fit' (1999: 51). In Tajfel's (1981: 240) words, this process is called depersonalization (the next stage often being dehumanization) of the members of the out-group. In the case of the villagers, the nature of their relations shifted on the continuum from *inter-personal* (interaction between people is determined by their personal relationships and their respective individual characteristics) to *inter-group* (the behaviour of individuals towards each other is determined by their membership of different groups). Explaining how societies end up at the inter-group extreme of the continuum will importantly enhance our understanding of conflict.

Returning from the above views to the comparison principle, we note that if comparison (whether inter-personal or inter-group) serves the purpose of (uncertain) status evaluation (who is the better swimmer?) we will see competition only starts when group members view the 'other' as relevant for purposes of social comparison. Only then will they begin to try to develop a positive identity in relation to the out-group. Consequently, the better the 'other' is judged to be, the worse our self-evaluation. This is then how comparison turns to competition: positive self-evaluation can only be achieved at the expense of the other.

From competition to aggression

Social identity theory holds that although economic inequality, grievances, resource deprivation or any other incompatible group interests undoubtedly enhance our understanding of inter-group tensions, they cannot sufficiently explain the step to overt conflict. Group hostility and aggression will only occur when the subordinate group begins to view the dominant group as relevant for purposes of social comparison and begins to develop a positive relation to it. In other words, conflict is very unlikely in the absence of inter-group identity competition (Tajfel and Turner 1986). However, the step from competition to aggression is not automatic. When comparison results in a negative group evaluation, group members respond to this psychological discomfort in different ways, ranging from assimilation to violence. In order to explain this coherently, we have to bring in another component of social identity theory: the notion of belief structures (Tajfel 1981). People may engage in a variety of strategies to enhance self-esteem. The choice of strategy will depend on perceptions of the relationship between their in-group and out-group(s). The boundaries between groups may be seen as permeable or impermeable, the status differences as legitimate or illegitimate, and the nature of these differences as stable or unstable. When status differences are seen as legitimate and stable, the differences between groups are secure. If group boundaries are permeable, and if group members believe that their situation in relation to 'dominant' groups can be improved, they will try to become part of that group, and leave their 'lower status' group. In this case individuals act according to a *social mobility belief structure*. Exit from the group, however, is not always possible. This is for instance the case when social identity is based on persistent social constructions (such as for example one's skin colour, or gender), or, for many, when it involves deeply felt religious convictions or ethnic attachments. In this case of impermeable boundaries, members consider that their social identity can only be improved by changing the relationship between in-group and out-group as a whole: this then is a *social change belief structure*. So, if people feel locked up in their group, they will look for collective ways to enhance self-worth. One response is what is dubbed 'symbolic inversion' in the field of Subaltern Studies, that is, group members attempt to recast the in-group's 'negative' features into 'positive' strong points. A famous example of this is the 'black is beautiful' slogan of the African-American civil rights movement. Other examples are the ways by which many indigenous groups create new dimensions of inter-group comparison, contrasting their 'spirituality' or 'native wisdom' with the 'greed' and 'emptiness' of the urban middle-classes. Another reaction, identified by Tajfel, is clearly more activist, that is, 'to engage in social action which would lead to desirable changes in the situation' (1981: 256).[2] The most radical form of social action in response to negative group evaluation is violence: group members try to restore their self-worth by destroying or severely weakening the out-group. Again, although inter-group identity competition does not inevitably lead to group conflict, Tajfel and Turner argue that it is 'plausible to hypothesize that, when a group's action for positive distinctiveness is frustrated, impeded, or in any way actively prevented by an out-group, this will promote overt conflict and hostility between the groups' (1986: 23). Importantly, their research points out that this may be so even in the absence of incompatible material group interests.

As soon as inter-group identity competition provokes overt conflict, an escalatory dynamics is evident. People perceive attacks on in-group members as an attack on themselves, and start to act accordingly, enhancing processes of group closure and 'group think'. 'This escalatory dynamic, and the continually increasing consolidation and intensification of individual and group identities that it produces, may partially explain the high degree of intractability that seems to characterize so many conflicts' (Seul 1999: 558).

The same, but different: Brewer's theory of optimal distinctiveness

In her work on inter-group conflict, Marilynn Brewer argues for a careful re-examination of the steps that lead from 'in-group love' to 'out-group hate'.

She agrees with SIT that it is the social and psychological processes of in-group attachment and loyalty that lay the groundwork for inter-group conflict, and not competition over resources, or any other realistic, material, objective incompatibility. She has, however, a different view on how these processes of group formation escalate into out-group aggression. Brewer claims that there are a number of steps to take before social categorization and group competition turn into hate and hostility. She focuses on the role of emotions in inter-group contexts to explain the step to violence: in particular the combination of feelings of *contempt* and *anger*.

Brewer begins her analysis by questioning the explanation given by Tajfel (1978) and Turner (1975) that individuals are motivated to categorize, and, more importantly, to identify themselves as members of a social group in the interest of enhanced self-esteem. In other words, she critiques the idea that group membership is the consequence of a search for self-esteem. Brewer argues that research on the causal role of self-esteem in social identification is far from convincing. Group evaluation is not always positive, or self-aggrandizing, and identification with the group often involves assimilation of group failures as well as successes. There is even good reason to believe that the causal relation works in the opposite direction, that is, attachment of the self to the group leads to a positive evaluation of the group, and not the other way around. So, if in-group identification is largely independent of in-group status, then motives other than the self-esteem principle must be implicated in why individuals would attach (some measure of) the self to the fate of a collective. As an alternative, Brewer proposes the 'optimal distinctiveness theory' (1991, 2001). At the core of this theory is the recognition that 'group living' represents the fundamental survival strategy that characterizes the human species. Her argument is that humans evolved, not as isolated individuals or even in families, but as members of larger social groups. In order to be able to cooperate and learn from each other, people had to trust other humans. However, simply trusting all others would be risky and even dangerous. As a consequence, humans developed a predisposition to trust only their in-group members. Since all humans act according to this universal tendency, this gives rise to in-group–out-group formation. Building on this evolutionary perspective, and the sameness–uniqueness dichotomy of the identity concept (see chapter one), Brewer argues that human beings have two powerful social motives: they have a need for inclusion (satisfied by in-group assimilation) and an opposing need for differentiation (satisfied by inter-group contrast). Hence, optimal distinctiveness theory argues that social identification is the product of the search for inclusion and differentiation, rather than a consequence of the search for self-esteem (Brewer 2001).

> When a person feels isolated or detached from any larger social collective, the drive for inclusion is aroused; on the other hand, immersion in an excessively large or undefined social collective activates the search for differentiation and distinctiveness. ... Groups that have clear categorical boundaries satisfy the need for inclusion (intragroup assimilation) at the same time that they provide a basis for satisfying the need for differentiation (inter-group contrast). ... In-groups that meet these simultaneous conditions become an integral part of the individual's sense of self and the basis for a secure and stable self-concept.
>
> (2001: 22)

From this perspective there are two fundamental sources of potential threat to a person's social identity. First, loss of a secure sense of inclusion and, second, loss of distinctiveness. The first threat stems from feelings of marginalization from the in-group. For a variety of reasons, a person may fear he or she is 'left out' of the desired in-group and suffers from a loss of a secure sense of fit. An effective strategy to re-establish secure inclusion is the derogation of out-groups. By emphasizing the inferiority of the others, the contrast between 'us' and 'them' increases. This then may enhance the relative similarity between the self and the in-group and restore a sense of inclusion. Emphasizing the role of emotions in group relations, Brewer thus argues that 'threats to inclusion are predicted to heighten feelings of moral superiority, intolerance of difference, and concomitant emotions of contempt and disgust toward relevant out-groups' (Brewer 2001: 32). Contempt and disgust, however, are not enough to produce violent conflict. They may feed negative discrimination against the 'other', but generally these kinds of emotion are associated with avoidance rather than attack. Groups may live in a state of mutual contempt without ever going to war over their differences. A more unstable situation occurs, however, if feelings of fear and anger arise. These emotions generally flare up when the second fundamental social human need is in danger: the need for secure differentiation. This may occur in situations of social change that involve (the prospect of) close contact, integration with, or dominance by the out-group. These changes may lead to a fear of invasion, and propel emotions of anxiety and anger, which have a tendency to lead to actual acts of aggression and violence towards the 'invaders'. Brewer's theory hence suggests that:

> the combined emotions of contempt (engendered by moral superiority in the service of secure identity) and anger (engendered by fear of invasion and loss of distinctiveness) provide the potent ingredients that are sufficient to kindle hatred, expulsion, and even ethnic cleansing.
>
> (2001: 33)

In addition, Brewer refers to a number of escalatory factors, which although not fundamental, still may exacerbate the dynamics leading up to out-group hate. These are, for instance, political elite's triggering of group hostility, group culture and the level of social structural complexity of a certain society (that is, the level of social segregation or diversity, the extent to which people make out part of a variety of social categories). She emphasizes that any relationship between in-group differentiation and out-group hostility is 'progressive and contingent rather than necessary or inevitable' (2001: 35). Nonetheless, critics of the theory of optimal distinctiveness state that it does seem to attach a certain measure of naturalness (and hence, inevitability) in the lead-up to inter-group violent action. Below we will look at a number of critical reflections on SIT and the theory of optimal distinctiveness.

Critique: a propensity for group hostility?

The aim of this book is to review a selection of prominent research traditions of violent conflict by tracing their underlying assumptions, their ontological and epistemological stances, and to identity the affinities and contradictions between them. The agenda of the book inevitably involves having to *simplify* the theories under discussion to a certain extent. It is impossible to do justice to the rich complexity and variation within the research traditions considered here. While simplifying one always runs the risk of *caricaturing*. When it comes to discussing social identity theories of conflict I have noticed a certain temptation among its critics to portray these as reductionist, a-historical, a-political or out-and-out social Darwinist. Although of course a theory should be assessed by its overall explanatory power, it is important to recognize that different theoretical approaches revolve around different puzzles. In addition, our assessment is helped by specifying what a theory does, but also what it *does not* intend to explain or understand.

Social identity approaches to violent conflict paint a rather grim picture of the human collective. Although it is repeatedly stressed that inter-group violence and hatred is neither inevitable nor necessary, it is implied that human groups have some sort of in-built propensity for identity group hostility. Dressed down, social identity approaches do tell us that it is the human need for social identity differentiation that, not always, but at times, produces an escalatory group dynamics – from comparison, to competition – that leads groups into violent conflict. It is this naturalness that again forms the basis of the theory of optimal distinctiveness. If group living is the 'fundamental survival strategy characterizing the human species' then it is only a logical impulse for people to rise to anger and hatred if they feel their sameness and uniqueness are under attack. It is not surprising that critics take issue with the 'nature argument' of social identity approaches, for the implications of this way of theorizing are significant. Through the lens of social identity approaches phenomena such as xenophobia, prejudice and discrimination seem to stem primarily from a set of natural impulses. But how valuable are these laboratory findings for the analysis of actual violent conflict? Surely, real world violence is more complex than this? Why and when do certain identities become pervasive in conflict? How do some forms of identity come to dominate others? Why and when do people 'perceive' they are threatened, or invaded? Many conflicts break out in societies with a high social structural complexity; with cross-cutting category distinctions. We make out part of many different social categories and groups (professional, political, ethnic, cultural, religious, regional). How and when and why do mono-identity group formations begin? Or, more concretely, in the case of our school-going, soccer-playing, befriended Bosnian villagers: how and why did they begin to depersonalize their neighbours along ethnic lines? How was it that ethnic identification became so pervasive in the post Tito, post-communist era? And even if we accepted that group hostility stems from identity insecurity, how then do these emotions transform into *sustained* violent conflict? Let us turn to the core questions of the book as a way to organize the discussion on the explanatory power of social identity approaches.

What makes the group?

Social identity approaches define the group cognitively: in terms of people's self-conception as group members (Hogg 2006). Although social identity approaches aim to provide a link between the individual and group levels of analysis, they are individualistic in orientation, focusing on the thoughts and feelings of individuals, and the ways the individual interacts with his or her social environment. The group, then, seen from a social identity perspective, emerges from individual cognitive processes which stem from the human need for consistency, order and simplification, and in some interpretations, positive self-imagery. It is these individual cognitive imperatives that form the core of the approach. It is not the task of social identity theorists to study why people are categorized in certain ways, but rather to explain what possible social dynamics result from group attachments, and what are the forces driving this dynamic (e.g. the need for categorization, the need for self-esteem and the need for optimal distinctiveness). From this we can understand that the social identity perspective does not aim to be able to answer most of the above questions. When it comes to explaining the

Serb–Croat violence waged by villagers in Bosnia, social identity scholars most probably would say: we cannot explain the how or why of the cleavage, we can only explain the socio-psychological processes that make people identify, attach and engage in a social dynamics of identity outbidding at the expense of the other. Hence, the approach is not interested in the politics of identity group formation and boundary drawing, as are for instance the political anthropological theories of ethnicity discussed in chapter one. It is thus important to recognize that it is not considered the job of the social identity theorist to explain the origin, development or content of the social group or category. Rather, the social psychologist takes these as point of departure and focuses on the consequences of group categorizations. This scholarly division of labour is clearly explained by Tajfel:

> The content of the categories to which people are assigned by virtue of their social identity is generated over a long period of time within a culture, the origin and development of these ideas are a problem for the social historian rather than for the social psychologist. The task of the social psychologist is to discover how these images are transmitted to individual members of a society.
>
> (1981: 134)

In a similar way, Hogg and McGarty acknowledge that although the incorporation of social context is considered important to social identity theory, it is only mediated through the individual's mind: 'While the reality of social groups and institutions is accepted as matter of course, it is nevertheless the case that we as social psychologists are concerned with such institutions to the extent to which they are psychologically represented' (1990: 24). Hence, the 'why' of identity group formation is answered by looking at the human need for categorization, order and self-esteem (or, for instance, optimal distinctiveness). Not by looking at the historical and political contexts that generate exclusionist groupings, or the political functions served by group formation. If we try to visualize this difference on an imaginary conflict map we see how instrumentalist theories of group conflict are intrigued by how and by whom the boundaries of the group 'balloon' are drawn/erased (focusing on power, violence, discourse), whereas social identity scholars are interested in what happens within the group balloon: the cognitive, evaluative and emotional processes that 'hold' the balloon together.

How and why does a group resort to violence?

Social identity approaches emphasize how the individual's need for social identity differentiation lies at the core of a series of escalatory group dynamics that, in some cases, may lead to inter-group violence. Ultimately, group aggression is seen as a collective coping strategy in the service of maintaining or restoring identity status. Social identity approaches aim to produce a general theory of inter-group conflict through a step-by-step elaboration of a small set of ordered hypotheses. Ontologically, the approach takes an individualist stance. It starts with the individual and aims to identify and order the cognitive, evaluative and emotional factors that set the stage for in-group attraction and out-group hostility. Epistemologically, the theory aims to 'explain' rather than 'understand' inter-group hostilities and violence: it seeks to build a socio-psychological theory of inter-group relations from which predictions can be made about certain uniformities in the behaviour and attitudes of members of some social groups (or categories) towards other social groups (or categories). Through a careful testing of a series of hypotheses in laboratory settings, researchers aim to produce general explanations of group behaviour. The underlying view here is of human behaviour as essentially predictable, and of actors as acting upon a set of psychological laws.

The focus on individuals helps clarify the deep and passionate feelings that tend to accompany acts of inter-group violence. As Horowitz argues in his classic *Ethnic Groups in Conflict*: 'The sheer passion expended in pursuing ethnic conflict calls out for an explanation that does justice to the realm of feelings. ... A bloody phenomenon cannot be explained by a bloodless theory' (1985: 140). This is indeed what social identity approaches offer: by stressing how the human need to belong may propel strong passions and emotions. But such an individualistic position also has its limitations. It tends to strip individual action away from social context, thereby assuming as universal certain sentiments, emotions and ways of thinking that might, in fact, be variable across time and place. Ontologically, the question is whether complex phenomena such as violent conflict can be analysed through recourse to such individual cognitive imperatives. The cognitive approach underlying social identity theory explains inter-group conflict as integral to the human need for consistency and simplified information processing. It leaves unanswered the question of how group hostilities are socially and politically constructed throughout time and space, and how group conflict is planned and organized. By contrast, authors such Susan Condor (1982) and Vivienne Jabri (1996) argue that the categorization of self and other is more than just a product of cognition and information processing and derives from discursive and institutional continuities. Some critics therefore point at the need to consider inter-group violent conflict as a social, rather than an individual, phenomenon. We will elaborate on this in chapter six.

Ironically, Tajfel himself is often portrayed by his students and collaborators as a fervent opponent of reductionism and 'out of context' psychology. According to John Turner (1996: 20–1):

> Tajfel's discussions of social identity theory, inter-group relations and the social functions of stereotypes show how he tried to put these ideas into practice. He also discussed the social normative character of social conduct, its relationship to socially created rules, norms and values, as a fundamental argument against reduction to biological or asocial/pre-social psychological theory. ... His general point is that human conduct is fundamentally rule-governed. People seek to act appropriately (and evaluate themselves positively) in terms of the social norms and values of their social groups and the wider society. Such norms and values derive from social systems and ideologies. Thus social conduct is not based on a 'hedonistic algebra of self-interest ... based on a few universal human drives' (Tajfel 1981: 36), as so many so-called social psychological theories seem to suppose.

Turner reminds us of the importance of reviewing and reading 'theories in context' and taking their genesis into account. One of Tajfel's aims at the time was to create a social psychology that was genuinely 'social' and capable of addressing serious social problems. His idea that ordinary cognitive processes of social categorization underlie prejudice and group hostility went against the prevailing views of the time. He refused to see group hatred and prejudice as stemming exclusively from human instincts, frustrations or personality traits as had Freud, Lorenz and Adorno before him. With this he shifted the focus to the 'normality' of collective violence. Very much in line with the findings of scholars such as Sherif (1961), Milgram (1963) and Arendt (1963), Tajfel shows that it is not the psychopaths and retarded, but largely the ordinary, plain and average who, through a series of escalatory dynamics, end up supporting or committing violence against what they perceive as the out-group. He thus importantly contributed to the discussion on the role of silent bystanders in times of war. This of course does not in any way invalidate later critiques of social identity theory as not social (or rather: political) *enough*. Tajfel emphasized the limitations of social psychology in one of his later writings, the classic *Human Groups and Social Categories* by stating that 'it would be no less than ridiculous to assert that objective rewards (in terms of money, standards of living, consumption of goods and services) are not the most important determinant of … conflicts'. Socio-psychological forms of analysis 'cannot *replace* the economic and social analysis, but must be used to *supplement* it' (1981: 223).

How and why do they (not) stop?

In purely abstract terms, and by reading social identity theory 'in reverse', we could argue that inter-group violence ends when individuals perceive that their social identity needs are met. That is, when status differences are seen as legitimate and stable, and people's needs for secure inclusion and differentiation are satisfied. In practice, of course, this makes little sense. Authors widely acknowledge that as soon as group violence sets in, and people are killed because of their identity, an escalatory dynamics will feed into an intensification of us/them divides, oscillating toward (more) hatred and protractedness. Clearly, this profoundly disrupts any chances for the restoration of secure identity. What is perhaps true for a pride of lions does not apply to humans: inter-group violent conflict is not likely to produce a new, stable group balance, at least not in the short or medium term. However, if we wanted to draw lessons from social identity approaches for the field of conflict resolution, it is this centrality of the psychological need to (re)establish secure, legitimate and stable group identities that seems most prominent. Although the approach does not provide the conflict analyst with toolkits of how to achieve this, Brewer warns us to not fall into at least one trap: the strategy of common goals. Before we turn to the conclusions, we will briefly look into the conflict resolution implications of her theory of optimal distinctiveness.

It is a much researched human tendency: intra-group cohesion is increased in the face of shared threats or common challenges. It is this finding upon which all 'team-building' and 'human resource management' courses are built: *Together Everyone Achieves More*. An extrapolation of this general finding is the widely held belief that the presence of common goals or common threats also can provide the conditions to bring *different* groups together, and so support cooperation and reduce conflict. This belief is reflected in the rhetoric of politicians in their addresses to 'the people' when faced by real or imaginary outside threats, be it tsunamis, terrorist attacks, war or 'foreign cultures'. The mantras on 'closing ranks' and 'leaving our differences behind' are well known to us. This language is also used in discussions on peace-building and reconciliation: how in a post-conflict setting hostile group relations can be 'repaired' by bringing in overarching goals, projects, even identities. Brewer (2001), however, in her work on inter-group cooperation argues for the complete opposite. She claims that the anticipation of positive interdependence (cooperative joint action) with an out-group rather *promotes* than reduces inter-group conflict and hostility. The main reason for this is the fundamental difference between dynamics of interdependence *within* and *between* groups. Within the context of the in-group, engaging the sense of trust needed for cooperative collective action is relatively easy. In an inter-group setting, however, perceived interdependence and the need for cooperative interaction make the absence of trust painfully apparent. It is exactly this sense of mutual and depersonalized trust based on common identity that is a necessary requisite for joint action. 'Without the mechanism of depersonalised trust based on common identity, the risk of exploited cooperation looms large and distrust dominates over trust in the decision structure' (2001: 33). From the perspective of the theory of optimal distinctiveness, it is thus counter-productive to try to reduce conflict by bringing in super-ordinate goals or threats: this will only propel people's fear of a loss of secure inclusion and differentiation, and produce further conflict.

When it comes to the *prevention* of inter-group conflict the approach has a perhaps more optimistic, although largely hypothetical, contribution to make. Societies that are segmented along strong and primary categorizations, such as religion or ethnicity, seem prone to dynamics of in-group favouritism and out-group hostility. Such segmentation, particularly if it is dichotomous (splitting up society into two main groups), gives rise to social comparison and perceptions of incompatible interests, and hence conflict. However, the opposite may be true as well. Societies that are more complex and differentiated along multiple dimensions may show greater conflict resilience. Their high 'social structural complexity' enhances cross-cutting category distinctions and allows individuals to be part of many cross-cutting in- and out-groups. One can, for instance, play in an orchestra with musicians of different ethnic backgrounds, go to church with people with varied occupations and income-levels, and find colleagues at work with different religions and regions of residence, and so forth. Such cross-cutting memberships make the individual less dependent upon one single in-group for the satisfaction of his or her psychological needs and less vulnerable to polarization. Returning to Freud: this complexity will perhaps make us less willing to pay the 'psychic price of group belonging', and less conformist.

Conclusion

The cognitive processes at the core of social identity approaches help us to answer the question of why ordinary people turn against each other. The approach gives us insight into why and how the individual's group attachments at times can trigger an escalatory dynamics that make in-group members accept and support violence against 'the other'. It tells us that without insight into these socio-psychological processes, any analysis of violent group conflict is incomplete. Certainly, the role of ethnic entrepreneurs, economic exploitation or ethno-symbolic mythologies is not dismissed, but violent conflict is unlikely to evolve without the support of ordinary people, acting upon a series of deep-seated cognitive imperatives. As was discussed, the transmission of laboratory findings to real life conflict is not without its hazards. Nevertheless, the ideas produced, such as the cognitive aspects of prejudice and the narcissism of minor difference, certainly add to a more comprehensive analysis of inter-group conflict. For an assessment of the complementarities, or rather, the contradictions between the various conflict theories reviewed so far, let us conclude by trying to position the social identity school in the Hollis matrix.

In contrast to culturalist understandings of the masses as passively receiving and internalizing cultural models, including categories of ethnic belonging and predatory mythologies, social identity approaches explain human conduct, including out-group aggression, as stemming from cognitive processes underpinned by the individual's need for group living, differentiation and inclusion. Whereas the former places the source of human action at the level of the normative structure of society, the latter places it at the level of the individual. So, as mentioned, ontologically, the approach takes an *individualist* stance.

Social identity approaches also differ rather fundamentally from elite theories of violence, such as constructivist instrumentalism. As we have seen in the previous chapter, an important outcome of the instrumentalist approach is that war, and the antagonistic group identities in whose name war is waged, are constructed. Wars are made to happen, and because of that, they can also be unmade, implying that war is by no means inevitable, or natural. The social world is what people make of it, and only through studying the specific ways of 'world making' from within can we understand human action (including violent action). From this interpretative stance, we as students of violent conflict are to seek the meaning of action. And since actions only derive their meaning from the shared ideas and rules of social life, we need to view them from within: through the actors' interpretation. This is called the 'double hermeneutic': to make an interpretation of an interpretation (Hollis 1994: 146). Only by studying the way in which a specific group of people produces specific meanings can scholars, in turn, make sense of their actions. By contrast, social identity theory, despite claims that the relation between social identity and inter-group violence is contingent rather than inevitable, is built on the assumption that the sources of group violence are located at the level of the individual's cognitive imperatives. This emphasis on conflict as stemming from rather predictable psychological 'laws', that can be detected by studying the uniformities in behaviour and attitude of members of groups, shows how social identity approaches fit the left column of the Hollis matrix: with its emphasis on *explaining* human action from without, rather than understanding it from within (right column). The matrix highlights how the theories discussed so far, although sharing a focus on group formation and belonging as possible sources of violent conflict, start from radically different underlying assumptions about conflict as specific and constructed versus conflict as universal and in-built. Any attempt to engage in cross-disciplinary theorizing should start from these oppositions.

Table B

Ontology/Epistemology	**Explaining (positivist)**	**Understanding (interpretative)**
Structuralism	*Primordialism*	*Ethno-symbolism* *Culturalism*
Individualism	Social Identity approaches	*Elite theory*

Further reading

Ashmore, Richard et al. (2001) *Social Identity, Intergroup Conflict, and Conflict Reduction*, Oxford: Oxford University Press.
Ignatieff, Michael (1999) 'The Narcissism of Minor Difference' in *The Warrior's Honor*, London: Vintage, pp. 34–71.

Seul, Jeffrey R. (1999) '"Ours is the Way of God": Religion, Identity, and Inter-group Conflict', *Journal of Peace Research* 36 (5): 553–69.
Tajfel, Henri (1981) *Human Groups and Social Categories*, Cambridge: Cambridge University Press.

Recommended documentaries

We Are All Neighbours (Tone Bringa, Granada TV, 1993).
A Class Divided (PBS Frontline, 1985).

3   Violence and structures

The news of 6 April 2009. The first item takes the viewer to the village of Mbyo, Rwanda. Two men, Frédérique Kazingwemo and Félix Habiyamana, look back at the Rwandan genocide, which began exactly 15 years ago. The voice over tells us that one is Hutu and the other a Tutsi, driven apart by the war. Frédérique participated in the genocide, 'I am a murderer' he admits. Félix fled to Burundi, and upon returning to his village he found out that most of his family had been killed. Now the two men are friends again. They stand close to each other, they shake hands. 'It was not our fault' they explain. 'It was the system'. The next item shifts to the banking crisis and its causes. A young banker, in front of a glass building, pitches his truth: 'it is not the individual bankers who are to blame for this, it's the system'.

Frédérique's and Félix's explanation of the genocide, and – although of little case relevance here – the banker's reaction to the financial crisis, take us back to the discussion on framing and blaming of the introductory chapter: by categorizing and labelling acts of violence (such as in Rwanda) we, intentionally or not, become engaged in discussions on blame and responsibility. Although recognizing Frédérique's role as perpetrator in the Rwandan genocide, the two men from Mbyo point out that it is the system that is to blame for the genocide, not the individual or collective agent. By implication, they state that they – both perpetrator and victim – merely followed the rules of the system: they were forced into certain positions and merely 'played their part'. Similarly, the banker points out that neither he, nor his colleagues, were responsible for the banking crisis that hit the world in 2008: they just went along with the system. These everyday observations on the distinction between 'the individual' and 'the system' bring us to a fundamental ontological divide in the social sciences between approaches that claim that human action can only be accounted for by appealing to some larger whole (structuralism) and orientations which claim that structures can only be accounted for by appeal to individual agents (individualism). Simply put, is it agency or structure that is most important to explain human action? Does the 'structure of the social system' determine the actions of individuals, or vice versa? And do these positions stand in a radical, and insoluble 'chicken-or-egg' relation to one another, or can they perhaps be complementary? Although a truly elaborate discussion of these issues is beyond the scope (and capacity) of this book, the agency–structure debate is inescapable in the study of violent conflict. Throughout the book, we will turn to insights from the philosophy of social sciences to help us position the various conflict approaches in their proper 'ontological boxes'. Roughly, we can state that agency-based approaches locate the sources of violent conflict at the level of individual agency. Structure-based approaches, by contrast, locate the causes of violent conflict in the organization of society. It is this latter category which will be at the core of this chapter on structures and violence.

In their analysis of the connection between structure and violent conflict the approaches discussed in this chapter draw on two different sociological traditions: Marxian and Durkheimian.[1] Roughly, the Marxian tradition places emphasis on the *material conditions that shape social relations*. The essence of Marxian thought is that social change is firmly rooted in material, economic conditions. Conflict, in this view, results from the inherent contradiction in the structure of the capitalist system, where those who control the means of production (the dominant class) stand in direct opposition to those whose only property is their labour time (the workers). The task of conflict analysis is to identify the main social classes and interests which emerge from the organization of production, examine the resulting conflicts of interest, and consequently, the readiness and capacity of each class and its representatives to act on its interests. By contrast, Durkheimian traditions focus on *what holds societies together*, that is, on the structure of 'social rules' that function to bring society (back) to order and social equilibrium. The classic Durkheimian idea presents society as characterized by a continuous struggle between forces of integration and forces of disintegration. Society, in this view, exerts its control over individuals through their participation in a shared consciousness. 'The totality of beliefs and sentiments common to average citizens of the same society forms a determinate system which has its own life; one may call it the collective or common conscience' (Durkheim 1933: 79). Rapid social change (e.g. industrialization, urbanization, modernization) weakens the controls and attachments which normally sustain these shared beliefs and keep people in their places. From this, Durkheim derives models of three different kinds of collective action: routine, anomic and restorative. If all is stable and a society is characterized by high levels of shared beliefs these will be sustained routinely. If shared beliefs are shaken, however, this translates into a set of undesirable results: individual disorientation, destructive social life and conflict (anomie). Disorder and conflict are thus seen as the outcome of a process in which social change weakens the system that holds people in their places. It is only through restorative collective action that societies can move back to stability and a new or renewed commitment to shared beliefs.

The structure-based approaches under review here all aim to show the interconnectedness between the organization of society and violent conflict. Conflict is explained as deriving from violence *inherent* to political, economic, cultural and geopolitical structures. The influence of the above sociological traditions can be recognized in the analysis of how the incapacity of political institutions such as the state (not society in general, as Durkheim would argue) to deal with rapid (economic) change translates into anomic collective action, but also in the Marxist idea of false consciousness as discussed by Galtung, or the references to Gramsci's views on the role of hegemonic culture in 'mainstreaming' the values of the dominant classes as commonsense values of all.

This chapter has a threefold aim. First, it discusses the work of the Norwegian sociologist Johan Galtung, one of the principal founders of the field of Peace and Conflict Studies, and in particular his notion of structural violence and the conflict triangle. Second, this chapter aims to bring to life abstract structuralism by reviewing more applied structure-based analyses that examine the interconnections between the structure of *global* systems and *local* conflict. This second part of the chapter addresses the 'political economy of violent conflict'. It examines in particular the connections between structural contradictions inherent to the modern state system, global capitalism and global governance and contemporary violent conflict. In the third and final part of the chapter, we briefly return to the role of 'framing' by means of Mark Duffield's work on the representation of the 'borderlands' and the biopolitics of the new interventionism of the post Cold War era. With this, we clearly move away from the focus on group formation and group dynamics so dominant in the previous chapters. Where, for instance, social identity theory does not incorporate historic, economic or political contexts into the analysis, to its structuralist counterparts context is everything.

Manifest violence and structural violence

I think it is safe to say that the large majority of theories that fall under the heading of Conflict Studies focus on what could be named 'manifest violence': violence as visible, instrumental and expressive action. It is this kind of violence that is generally defined as 'an act of physical hurt'. Since the violent act is visible and concrete, it is an efficient way of staging an ideological message before a public audience (Riches 1986: 11). It is the kind of 'breaking news' violence that comes to us from our television and computer screens. That both seems to fascinate and appal audiences worldwide: the suicide attacks, urban riots, precision bombings and mass murders of our times. It is the kind of violence that is performed by identifiable individuals such as Frédérique, that made Félix flee his village, and that killed his family. It is also this violence that provokes humanitarian interventions, NGO negotiation, PhD research, humanitarian aid, weapon trade and war journalism: what can be cynically referred to as 'the conflict industry'.[2] If episodes of manifest violence end this is often termed peace. Although acknowledging the importance of the study of manifest violence, structure-based approaches of violent conflict argue for a much broader understanding of violence. Manifest violence is just the *visible* component of the phenomenon. Underlying these 'acts of physical hurt' are other forms of violence, sectioned into structural (or systemic) and cultural (or symbolic). This is the violence done to people in much more diffuse and indirect ways such as the subtle forms of coercion that sustain relations of exploitation and repression.

In an influential article published in the *Journal of Peace Research* in 1969, Johan Galtung, seen by many as the founding father of Peace and Conflict Studies, argued against the empiricist and behaviourist models of his time and in favour of a radical new understanding of violence. Galtung argues that violence is built into unequal, unjust and unrepresentative social structures (imperialism, capitalism, caste society, patriarchy, racism, colonialism) and should hence be defined as a situation in which actual realizations of human beings are below their potential realizations. In a reframing from 1996 he defines violence as:

> avoidable insults to basic human needs, and more generally *life*, lowering the real levels of needs satisfaction below what is potentially possible.
>
> (1996: 197)

The difference between actual and potential needs satisfaction can be defined by the actors themselves or by others (e.g. researchers), but it can only be seen as indicative of

violence if the perceived difference is *avoidable*. Thus, if a person dies from tuberc
in the eighteenth century it would be hard to conceive of this as violence since it
have been quite unavoidable, but if he dies from it today, despite all the m
recourses available, then this is what Galtung would call structural violence. People are
caught up in structures of exploitation and repression that are harmful and damaging
to them, hence – physically – hurtful, and *violent*. With this, the terrain of conflict
research is extended substantially, including into the analysis the processes and
mechanisms that prevent people from realizing their potential, that is, the silent violence of poverty, low education, poor health and in general low life expectancy inherent
in the way societies are organized. Clearly, by drawing this new definitional boundary,
Galtung aims to politicize and bring to the fore what is largely taken for granted. By
labelling poverty and underdevelopment as violence, he is casting blame and responsibility, pointing at the underlying forces supporting and legitimizing this. He draws our
attention to violence in the normality of things, for we are so obsessed and distracted
by the spectacular forms of violence (the killing, maiming, war rape), that we fail to
address the much less visible, but massively destructive force of structural violence that
lies underneath (people dying from lack of health care, malnutrition, slavery). This
profoundly rocks the analytical boat of violent conflict studies and commonsensical
dichotomies of war versus peace. For what we hitherto recognized as a state of 'peace'
(the absence of protracted manifest violence) may actually be a state of conflict.
Through Galtung's analytical lens, peace may very well be sustained by highly
destructive forms of structural violence. He clarifies this by making the distinction
between *negative peace* and *positive peace*. Whereas negative peace is defined as the
absence of manifest violence, positive peace is defined as the overcoming of structural
(and cultural) violence as well. Slavoj Zizek in his introduction to *Violence* (2008: 2)
eloquently addresses the 'violent peace' paradox as follows:

> The catch is that subjective and objective violence cannot be perceived from the
> same standpoint: subjective violence is experienced as such against the background
> of a non-violent zero level. It is seen as the perturbation of the 'normal', peaceful
> state of things. However, objective violence is precisely the violence inherent to this
> 'normal' state of things. Objective violence is invisible since it sustains the very
> zero-level standard against which we perceive something as subjectively violent.
> Systematic violence is thus something like the notorious 'dark matter' of physics,
> the counterpart to an all-too-visible subjective violence. It may be invisible, but has
> to be taken into account if one is to make sense of what otherwise seem to be
> 'irrational' explosions of subjective violence.

It is indeed this connection between structural violence (or Zizek's systemic violence)
and the 'explosions' of manifest (subjective) violence that needs further exploration. It
is the *interconnectedness of violence* that is at the core of the approaches under review
in this chapter. Galtung's canonical 'conflict triangle' will serve as entry point.

Galtung's conflict triangle

Manifest violence is only one of three components that together form Galtung's conflict triangle. It certainly is the more spectacular and *visible* of the three and the one
that attracts most attention, but for any situation to be a conflict this 'behavioural'

(B) component must be linked to two *invisible* components: attitudes and assumptions (A) and contradiction (C). I will here explain Galtung's conflict triangle in two steps. First, we look at the triangle as a model to describe the life-cycle of conflicts. Second, we discuss how the triangle can serve as a model to grapple with the distinction between what Galtung coined 'actor conflict' and 'structural conflict', and ultimately, the relation between manifest and structural violence.

The triangle as conflict life-cycle

Conflict, according to Galtung, is a triadic construct. Only if we have A, B and C do we have fully articulated conflict. There is thus a manifest (B) and a latent side (A and C) to conflict. The *manifest*, empirical and observed side is identified by B for behaviour (violence, discrimination) and the *latent*, theoretical, inferred aspect of conflict is identified by A for attitude/assumptions (fear, prejudice) and C for contradiction. Whereas A and B speak for themselves, what Galtung means by C needs perhaps a bit more elaboration. Contradiction (C) has to involve 'something wanted', named a 'goal', and its attainment a 'goal state'. This is what Galtung identifies as the content of the conflict: 'Deep inside every conflict lies a contradiction, *something standing in the way of something else*' (1996: 70, emphasis added).

In most readings (e.g. Miall et al. 1999) Galtung's triangle is primarily seen as a model to describe the escalatory and de-escalatory dynamics of a conflict. It is emphasized how it can be used to trace flows in all six directions, starting anywhere. A conflict spiral may, for instance, start in C. Let us say someone's access to land is blocked by someone else (C). This may be experienced as frustration (A), and this frustration may lead to aggression (B). In return, aggressive behaviour may bring a new contradiction into the relation (for instance, the aggressive behaviour of the frustrated party may be incompatible with the other party's concept of happiness). Hence, we have a new C, which may give rise to a new round of attitudes and behaviours, which may lead to new contradictions and so on and so forth. Violence breeds violence, and we may see an escalatory dynamics that runs its course like a fire: only stopping when the house is burnt down. Galtung describes how the parties may burn out in the A corner from emotional exhaustion, or in the B corner from physical fatigue. However, A and B may also be restrained, and the contradiction may be superseded.

Some conflicts, however, run their course in less obvious ways. The spiral may also start in A or B. A party may have accumulated a certain aggressiveness (e.g. from bad experiences in the past) and 'when something comes along' that looks like a problem (C), this negative energy is hitched on to this contradiction, unleashing a negative conflict spiral, with newly developing A > C > B dynamics. Used in this way, the

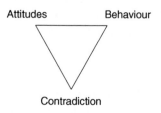

Attitudes   Behaviour

Contradiction

Figure 3.1 Galtung's conflict triangle

triangle serves as a model to describe how conflict is a dynamic process in which contradictions, attitudes and behaviours are constantly changing and influencing one another. In sum, the triangle helps us to study the life-cycle of a conflict.

There is, however, more to the triangle than conflict dynamics alone, and it is this discussion, which deals with the dialectics between the manifest and the latent components of the triangle, that brings us back to the discussion on structural violence.

Actor conflict and structural conflict

Galtung makes a distinction between *actor conflicts* and *structural conflicts*. In an actor conflict, the actor has agency, he or she is fully aware of the 'real' incompatibility underlying the conflict (C), and is ready to act with purpose. The actor is conscious of 'what is' (cognition), what (s)he wants (volition) and for that reason 'ought to be', and how (s)he feels (emotion). Simply put, A and C are fully conscious. And because A and C are clear and conscious, the actor can act (B) in accordance with them, that is, purposefully. This type of conflict is called 'actor conflict'. The metaphor here is that of the actor as driver, in control of the car, clearly seeing all obstacles in his or her way. Most conflicts, however, are not as 'conscious'. Very often, individuals have a false image of C, of what goal-states stand in the way of each other. A group of workers may for instance think that migrants are to blame for the rising levels of unemployment they experience (C) and start building up feelings of envy and hatred (A) towards them, which result in acts of aggression and discrimination (B). However, this may not be a realistic image of what is at hand. Instead, it may not be the migrants but the structure of the global economy that increasingly forces local corporations to relocate their businesses to low-tax and cheap labour regions that is causing unemployment (C). Only if they become aware of the 'real C' can the workers begin to act purposefully and try and resolve their conflict. When addressing the notion of false consciousness Galtung (1996: 74–5) explicitly refers to Marx, but takes a less objectivist view on what in the end determines the 'true' and the 'false'. What his theory seems to imply is that by trial and error ultimately a realistic image of A, B, C will appear:

> We, party to the conflict or not, construct an image of the conflict, complete with A, B, and C of ourselves and the other party. Whether this is done by the participants or by the observer, that image will always remain a hypothesis, to be tested again and again and to be revised. False consciousness means a disconfirmed hypothesis, an unrealistic image, and that can happen to all of us. ... The test lies in what happens later.

If actors are not aware of A and C, this is what Galtung calls a structural conflict. Actors are caught up in structures of repression and exploitation but fail to recognize them as such. A and C are embedded in the subconscious: there is a contradiction but no awareness of it. There is not even false consciousness.[3] People may feel frustrations, and even at times act upon these frustrations, but in random, senseless ways. But, we may ask, is then the term structural conflict not a contradiction in terms? What determines a conflict if not the actors themselves? With what right do we talk about a conflict at all? What is the C in structural conflict, and how are parties involved in it? Galtung's reply to this is that the contradiction lies in the system tying them together, or to use another formulation, C lies in the *structure of the social system*. Actors are unconscious of what is happening to them in the structure of the social system. They fail to see what it is that is standing in their way: what it is that prevents them from reaching their potential levels of needs satisfaction. While doing social life, people actually do harm to themselves. As the famous definition of ideology has it: 'they do not know it, but they are doing it'. They fail to see the larger picture. This is what Galtung calls structural conflict. The archetypical structural conflict, in his view, has exploitation as a centre-piece. This simply means that some (the 'top dogs') get much more out of the interaction in the structure than others, the underdogs (1996: 198). Clearly, this relates straight back to a Marxian critique of capitalism as inherently exploitative and as defined by a fundamental conflict of interests between those in control of the means of production (the capitalists) and those who only control their labour (the workers). But what prevents people from seeing the larger scope of what is at stake? And what is required to transcend from structural to actor conflict?

Cultural violence

'Just as political science is about two problems – the use of power and the legitimation of the use of power – violence studies are about two problems: the use of violence and the legitimation of that use' (Galtung 1996: 196). Galtung introduces the notion of cultural violence to highlight how exploitation is legitimized and why people fail to see 'what is standing in their way'. Culture (or rather certain aspects of culture) teaches and dulls us into seeing repression and exploitation as normal, or, rather, *not see it at all*. By cultural violence, Galtung (1996: 196) means:

> those aspects of culture, the symbolic sphere of our existence – exemplified by religion and ideology, language and art, empirical science and formal science (logic, mathematics) – that can be used to justify or legitimize direct or structural violence.

The study of cultural violence focuses on the way in which forms of both manifest violence and structural violence are legitimized and thus rendered acceptable in society. This idea of culture as sustaining and misrepresenting social structures of domination as 'natural' can be traced back to the work on cultural hegemony of the Marxist philosopher Antonio Gramsci (1891–1937). Capitalism, Gramsci famously argued in his *Prison Notebooks*, is capable of sustaining itself not just through violence, economic coercion and political repression, but also ideologically, through a *hegemonic culture* in which the values of the dominant classes have become the 'commonsense' values of all. People, lost in their daily routines and worries, and guided by symbolic orders and notions of normality and commonsense, are incapable of perceiving the greater, systemic nature of socio-economic exploitation that cultural hegemony makes possible. Gramsci's thought importantly influenced later thinkers such as Michel Foucault, Pierre Bourdieu, Zygmunt Baumann, Noam Chomsky and Judith Butler, and his influence is also clearly evident in the work of Galtung. We will return to the discussion on the legitimization of violence, under the heading of discourse theory, in chapter six.

We have so far identified three types of violence: manifest, structural and cultural. These forms of violence have a dialectic relation, constantly influencing and legitimizing one another. Despite the symmetry of Galtung's violence triangle, there is nonetheless a basic difference in the time relation of the three concepts. Manifest violence is an *event*; structural violence is a *process* with ups and downs and cultural violence is *permanent*, remaining largely the same for long periods of time, given the slow transformation of basic culture. In describing how the three types of violence enter time differently, Galtung uses a metaphor from geology: with the earthquake as event, the movement of the tectonic plates as a process and the fault line as a more permanent condition (1996: 199). Just as was the case with the conflict triangle, causality flows in all six directions and cycles connecting manifest, structural and cultural violence may start at any corner, invoking different stories.

One such story is the way in which cultural violence both legitimizes the 'fact' of structural violence and the 'act' of manifest violence. Or how a causal flow can be identified from cultural to structural to manifest violence. Galtung gives the example of how the 'criminalization of the poor' is a form of cultural violence. Victims of structural violence (the exploited poor) are branded as evil aggressors when they try to break out of the 'structural iron cage' through the use of direct violence (see Loic Wacquant's *Punishing the Poor*, 2009). The story of slavery shows us how the vicious cycle of violence can also start in the manifest violence corner, leading to structural and eventually cultural violence (1996: 200):

> Africans are captured, forced across the Atlantic to work as slaves; millions are killed in the process – in Africa, on board, in the Americas. The massive direct violence over centuries seeps down and sediments as massive structural violence, with whites as master topdogs and blacks as the slave underdogs, producing and reproducing massive cultural violence with racist ideas everywhere. After some time, direct violence is forgotten, slavery is forgotten, and only two labels show up, pale enough for college textbooks: 'discrimination' for massive structural violence and 'prejudice' for massive cultural violence. Sanitation of language: itself cultural violence.

What is repeatedly made clear here, and what is at the core of Marxian structure-based theories of violent conflict, is the violence *in* structures. The rules and regulations, cultural codes and norms that together make up the organization of societies, and that are largely taken for granted, are inherently violent. They are, however, often not recognized as such. The overwhelming complexity of social life and the individual's dual structural role as both player and maker of the game, however, mean that he or she is caught up in a Gramscian hegemonic limited 'state of focus', where one cannot see out of the box.

Conscientization

Are we forever locked up in our boxes, or is there a chance of breaking out? In answering our second question (can we go from structural to actor conflict?) we run into the programmatic (transcendental) character of Galtung's work. Indeed, according to Galtung it is possible 'to lift C up from the subconscious and into the daylight'. This is called *conscientization*, a concept taken form Paulo Freire. Again, the link to Marxist calls for the 'awakening of the proletariat' and Gramsci's 'educating the masses' is obvious. Often, Galtung argues, actors, unconscious of the contradiction in the structure of the social system (be it on the personal, social or world level) have a 'frustration image' as a passing stage before the more realistic image of the conflict emerges. Women may feel frustrations at not being in control of their lives, working classes at never reaching middle class incomes, and these frustrations may trigger occasional acts of violence. But only when women and workers become aware of the contradiction in the social system (patriarchy, capitalism) will they be able to act purposefully, and see the very concrete actors on the other side. It is only then that they enter the arena of 'actor conflict' and can begin to work on conflict resolution. Galtung remains somewhat enigmatic about what exactly triggers conscientization, except in references to 'the spirit', and the 'reflective capacity' of conflict parties. He hints at the role of emotions, particularly frustration, as a guiding force. 'The frustration phase becomes like a crust of ice on a frosty day as the consciousness passes from the cold waters underneath into the clear air above' (1996: 77). In chapter four we will address the notion of *collective action frames* as a more focused analytical concept to study what Galtung refers to as conscientization. 'Collective action frames redefine social conditions as unjust and intolerable with the intention of mobilizing potential participants, which is achieved by making appeals to perceptions of justice and emotionality in the minds of individuals' (Tarrow 1998: 111).

Galtung is theoretically omnivorous, and mostly interested in how we get from being puppets on a string, to true actors. He calls for the 'freeing of the spirit', 'escaping the realm of the subconscious', to become value-directed, aware and capable of seeing the 'real' incompatibility in the structure of the social system. At times he supports an interpretative epistemology ('the statement "this is a conflict" should always be taken as an *hypothesis*' (1996: 70, my emphasis)) but he also hints at objectivism by stating that actors only know what they want subconsciously: 'they want it but they do not know that themselves' (1996: 80). Above all, his work is programmatic. He clearly argues for a movement: down from the 'rule follower' living in the upper right quadrant of our matrix to the purposeful 'actor' of the bottom right box. Although repeatedly referring to Marxist thought, he keeps his distance from the more objectivist or deterministic approaches to what constitutes the real contradiction. He calls for a constructive peace studies, which builds upon both empirical peace studies (informing us only about patterns and conditions for peace or violence in the past) and critical peace studies (as pointing out what is wrong) to do just what architects and engineers are doing: take theories about what might work and bring them together with values about what ought to work in order to build new habitats and constructions. For Galtung, Peace and Conflict Studies should be understood as a socially 'productive' discipline only feasible in terms of investigation-action, thus breaking the barrier between theory and practice. This pedagogy of dividing academic training into three stages of (1) evidence-based analysis; (2) critique; (3) creation has become quite influential.

Structure: force without a face

Galtung's work can be positioned in the wider 'structuralist turn' of scholarly thought of the 1960s and 1970s. Structure-based analysis, in particular Marxian understandings of the global political economy, exemplified by for instance the Latin American Independencia school and the rise of the field of Development Studies, was important in the shaping of academic thinking on issues of peace and war. Galtung's definition of structural violence is operationalized at state and sub-state levels by a variety of authors (Jacobs and O'Brien 1998; Preti 2002: Farmer 1996; Kent 1999, for an overview see Jacoby 2008). Likewise, the idea of 'false consciousness' is, in a broad variety of ways, implied in structure-based conflict analyses. Authors arguing from a structure-based approach have, for instance, repeatedly critiqued dominant representations of contemporary conflicts as 'ethnic' as distorted, as a false image (e.g. Woodward 1995; Storey 1999). These distorted images can be understood as being brought in intentionally: 'top dogs' have an interest in framing the frustrations of 'underdogs' as deriving from religious or ethnic antagonisms, where the real contradiction is economic exploitation. However, the top dog/underdog dichotomy seems simplistic, and it is hence acknowledged by many structure-based analysts that although in the end elite machinations are essential, often the actors involved (both top and underdog) operate according to a much more implicit and ambiguous practical logic and 'feel for the game' (as in Bourdieu's *Logic of Practice*). It is here that the Gramscian notion of cultural hegemony comes in with its emphasis on how difficult it is for us to see the 'larger picture' shaping our routines and relationships. In our times of 'high globalization' this picture is indeed complex. Partly, this complexity explains the tendency – of both political leaders and audiences – to target concrete 'evil others' as the source of misery and suffering rather than 'structures', for these are not only hard to substantiate, they are also seen as uncontrollable. As Appadurai (2006: 44) puts it 'globalisation is a force without a face', and although the changes it brings may give rise to deep anxieties and social uncertainties it cannot be targeted in any 'satisfactory' way. 'Ethnic others', by contrast, can.

Structure-based approaches to conflict try to steer away from the emphasis on violent agents (perpetrators and victims) and focus the analysis on the underlying organization of society as shaping and sustaining violent conflict. In this, they are confronted with the question 'what structures do we see at work?' and the empirical difficulty of substantiating causal relations. Most structuralist theories require no clear subject–action–object relationship (I hit/shot/killed you) but a diffuse subject–object relationship, something we will discuss further in chapter four. Another important issue is how to define this 'abstract force' often referred to as 'structure'. As explained in the introductory chapter by means of the Hollis matrix the authors under review in this chapter understand structures as 'sets of meaning rules' rather than objective, external 'laws' determining social behaviour. That is, they understand structures as 'games' with specific constitutive and regulative rules and practices. These 'games' are *external* to each individual player, in the sense that we as individuals have a tendency to follow the rules of the game obediently. But 'games' are seen as *internal* to the players collectively. Ultimately, games are socially constructed, and inter-subjective. Giddens (1979: 64) defined structures in this sense as 'rules and resources recursively implicated in the reproduction of social systems'. Structures are thus 'rules that are articulated in social interaction and tell people how to "do" social life, and the resources on which people can call to achieve their objectives' (Wallace and Wolf 1999: 181). Structures are hence relational, shaped by power differences (access to resources) and both enabling and constraining (telling us how to do, but also how not to do social life).

There is no set level for how to apply structure-based theory. The core assumption of structure-based approaches is that systems largely shape the actions of their units, be it at the global, regional, state or community level. The key question of this chapter on structure-based approaches to violent conflict revolves around the interconnection between structure and (collective) action. In the remainder of this chapter we will discuss the work of a selection of prominent conflict scholars who explore the connection between global structures and local violent conflict. I have deliberately selected authors who work from a global perspective, for this allows us to extend our levels-of-analysis approach by drawing in national, regional and global levels. Although they see different structures at work differently, all authors explore the connections between violent conflict and the organization of society. Three global systems are highlighted: the modern state system, global capitalism and global governance. Notably, the authors under review here are not just single voices but represent strands of thought within the academic literature on global development and conflict.

Unending failure: the state-making paradox

In his work on 'state-making and state-breaking' Mohammed Ayoob (2007) understands contemporary violent conflict in the global South in the context of the process of state formation. More precisely, in the context of a crisis in state formation. His main point is that postcolonial states are expected to replicate in a few decades a process that took developed states a couple of centuries and a long series of bloody wars, that is, the establishment of relatively stable, centralized modern states. Both the enormity of the time lag, and the radical difference in international norms and political contexts highly complicate state formation. It is this crisis of 'state-making' that is the source of most contemporary violent conflicts in the underdeveloped world.

At the core of Ayoob's work is the argument that the democratic nation-states of the developed world, with their relatively high levels of legitimacy and consent, did not evolve overnight. The process of sovereign state-making that took shape in sixteenth-century Europe was a top-down, elite-driven and lengthy process, by which disparate populations were cajoled and coerced to ultimately accept the legitimacy of the state and its institutions to extract resources, set territorial boundaries and control the monopoly over the use of violence. As Charles Tilly points out, this was by no means a peaceful process:

> The building of states in Western Europe cost tremendously in death, suffering, loss of rights, and unwilling surrender of land, goods, or labour ... The fundamental reason for the high cost of European state building was its beginning in the midst of a decentralized, largely peasant social structure. Building differentiated, autonomous, centralized organisations with effective control of territories entailed eliminating or subordinating thousands of semiautonomous authorities ... Most of the European populations resisted each phase of the creation of strong states.
>
> (Tilly 1975: 71 in Ayoob 2007 :130)

This process of state-making antedated the formation of nation-states by at least a couple of centuries. The distinction between *state* and *nation-state* is crucial here. A state is a 'relatively centralized, differentiated, and autonomous organization successfully claiming priority in the use of force within a large, contiguous, and clearly bounded territory' (Tilly 1990: 43). The notion of the nation-state, however, entails the idea of a state whose inhabitants form a nation: a 'shared culture' (Gellner 1983) or 'imagined community' (Anderson 1991). The idea of the nation-state, and hence nationalism as the principle that 'the boundaries of the state and nation should be congruent' emerged in the nineteenth century, when the rise of capitalism and industrialization created the need for a more homogeneous, standardized society. It was only then that people began to imagine themselves as being part of a nation, and that the process of national identification began to take shape. Although there is debate among scholars about the when and why of the rise of the nation-state, there is ample agreement on how it took centuries of uncivil wars, coercion and bloodshed before European states could overcome their weaknesses, remedy their administrative deficiencies, and bring 'lukewarm loyalty up to the white heat of nationalism' (Ayoob 2007: 131).

In the post WWII era, the imaginary of the socially cohesive, political responsive and administratively effective nation-state of the developed world became the standard ideal type. State-makers in postcolonial (but also postcommunist) countries who fail to live up to this ideal-typical template risk international ridicule and permanent peripherality within the system of states. Their states are labelled as 'failed', 'fragile' or 'collapsed'. Ayoob argues that in order to copy the process of nation-state building, state-makers in developing countries need above all two things: lots of time and a relatively free hand. Of course, neither of these two commodities is available. For developing countries are not only under pressure to demonstrate adequate statehood quickly, in an era of mass politics and democracy, they are also confronted with a set of international norms and regulations that pressure them to do this in humane and civilized ways. In fact, developing state-makers are confronted with contradictory contemporary international norms. They have to cope with the paradox of the inalienability and 'sacredness' of colonial state borders in international law on the one hand, and the principle of human rights, including the right to ethno-national self-determination on the other hand. This often poses a great threat to the competence of the state. State governments are pressured to force a diversity of populations (whose ethnic antagonisms often stem from the divide-and-rule strategies of colonial rulers) to remain within the territorial boundaries of the often rather arbitrarily drawn borders of the colonial state. In contrast to earlier centuries, in the current era individuals and groups can claim rights that are independent of their memberships of individual states and that derive not from their national status but from their status as members of the human species. At the same time, newly independent states are incapable of accommodating political and economic demands from dissatisfied groups, either because they lack the necessary resources or because doing so could seriously jeopardize their territorial integrity. In particular the international recognition of the doctrine of ethno-national self-determination increases the challenge to the legitimacy of the principle that postcolonial states are territorially inviolable. Ayoob describes the core of the problem as follows:

> The major problem is that standards are set by Western Europe and US, states that have successfully completed their state-building process, they can therefore afford to adopt liberal standards in relations to their populations, because they are reasonably secure in the knowledge that societal demands will not run counter to state interests and will not put them in jeopardy. However, these standards are in the Third World often in contradiction with the imperatives of state making.
>
> (Ayoob 2007: 133)

In sum, it is the contradictions inherent to the organization of the modern state-system, in particular the unevenness in state-making processes, that importantly constrain the ability of state-makers in developing countries to reach levels of nation-statehood similar to the western world. Before we turn to the question of how this structural imbalance translates into violent conflict we first turn to another system: global capitalism.

Global neoliberalism

Contemporary thinking on the connection between the global economy and local violent conflict is characterized by a controversy between two common perspectives. The first is the 'liberal peace' interpretation, according to which free market reforms and good governance contribute to stability and the resolution of conflict through the promotion of economic growth. From this point of view globalization and market deregulation are seen to furnish the basis of stability. Underlying this view is the assumption that through the mechanism of the free market labour, production and raw materials will be automatically adjusted in ways that will rationally secure the optimal benefits for all. The free market is understood as the ultimate driving force behind rationally calculated and hence superior forms of organization and order. This position is contradicted by proponents of the second view, stemming from political economy. This interpretation claims that the doctrine of neoliberal globalization that swept the world in the 1980s, and has since become hegemonic, tends to encourage new and durable forms of division, inequality and instability. In the encounter with national and local contexts, the neoliberal market reforms of the 1980s are seen as having produced unexpected and at times unwanted outcomes, including violent conflict. Neoliberalism has deepened poverty, increased economic inequality, and has exacerbated the division of the world into 'core' and 'periphery', or 'metropolitan' and 'borderland' zones. In particular, the shift from an inclusionary to an exclusionary capitalist logic is seen to have had profound implications. Authors such as Castells (1996, 1998) and Cox (1995) have argued that with the rise of the modern informational economy of the 1980s, the logic of capitalist development is better characterized by consolidation and exclusion than by – classic – expansion and inclusion. Since this time, the tendency has been for production, finance, investment, trade and technology networks to concentrate in and between the metropolitan blocks of mass consumer societies at the expense of the outlying areas. The present system is driven much more by commercial investment and technology networks than by a thirst for cheap labour and raw materials. As a result, apart from 'enclave economies' revolving around a number of high value commodities (oil, diamonds, coltan, gold, timber) much of the 'South' is deemed 'structurally irrelevant' from an economic point of view (Castells 1996: 135 in Duffield 2002: 1054).

Proponents of the liberal peace approach recognize the rise in internal violent conflict of the 1990s. They also acknowledge the fact that the process of global neoliberalization coincided with an overall rise of parallel economies, severe financial crises in Asia and Latin America, and high levels of poverty and inequality. However, where scholars from the political economy tradition argue that these instabilities are inherent to the logic of the global capitalist system, advocates of the liberal interpretation have a quite different reading. In their view, it is not the neoliberal model that is to blame for the serial market failures and lack of progress, but rather the immature, corrupt and inefficient state administrations of developing countries and transition economies themselves. It is emphasized that global neoliberalism can only successfully proceed in a 'sound' governance environment. Whereas the idea of 'more market and less state' was the prime objective of both the stabilization programmes that started in the 1970s and the Structural Adjustment Programmes (SAPs) that were vigorously enhanced and extended in the 1980s, the call for *less state* of the Washington consensus has been gradually substituted by a call for a *better* state. So, where the liberal interpretations locate the sources of civil war and instability at the level of 'bad actors' (greedy rebels, corrupt leaders, criminalized regimes) who rationally calculate the costs and benefits of war and rebellion, the political economy approach emphasizes the need to grapple with the complexities of the relation between local war and the global capitalist logic. The argumentation of the first will be further explored in chapter five. The remainder of this section will deal with how political economy approaches understand the connection between neoliberal globalization and violent conflict. As we will see, the state again plays a leading role in this analysis.

Global structures and local conflict: the interconnections

It is at the level of the state, and state-making efforts, where the impact of economic, geopolitical and political transformation become manifest and hence researchable. It is not surprising that many structure-based approaches to violent conflict focus on this level of analysis. The argumentation followed by authors such as Mohammed Ayoob that contemporary violent conflict should be understood in the context of a crisis of (postcolonial) state- and nation-making, and how the international standards set by established, western nation-states importantly aggravate this crisis, is acknowledged by authors arguing from a political economy stance. However, they point out, this crisis is exacerbated by an even more fundamental problem. New states are not only hampered in their efforts to monopolize national territory, they also lack control over their national economies. They are not only enfeebled politically, but also, and more importantly, economically. Whereas states in Europe went through a process of state and nation building based on the idea of the national economy and state territory as viable economic unit (the so called 'threshold principle'), and went through phases of strong economic protectionism, thriving on colonial exploitation and a strategy of primitive accumulation, the state- and nation-building processes of developing countries are marked by very different contextual realities. Not only do they suffer the consequences of a history of extraction and exploitation, they also often have only experimented briefly with economic models of state-led growth. Clearly, the economic development and trajectories of developing countries show massive differences, from the long history of import substitution characterizing many Latin American states, to the postcolonial neopatrimonial state in Africa, the newly industrializing countries (NICs) of southeast Asia, and the economic protectionism in post-independence India and Indonesia. A central argument, however, in the political economy tradition is that although the 'neoliberal revolution' of the late twentieth century played out differently, it went with a worldwide erosion or disintegration of state structures. The incapacity of governments to monopolize national territories and control economic dynamics has eroded the decision-making power and legitimacy of the state in many developing countries (but also in more advanced industrial countries). Processes of state and nation building are either weakened and delegitimized, or frustrated and impeded. The effects of this are twofold: the emergence of identity conflicts and network wars.

Identity conflicts

Mary Kaldor's book *New and Old Wars: organized violence in a global era* (1999) was a strong influence on the discussion of globalization and local violence. What she coined as 'new wars' were 'to be understood in the context of globalisation' (1999: 3). Kaldor contrasts the old 'politics of ideas' that had characterized conflict throughout most of the twentieth century, with what she identifies as the rise of a new 'politics of identity' of recent decades, which emerged out of the disintegration or erosion of modern state structures, especially centralized authoritarian states. 'The collapse of communist states after 1989, the loss of legitimacy of post-colonial states in Africa or South Asia, or even the decline of welfare states in more advanced industrial countries provide the environment in which new forms of identity politics are nurtured' (1999: 78). In a context where decision-making powers have shifted from the state to the market, and where the neoliberal framework has been more or less fixed by external international financial institutions (such as the World Bank, the International Monetary Fund, the World Trade Organization) and donor agencies, and where transnational activities abound, political classes suffer from growing impotence and declining legitimacy. In the process of global market integration, national governments have been stripped of their powers to determine policies in the socio-economic realm. The inability of the state to impose rules and regulations to keep market power in check has posed problems for both democratic accountability and political legitimacy. The lack of control of the economy leaves the cultural field as the main battleground for political constituency building and opens a 'market' for identity-based politics. As a consequence, minorities, migrants and 'ethnic others' become the flash point of exclusionary discourses and are scapegoated as invaders and the source of all evil. In this sense, identity politics can be seen as a survival tactic for politicians in contexts of declining economic decision-making powers. It is hence the weakening and delegitimization of the state set in motion by the neoliberal globalization project that is at the base of contemporary ethnic conflict, nationalism and xenophobia (see also Appadurai 2006). This process is certainly not exclusively characteristic of the underdeveloped world. More than anything it is the rapidly neoliberalizing former welfare states of western Europe and Scandinavia that witness the rise of populist and xenophobic repertoires. In places such as the Netherlands, Sweden and Denmark, where the neoliberal project has, largely unnoticed, abolished the collective standards and solidarities of the post WWII era, the faces of immigrants have served as ideal, identifiable targets for new narratives of othering and belonging (Demmers and Mehendale 2010).

Network wars

The political economy position implies that contemporary conflicts need to be understood in the context of the economic transformations of the late twentieth century. These transformations trigger not only identity politics, but also new forms of resource competition. The rise of the so called 'war economies' in many developing countries is linked to the decline of state formation as a political project in the context of the worldwide trend of globalization and liberalization. Keen (1998), for instance, with a wink at Von Clausewitz, states that internal forms of war are now better understood as the continuation of *economics* by other means. The war economies that emerged after the Cold War, revolving around illegal trade in diamonds, arms, drugs, timber, and coltan and oil bunkering in Africa, Eastern Europe and Central Asia, and the production of poppy (e.g. Afghanistan, Pakistan) and coca (e.g. Colombia, Bolivia) are understood to be perpetuated by local and global networks of producers, traders, warlords, corporations and consumers. Increasingly, actors move beyond the state in pursuit of economic power. The result of this is the so called 'post state conflicts' or 'network wars' (Duffield 2002). These are often internal forms of war in which actors find it no longer necessary to project power through the juridical or bureaucratic control of a relatively fixed territory. The state has been replaced by multiple centres of authority, often controlled by warlords and local business networks who no longer consider the state the main 'trophy' in conflict, except perhaps as a means to solidify their commercial activities. The interconnectedness between these local economies of war and the international market is expressed in the term 'network war'. In their aim to control strategic assets local warring parties strike deals with multinational corporations that have a vested interest in access to natural resources. In Columbia, for instance, with the growth of oil concessions foreign companies developed a complex strategy engaging the state, rebel forces and para-military (see Richani 2002). Often enough, however, local and global parties become engaged in violent competition over oil or timber. In Nigeria and Sudan, the energy security strategies of China, the US and Europe have resulted in what Watts (2008) names the 'scramble for African oil'. This has only been exacerbated by the War on Terror. 'It is in the intersection of a more aggressive scramble for African oil by China, and the U.S. twin concerns of secure oil supply (national energy security) and the global War on Terror that a perfect storm of political volatility is created' (2008: 33). Together with local ethnic antagonisms, youth militancy and state repression this accounts for the Nigerian 'oil complex': a highly unstable and militarized corporate enclave economy. The rise of shadow economies is also enhanced in more indirect ways. International financial institutions such as the World Bank and IMF preach economic integration of all societies, but in practice primarily enforce trade liberalization in poor countries. This double standard of pushing poor countries to open markets and allowing rich countries to protect their markets is greatest in such sectors as textiles and agriculture. As is pointed out by Douma (2003: 50) the continuing protectionist measures, such as massive subsidies to farmers in the North and the existence of tariff barriers and import quota, have had a detrimental impact on the prospects of poor countries to gain access to important consumer markets, which, in turn, feeds into processes of criminalization and violent conflict. In a complexity of ways, international capital rewards reinforce local structures of violence (Willett 2010). In situations where there are few sources of livelihood, joining military groups, or shifting to coca and poppy growing or coltan and diamond mining may be essential survival strategies. For example, in the case of Colombia, peasants are known to shift from growing bananas (earning 16 dollars a month) to illegal coca production (earning 100 dollars a month). All these processes have an important impact on the existence and perseverance of war-related economic systems.

In sum, the changing competence – or outright impotence – of the state is of key importance to the understanding of the emergence and sustenance of internal violent conflict and disorder. From a political economy perspective it is the decline of state formation as a political project that results in a loss of legitimacy of political classes and nurtures new forms of identity politics. In addition, economic groups, both legal and illegal, global and local, increasingly operate 'around the state'. What results is a rather grim picture of large parts of the excluded South as caught up in a downward spiral of violent resource competition along often heavily politicized ethnic fault lines. It is exactly this picture of breakdown and decline, evoked by the political economy approach, that is contested by a more Durkheimian reading of violent conflict. Before we move to our third 'global system', we will here briefly look into this critique.

A critical note: the (dis)order of violent conflict

It is tempting, for the outsider, to view the larger part of the underdeveloped world, particularly postcolonial territories, as plagued by failure, breakdown and anomie. In line with the argumentation above, the majority of conflict approaches linked to political economy regard the many incidences of intra-state violent conflict in particular the South in terms of a *failure of modernity*. This view is contested by a group of scholars who propose to read the forms of collective action on the ground not as anomic, but rather as restorative. Duffield (2002), for instance, argues that the political economy approach has an important contribution to make when it comes to understanding the transformations in global capitalism, but fails to look beyond the truism of the 'failed state'. In its representation of the South as made up of 'multiple black holes of social exclusion' (Castells 1998: 164), it unintentionally reproduces the 'new barbarianism' discourse implicit in many conventional descriptions of contemporary conflict zones. The images of social regression and criminalized violence produced by the political economy analysis clearly articulate 'popular images of borderland barbarity, excess and irrationality' (Duffield 2002: 1054). Situations on the ground may prove to be much more complex and ambivalent than the images of failure and chaos suggest. Rather than a failure of modernity, the new shadow economies and network wars that emerged in the post Cold War era can also be understood as forms of *reflexive modernization*, as 'emerging political complexes' instead of 'complex political emergencies'. Political actors, institutions and social groups in places such as Sierra Leone, Chechnya, the Democratic Republic of the Congo and Colombia have appropriated and adapted the changes that came with globalization into new, and essentially non-legal and non-liberal forms of autonomy, protection and regulation. Although there is no need to romanticize these new forms of organization – including the organization of violence – it is worthwhile to take a more ethnographic approach to the ways by which the new shadow networks offer alternative forms of social regulation. In a similar way, Keen (2008), Cramer (2006) and King (2004) argue for a close examination of the reflexive systems supporting the 'new wars'. Rather than conceptualizing war as collapse, Keen, for instance, suggests investigating war as an alternative system of profit, power and protection. For Keen 'events, however horrible and catastrophic, are actually *produced*, they are made to happen by a diverse and complicated set of actors who may well be achieving their objectives in the midst of what looks like failure and breakdown' (2008: 15). Likewise, Cramer (2006) aims to show how war is not necessarily the absence of development, or 'development in reverse', and how war and capitalism have supported each other throughout history. What these authors argue for is that the all-too-simplistic branding of the large majority of contemporary violent conflicts as 'failure and implosion' leaves no moral space for different forms of reflexive and ambivalent modernity. The templates and taken-for-granted ideal types of 'nation-state' and 'development' against which any given state should be measured as having succeeded or failed are themselves in need of critical re-examination. This brings us to an analysis of the third and final global system discussed in this chapter: global governance.

Global governance as containment

Part of the discussion under the heading of global governance consists of an analysis that not so much aims to account for the phenomenon of internal war itself, but rather, its representation. This brings us to the systemic analysis of Duffield (2007, 2008, 2010a) on the relation between local 'borderland' wars and the power hierarchy of the global governance system. In a way, this third analysis includes a warning. It points to the slippery and controversial relationship between academic analysis on the one hand, and the 'reality call' of its ideological and practical implementation on the other. Put simply, academic knowledge on the 'new wars', as discussed above, is re-appropriated, both as a concept and in practice, by global governance institutions and turned into a legitimizing discourse. Stripped of its political economy components, the concept is used as a way to categorize contemporary violent conflict as uncivil, barbaric and excessive, and hence illegitimate. Cut off from its global and systemic 'sources' what is left of the 'new wars' concept is a label. This translation of an analytical concept into a policy concept perhaps seems meaningless at first sight, but may have serious consequences. Simplified, we see a shift from an analytical understanding of new wars as connected to global systems, to a policy understanding of new wars as primarily provoked by local actors.

By analysing the re-appropriation of the 'new wars' label, Duffield not only describes the shift in framing and the construction of new dichotomies, but also conceptualizes their *functionality* in what he sees as a global regime shift from geopolitics to bio-politics. Central to this analysis is the logic of representational transformation of parts of the global South from a series of 'strategic states' at the time of the Cold War into a 'dangerous social body' during the War on Terror era. What follows is an analysis of the contradictions inherent in the structure of this new system of global governance.

What is 'new' about the 'new wars', Duffield argues, is their alleged illegitimacy. What has changed, is not so much the nature of violent conflict, but the international denial of any *legitimacy* to warring parties within 'failed states'. For most of the twentieth century, supporting conflicts waged by irregular armies was an accepted fea-ture of international conflict – certainly during the superpower rivalry of the Cold War. Because a direct military confrontation between the two super powers was impossible, Moscow and Washington exported their geopolitical rivalry to the developing world. This resulted in the much discussed inter-state and intra-state 'proxy wars' and a merger of local and geopolitical antagonisms and alliances. The massive transfer of weapons to both governments and insurgents in the 'strategic states' of Central and South America, Africa and Asia greatly enhanced local insecurities and instabilities in these regions. Largely, however, local wars were seen as legitimate and were supported with funding, arms and political patronage. Importantly, during the Cold War devel-opment aid, and donor-led peacekeeping and conflict resolution activities were cir-cumscribed by state sovereignty, territorial integrity and the norms of non-intervention. The end of the Cold War, however, changed all this. Warring parties in internal conflict lost their geopolitical strategic functionality. The rapid withdrawal of financial and political support after 1989 forced warring parties in the former 'strategic states' to turn to other sources of income and support, such as the shadow economy and overseas diasporas. Rather than strategic allies, they turned into potential threats which needed to be contained (the quintessential example of this is of course the US relation to the Mujahedin in Afghanistan). It is against this background that the 'new wars' label gained prominence in the countless reports of the United Nations, World Bank, donor governments, regional organizations and NGOs. Duffield points out how these conventional descriptions create a series of 'us' and 'them' dichotomies (2002: 1052):

> *Their wars*, for example, are internal, illegitimate, identity-based, characterised by unrestrained destruction, abuse civilians, lead to social regression, rely on privatized violence, and so on. By implication, *our wars* are between states, are legitimate and politically motivated, show restraint, respect civilians, lead to social advancement and are based on accountable force. In describing their wars, by implication, such statements suggest a good deal about how we like to understand our own violence. They establish, for want of better terms, a formative contrast between *borderland* traits of barbarity, excess and irrationality, and *metropolitan* characteristics of civility, restraint and rationality.

By constructing the imagined space of the 'borderland', a powerful legitimation was established for the new western humanitarian and peace interventionism that came with the new hierarchy of power of the post Cold War era. The 'new war' label of chaos and barbarity was used as a moral justification for this increased interventionism (coined the New Humanitarian Order by Mahmood Mamdani). For, not only did internal wars cease to be politically functional, the emerging shadow economies and network wars were above all seen as *dangerous*, as seriously threatening western ways of life. This was of course greatly enhanced by the September 11 attacks and the Global War on Terror and resulted in the idea of underdevelopment as dangerous, and hence the *securitization of development*. For Duffield '(t)he bad forms of global circulation associated with non-insured surplus population penetrate the porous borders of mass consumer society, damaging its social cohesion and destabilizing its way of life' (2007: 122). It is in this light that Duffield argues for understanding the rise of 'human security' and 'state fragility' as *technologies of containment*. The renewed wave of western humanitarian and peace interventionism in the post Cold War period and its fashions of 'human security' and 'state fragility' are primarily technologies of power aimed at controlling people living on the margins of global society. The main development recipe in this context is the encouragement of local self-reliance (or 'sustainable development'). Whereas the notion of self-reliance began as a challenge to the world economy by advocating endogenously determined autonomous development, the term has been transformed over the past decades to mean support by international agencies for do-it-yourself welfare programmes in the periphery. These programmes aim to enable rural populations to achieve self-sufficiency, to contain the exodus from the borderlands to the metropolitan zones and hence create some sort of stability among populations which the global economy cannot absorb. In its transformed meaning self-reliance has become 'complementary to and supportive of hegemonic goals for the world economy' (Cox 1983: 173). Duffield applies Foucault's concept of 'biopolitics' in his critique of this liberal understanding of development. Simply put, where geopolitics is a form of politics where power is executed through a control over territories, biopolitics is the exertion of power through the disciplining and regulation of people.

Biopolitics is primarily about governing the life (and death) of the population. For Duffield, rather than a way to 'better' people, development has become a technology of security, aimed at containing the circulatory and destabilizing effects of underdevelopment's surplus labour (or 'waste life') upon the western way of life:

> Rather than moving towards global equity, for decades Western politicians have proved to be either unable or unwilling to moderate mass society's hedonistic thirst for unlimited consumption. ... The expectation that those excluded from the feast – the international surplus population – will be satisfied with basic needs is, at best, unrealistic and racist.
>
> (2007: 70)

'Human security' should not be understood by its common definition as 'prioritising people rather than states' but as a form of long-distance biopolitics – that is – as 'effective states prioritising the well-being of populations living within ineffective ones' (2007: 122). What follows is the emergence of what Duffield calls 'governance states' – that is, zones of contingent sovereignty where the west, through complex networks of public–private governance, shapes the basic economic and welfare policies. While its territorial integrity is respected, sovereignty over life is internationalized, negotiable and contingent.

In his analysis of the rise of the 'new wars' label, Duffield seeks to uncover how, in the post Cold War era, 'metropolitan' states established a new hierarchy of power through a series of public–private networks of global governance. Although he does not directly use the term, he addresses the violence inherent in the structure of the global governance system of the new humanitarian order, and the ways governments and NGOs, at times unknowingly, sustain and police the gap between mass consumer society and those living beyond its boundaries. When discussing the connection between globalization and violent conflict Duffield points out how the new inter-ventionism can be held partly responsible for the decrease in internal conflict after the 1990s. However, whereas the number of open violent conflicts diminished, global instability remained. According to the Human Security Report of 2005, if a wider view of human security is adopted – beyond death directly related to conflict – the number of people dying through generalized instability is increasing. Open conflict is now contained, not resolved. Clearly, Duffield's 'contained instability' is not far removed from what Galtung identified, in the first part of this chapter, as 'avoidable insults to life', that is, structural violence.

Conclusion

In this chapter we discussed authors who situate the source of violent conflict in the organization of society. The 'true contradiction', that is to say, *that which is standing in the way of something else*, is built into the structure of the system. It is built into the structure of the modern state system, where 'effective' states that have completed their nation-state building processes (often at the expense of the 'ineffective' ones) set the liberal standards that are in contradiction to the imperatives of state-making in large parts of the South. It is built into the structure of the global capitalist system, where international rules and regulations of market integration have stripped national governments of their power to control economic dynamics. It is also built into the global governance system where 'metropolitan' states through a new set of technologies of (bio)power keep 'borderland' populations in place.

The three questions

Let us now turn to the three core questions of the book to try and assess structure-based approaches to violent conflict. Again, we are forced to simplify a rather diverse and broad research tradition, and the answers to the three questions are clearly not unequivocal. However incomplete, the answers below do bring out a series of stark contrasts with those of the earlier chapters on ethnic boundaries and social identities. The most obvious contrast pertains to our first question: what makes a group? It is unsurprising that structure-based approaches do not indulge in long elaborations of what makes the individual or collective agent, for, as has been emphasized enough, they place the sources of violent conflict at the level of structures, not agents. Almost by implication, the group formations in zones of conflict do not fall in line with what Marxian approaches recognize as the 'real' parties in conflict. The 'real' groups in conflict are produced by the contradictions in the structure of the system. What is suggested by for instance the work of Galtung, and many of the authors in the political economy tradition, is that groups are individuals who share a similar position in the market economy. The dominant idea here is that of people having clearly defined interests. However, often people do not act in accordance with these interests (or, as in Galtung, they have no awareness of their joint exploitation). They fail to see what it is that is standing in their way. Their social anxieties and frustrations are projected onto 'false' enemies and threats, and hence translate into unrealistic forms of violence. The resulting conflict formations and violent actions in no possible way address, let alone resolve, the fundamental contradictions underlying them. It is this distinction between realistic and unrealistic violence which sets the structure-based approaches apart from other theoretical approaches to violent conflict. Even if people are aware of 'true contradictions', their room to manoeuvre is extremely limited and constrained by institutions, laws and regulations. Ontologically, structure-based approaches support a holistic stance. Holists contend that power resides in institutions and as such is beyond the control of the individual. People have little choice but to act according to the constitutive and regulative rules of the dominant social order. Particularly the orderings of the state (citizenship status, immigration laws) capitalism (consumption, production, job market, salaries) and global governance (international law and institutions, security doctrines, imperial powers) create robust and inescapable 'facts of life' that defy change. As long as the inherent contradictions in the organization of the modern state system, global capitalism and global governance remain, the violence that comes with them, both structural and direct, will remain as well.

The connection between structures and violence runs through the state. The fundamental contradictions in the structures of the modern state system, capitalism and global governance produce incompetent states that cannot accommodate needs and demands from society. This is the basic problem underlying contexts of instability in most of the global South. There is debate on whether this instability translates into either anomic or restorative forms of collective action, and whether the essentially non-legal and non-liberal forms of organization in conflict zones should be classified as 'breakdown' or 'reflexive modernization'. Structure-based approaches, however different, contend that the forms of structural violence done to people through the organization of society, in one way or the other, prepare the ground for direct violence. What is suggested, is that the violence inherent in the structure of the system, contains the intrinsic capacity to provoke direct violence. However, this cannot satisfy its critics. Structure-based approaches are much critiqued for their inability to produce an answer to the second of our questions: *how* do groups resort to violence? The connection between structural and direct violence remains under-theorized, and structure-based approaches cannot explain how particular violent conflicts occur. Although structural contradictions in the modern state system, the global economic system and the global governance hierarchy, and the concomitant changing competence of the state set the larger context, they by themselves cannot explain violent conflict. Why is it that in certain situations of structural violence we see no eruptions of violence, and in others we do? How do people organize for violence? Clearly, social uncertainties or frustrations, however deeply felt, by themselves do not 'make' wars. In the next chapter we will discuss approaches that specifically aim to explain how people mobilize for collective violent action.

In a way, we have already answered the last question: how and why do they (not) stop? It requires structural change to end or transform violent conflict. From a structure-based approach most peace-making, reconciliation and conflict settlement attempts are rendered insufficient. The elaborate attempts by the many global and local NGOs to 'bring conflict parties together' through inter-ethnic or inter-religious dialogue in places such as Kenya, Uganda, the DRC or Indonesia (but also in urban neighbourhoods in the west) overemphasize the 'attitude' component of conflict. Thinking back to Galtung's triangle, working on conflict attitudes (A) is primarily what reconciliation is about. Likewise, it is not enough to work on the B (behaviour) corner of the triangle. This is what conflict settlement efforts are about: to make parties refrain from fighting ('negative peace'). Whereas reconciliation efforts focus on A, and settlement is largely about B, conflict resolution only begins when C (the contradiction in the structure of the system) is addressed ('positive peace').

A few last words on epistemology and ontology. As has already been briefly discussed, most structure-based approaches to violent conflict take an interpretative epistemological stance. They do not understand structures as in some way external or prior to actions, and as determining them fully, as is claimed by objectivism. Structures are not seen as 'unobservable systems which exert purposive pressure on their parts' but as 'sets of meaning rules' or 'games' with specific constitutive and regulative rules and practices. A 'game' as explained by Hollis is:

> historically and culturally specific, with a real enough power to set the terms in which people think and relate but only in their own place and time. If so, it would not be surprising to find only overlapping or criss-crossing resemblances among the games of social life and no universal features which all normative structures have in common.
>
> (1994: 159)

The difference here is that structures are understood not as external (as envisaged in top left box of the Hollis matrix) but as forms of life that are inter-subjective and socially and historically constructed. That is, they are external to each but internal to all (and hence fit best in Hollis' upper right box). The approaches in this chapter all emphasize how in the specific era of the post Cold War certain 'forms of life' (free market capitalism, modern state systems and hierarchies of global governance) importantly shape the social world. Ontologically, structure is placed prior to agency, and collective action is largely explained as determined by the structure of social systems.

In this chapter we have focused on approaches which aim to explore the connection between the workings of global structures and local zones of violent conflict. These approaches primarily emphasize the global level of analysis, by addressing the constitutive and regulative rules supporting the systems of the modern state, capitalism and global governance. They examine the ways these rules structure relations particularly between actors in the 'metropolitan' and 'borderland' zones, and how this translates into different forms of collective action. Although the global analysis of violent conflict importantly sets the larger picture, there remains much to be said about the interplay between global structures and local realities. The following chapters will focus on approaches that see the structure-based approach to conflict as too broad. Although the workings of global systems give insight into the larger contexts of power (the so called 'opportunity structures'), they are not helpful in understanding how specific conflict trajectories come about. The question remains how and why distinct groups or parties become engaged in rebellion and collective violence against other parties, (groups of) civilians or the state. This is the key component of the following two chapters.

Table C

Ontology/Epistemology	Explaining (positivist)	Understanding (interpretative)
Structuralism		Structure-based approaches (Political economy)
Individualism		

Further reading

Cramer, Christopher (2006) *Civil War is Not a Stupid Thing*, London: Hurst & Company.
Duffield, Mark (2002) 'Social Reconstruction and the Radicalization of Development: Aid as a Relation of Global Liberal Governance', *Development and Change* 33 (5): 1049–71.
——(2010) 'The Liberal Way of Development and the Development – Security Impasse: Exploring the Global Life-Chance Divide', *Security Dialogue* 41 (1): 53–76.

Recommended documentaries

The Corporation (Mark Achbar, Jennifer Abbott, Joel Bakan, 2003)
Inside Job (Charles H. Ferguson, 2010)
Coca Mama (Journeyman Pictures, 2001)
Capitalism: A Love Story (Michael Moore, 2009)
Blood in the Mobile (Frank Poulsen, 2010)
Darwin's Nightmare (Hubert Sauper, 2004)

4   Mobilization for collective violent action
Multi-causal approaches

Although structural transformations such as the growth of the modern state system, the development of the global economy and the rise of global governance structures set the larger context, they by themselves do not make conflict. Conflict is made by human beings. By 'first movers', who one day may decide 'enough is enough' and begin to plan a rebellion, and by the active involvement of 'followers'. Hence, the question remains how and why people mobilize for collective violent action against other (groups of) combatants, civilians or the state. At this point in the book it may have become clear that both actors and contexts, and therefore agency *and* structure-based theories have something to offer to students of violent conflict. Why not combine the two? This is indeed the approach of the theories and models under discussion in this fourth chapter. They emphasize the salience of group identity and organizational capacity, but also look at state power, models of economic development and international linkages as importantly shaping violent conflict. The idea of multi-causality is self-evident. It is also fraught with difficulties. Mono-causal explanations of conflict are often implausible, and yet it is very difficult to weigh particular causes in multi-causal explanations, and to see how they interact. How is multi-causality theorized? How to make 'theoretical sense' of the interplay of structures and actors? One of the underlying questions of this chapter is to see if, and how, this can be done. Writing a chapter on multi-causal approaches is equally tricky: because of the variety of research traditions underlying the approaches under discussion such a chapter can easily become labyrinthine. The glue that should hold this chapter together is the shared emphasis of the reviewed approaches on *collective resentments*. That is, on how a collectively felt discrepancy between 'what is' and 'what ought to' translates in forms of discontent that in combination with a set of other factors explain the shift to collective violence. Simply put, what is emphasized is that engagement in collective violence is primarily *affective*, and not just calculative. The chapter's agenda is two-fold. First, it aims to review and situate the work of two classic 'conflict scholars': Edward Azar and Ted Gurr. Both scholars draw on human needs theory, and have constructed multi-levelled, and multi-causal conflict maps. They aim to identify key factors that determine group mobilization for protest or rebellion against the state or other groups. Since their approaches show resemblances to those of collective action theorists like Sidney Tarrow and Charles Tilly we will make a brief detour to contentious politics and collective action theory, and touch upon earlier discussions on identity, interests and rationality. The second aim of this chapter is to discuss issues of method and data, and to revisit the epistemological divide between *explaining* and *understanding*, and more specifically, quantitative and qualitative research methods. In the final part of the chapter, the somewhat 'grand scheme' models are complemented with more fine-tuned micro-political frameworks. These provide added nuance to our analysis by calling for a disaggregated approach to violent conflict and highlighting the variation of violence in war.

Protracted social conflict: an analytical framework

Many of the mantras of Conflict Studies today – conflicts are complex, multi-levelled and dynamic – can be traced back to the work of Edward Azar. In the midst of the Cold War, at the time when most scholars focused on the bipolar stand-off and classic models of inter-state war, Azar developed an understanding of what he called a 'new type of conflict', which, 'distinct from traditional disputes over territory, economic resources, or East–West rivalry ... revolves around questions of *communal identity*' (1991: 93, my emphasis). Drawing upon data-sets of violent conflicts compiled at the University of Maryland in the 1970s, Azar concluded that the key factor in – what he called – protracted social conflict (PSC) in places such as Sri Lanka, Northern Ireland, Cyprus, Nigeria, Sudan and the Philippines was the 'prolonged and often violent struggle by communal groups for such basic needs as security, recognition and acceptance, fair access to political institutions and economic participation' (1991: 93). Although Azar clearly placed *need deprivation* and, as we will see later, the *failure of governance* at the core of his analysis, he also strongly aimed to bridge conventional scholarly dichotomies by building a multi-levelled framework. In the first chapter of *The Management of Protracted Social Conflict: Theory and Cases* (1990) he criticizes the field of war studies for its high levels of compartmentalization. First, there is a tendency to understand conflicts through a rather rigid dichotomy of internal versus external dimensions, with sociologists, anthropologists and psychologists on the one side, and international relation scholars on the other. Second, there is a tendency toward the functional differentiation of conflicts into sub-categories: psychological, social, political, economic and military. Finally, there is almost exclusive focus on overt and violent conflict. Covert, latent, non-violent conflicts are rarely regarded as appropriate objects of study. Moreover, conflicts are understood from an organic cycle perspective. 'Every conflict is thought to go through a cycle of genesis, maturity, reduction and termination. The termination of violent acts is often equated with the state of peace' (1990: 6). In contrast, Azar argues, many conflicts do not fit into the above classifications: they are characterized by a blurred demarcation between internal and external sources and actors, there are multicausal factors and dynamics, reflected in changing goals, actors and targets, and, finally, conflicts do not show clear starting and terminating points. These insights have become somewhat of an orthodoxy today. Noting, however, that Azar wrote his last book at the closing of the 1980s, it is not surprising that he is often seen as one of the founding scholars of contemporary Conflict Studies (see Miall et al. 1999, 66–91). It is his work that has inspired others to develop levels-of-analysis approaches, in particular the framework developed by Miall, Ramsbotham and Woodhouse in their comprehensive textbook *Contemporary Conflict Resolution* (1999; 2006) and the related conflict mapping method (see Introduction).

The genesis of conflict: preconditions

Azar's model reads like a conflict map (see figure 4.1). At the core of the map is the identity group – racial, religious, ethnic, cultural and others. But there is ample room for the state, and international actors as well. The model begins by looking at the core

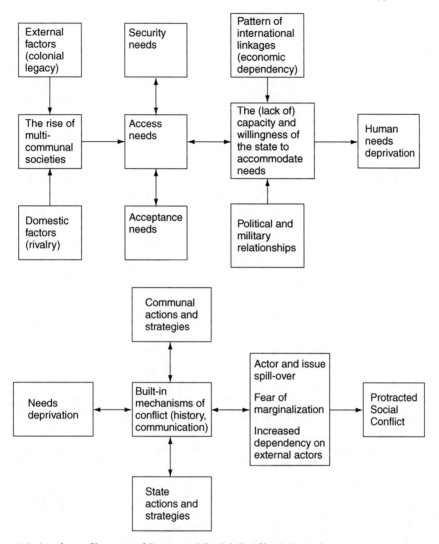

Figure 4.1 Azar's conflict map of Protracted Social Conflict (adapted)

ingredients for conflict, and then turns to conflict dynamics. Azar summarizes his main argument as follows:

> Protracted social conflicts occur when communities are deprived of satisfaction of their basic needs on the basis of their communal identity. However, the deprivation is the result of a complex causal chain involving the role of the state and the pattern of international linkages. Furthermore, initial conditions (colonial legacy, domestic historical setting, and the multicommunal nature of the society) play important roles in shaping the genesis of protracted social conflict.
>
> (1990: 12)

Azar walks us through his model in four steps. First, he emphasizes the *communal content* of protracted social conflict. 'If a society is characterized by multicommunal composition, protracted social conflicts are most likely to arise' (1990: 7). The multi-communal character of society in many parts of the world results from colonial divide-and-rule policies or historical patterns of rivalry and uneven access to state power. Multi-communal societies, whether formed through the colonizing process or through intercommunal struggle, are 'characterized by disarticulation between the state and society as a whole, with the state usually dominated by a single communal group or a coalition of a few communal groups that are unresponsive to the needs of other groups in society' (1990: 7). This 'strains the social fabric and eventually breeds fragmentation and protracted social conflict' (1990: 7). Second, Azar identifies the *deprivation of human needs* as the underlying source of conflict. As we will discuss later, his work clearly draws on human needs theory. Azar builds his model on the following assumptions. All human beings have a set of basic needs and individuals strive to fulfil these needs through the formation of identity groups. However, history shows us that human needs are seldom evenly or justly met. While one group may enjoy satisfaction of needs (such as nutrition, warmth, security, self-actualization) in abundance, others do not. 'Grievances resulting from need deprivation are usually expressed collectively. Failure to redress these grievances by the authority cultivates a niche for a protracted social conflict' (1990: 9). Although this is the essence of Azar's model, the step to conflict is not automatic and – as we will see later – depends upon the interplay of a variety of factors. Next to, and closely interrelated with, basic material needs (grouped together under the heading *security needs*) such as nutrition, housing, physical security, Azar distinguishes *acceptance needs* and *access needs*. We all have to secure our basic physical needs (security), a socially accepted and recognized communal identity (acceptance), and an effective participation in political, market and decision-making institutions (access). Azar shows how these three fundamental human needs are highly interconnected. For example, one has to have access to work or land in order to be able to feed one's family. The allocation of the means to satisfy basic material needs is thus highly dependent upon access needs: the effective participation in social institutions such as political authority or the market is a crucial determinant for satisfying security needs (clearly security in this context is understood in the broad sense of well-being). 'Effective participation may thus also be considered a developmental need, rather than merely an *interest* which can be negotiated or denied' (1990: 9). There are many examples of identity groups being denied security, acceptance or access needs. Exclusionist policies such as the Sinhala Only Act in Sri Lanka, which discriminated against Tamil-speaking professionals applying for public service jobs, or the racial segregation agenda of South Africa's Apartheid regime illustrate the interdependence of access and security needs. In turn, access to political and economic power is linked to the level of *acceptance* of each identity group. If the ruling political elites were to recognize and politically accommodate alienated communities, then discords over the distribution of political and economic power could be managed satisfactorily. In many cases, however, deprivation of physical needs and denial of access are rooted in the refusal to recognize or accept the communal *identity* of other groups. 'Formation and acceptance of identity thus may also be understood as a basic developmental need, with collective identity manifest in terms of cultural values, images, customs, language, religion, and racial heritage' (1990: 9). Clearly, the deprivation of one form of needs usually leads to problems in other areas. As Miall et al. (1999: 73) note, Azar's analysis of the causes of conflict in terms of human needs, rather than interests, is significant, for 'unlike interests, needs are ontological and non-negotiable, so that, if conflict comes, it is likely to be intense, vicious and, from a traditional Clausewitzian perspective, "irrational"'. The third component on Azar's conflict map is *the state*. Whether or not basic needs for security, acceptance and access are satisfied is largely dependent upon the state. In the modern world, the state 'is endowed with authority to govern and to use force where necessary to regulate society, to protect citizens, and to provide collective goods' (1990: 10). Ideally, the state should be able to satisfy human needs regardless of communal or identity cleavages, and promote communal harmony and social stability. In actuality, however, this is rare. Most states which go through protracted social conflict have 'incompetent, parochial, fragile and authoritarian governments that fail to satisfy basic human needs' (1990: 10). The likelihood for protracted conflict to break out is largest in societies where political authority is monopolized by a dominant identity group, using the state as an instrument to maximize their interests and exclude others. Next to the 'communal content of the state' Azar emphasizes 'regime type' and 'level of legitimacy' as important variables between needs and protracted social conflict. The domination of the state apparatus by one (or a few) communal groups is achieved through the distortion of modes of governance and often precipitate crises of legitimacy. Such crises diminish the state's ability to meet basic needs and lead to further developmental crises (1990: 11). Another important indicator of a state's ability to satisfy needs and prevent conflict is 'the availability of resources' and the 'policy capacity' of the state. Protracted social conflicts seem to be concentrated in developing countries, although certainly not exclusively. These countries are 'typically characterized by a rapid population growth and a limited resource base'. This combination of poor resource environments amid population expansion 'will constrain policy options'. Equally important is the nature of the policy capacity of the state, 'in which framework basic needs are evaluated and policies are formulated and implemented'. The policy capacity is about governance and effectiveness of the state (1990: 11). In most protracted social conflict-laden countries, policy capacity is limited because the state is unable to 'insulate the decision-making machinery from the political pressures of the dominant identity groups'. Again, the relative strength and autonomy of the state is directly linked to the level of accommodating basic needs. Although the disjunction between the state and society is at the core of Azar's model, this is not where his analysis ends. He identifies a fourth cluster of variables which precondition conflict under the heading *international linkages*. By drawing in the international context Azar emphasizes how the ability of the state to engender or prevent conflict is not determined exclusively from within, but also importantly from without: by the patterns of linkage within the international system. Economic dependency and political and military relationships impact state autonomy and independence, and at times force state governments 'to pursue both domestic and foreign policies disjoined from, or contradictory to, the needs of its own public' (1990: 11). Much in line with our discussion in chapter three, Azar relates the lack of means to satisfy basic human needs in countries in the global South to the nature of the economic development strategy adopted. 'Typically, an unbalanced, rapid-growth development strategy has distorted the allocation of resources, leading to sectoral and regional imbalances. Certain groups of individuals, especially minority communal groups, tend to be marginalized by such rapid development strategies' (1990: 9). Also politically and militarily, governments at times are forced into positions which go directly against the 'satisfaction of the national need for intercommunal trust and harmony' (1990: 12).

Process-level dynamics of conflict

Clearly, identifying clusters of preconditions is not sufficient. Whether or not in any one case these conditions *activate* violent conflict depends upon more contingent actions and events. In his PSC model Azar identifies as key determinants the interactive effects of three clusters of variables: 'communal actions and strategies', 'state actions and strategies', and 'built-in mechanisms of conflict' (1990: 12–15). Together they form the *process-level dynamics* of social conflict. The first, 'communal actions and strategies', involves the ways in which a specific event can trigger communal action and escalate into overt conflict. Initially, a trigger may, but need not be, a trivial incident (e.g. an insult to an individual with strong communal ties). But the moment individual victimization is 'collectively recognized' this incident may become an important escalatory 'turning point'. Azar emphasizes how 'collective recognition of individual grievances (or incompatible goals) *naturally* leads to collective protest' (1990: 12, my emphasis). This assumption importantly underlies his model of PSC (and is something we need to discuss more fully later on). Escalation continues if collective protest is met by suppression or repression from the ruling elites and their constituencies, as is often the case. Issues begin to broaden, and victimized groups begin to link the triggering incident to more fundamental grievances over communal security, acceptance and access. In addition, groups often seek external support from neighbouring nations and/or strategic partners, which then blurs the distinction between internal and external demarcations of conflict. Together, rising tensions and spill-over in actors and issues 'increases the momentum for organizing and mobilizing resources'. In sum, the type of initial condition, the organization and mobilization of communal groups, the emergence of effective leadership, the scope and nature of external ties, and the strategies and tactics (civil disobedience, guerrilla warfare, secessionism) importantly determine the dynamics of conflict (1990: 14). Of course, communal actions and strategies are shaped by the responses of political authorities. These 'state actions and strategies' then are the second crucial determinant of protracted conflict dynamics. Governing elites can react in a variety of ways to collective protest. If they choose to *accommodate* communal grievances and manage to improve the satisfaction of communal needs, conflict can be resolved or 'at least kept latent'. However, this is generally not the case: not only because of the political and economic costs involved, but also because of the 'winner-take-all' mentality 'which still prevails in multicommunal societies' (1990: 14). Accommodation is often perceived as a sign of weakness. In many cases, the state resorts to coercive repression or instrumental co-optation. Such a hard-line strategy in turn invites equally militant responses from the repressed groups, leading to an upward spiral of violent clashes. If the state (or, rather, the dominant actor that monopolizes state authority) is not capable of containing a conflict situation it may seek its own external assistance. 'The existing dependency and client ties facilitate direct or indirect intervention of external powers, which not only amplifies the scope of the conflict, but also makes it more protracted' (1990: 15). Finally, Azar distinguishes various self-reinforcing 'built-in mechanisms of conflict'. The 'history of experience in the conflict' and 'the nature of communication' among hostile contestants are also responsible for the shaping of the behavioural properties of protracted conflict. Conflicts associated with communal identity (fear of marginalization or loss of communal integrity) tend to involve strong and enduring antagonistic perceptions of the other. The perceptions and motivations behind the behaviour of the state and communal actors are conditioned by the experiences, fears and belief systems of each group. In a situation of limited or proscribed interactions, the worst motivations tend to be attributed to the other side, and due to a lack of falsification this feeds into 'reciprocal negative images'. Parties subject to the stress of violent conflict tend to become close-minded: 'hostility begets hostility and the process becomes institutionalized'. Importantly, Azar stresses how 'this mechanism of a conflict spiral, set in motion by communal fear and hostility, gains velocity with the deepening of the deprivation of basic needs'. Outcomes (military victories, negotiated settlements), as long as they do not satisfy basic needs, contain latent conflicts which in turn cause further cycles of violent conflict. The experience of conflictual interaction further reinforces perceptions and cognitive processes such as stereotyping, tunnel vision, misattribution of motives, bolstering and polarization.

Due to their innate behavioural properties of *protractedness*, *fluctuation* and *actor and issue spill-over* the above described social conflicts easily become intractable. This makes them different from most other conflicts, according to Azar. 'Most conflicts, classically understood, involve zero-sum outcomes in which winners and losers can be differentiated' (1990: 15). Conversely, protracted social conflicts have negative-sum outcomes: in the end all parties are sucked into a downward spiral of physical insecurity, institutional deformity, psychological ossification and increased dependency on external actors. Fear is the one element that is most fundamental to these dynamics of polarization and implosion. As Azar puts it: 'Protracted Social Conflicts are rooted in fear of marginalization' (1990: 16). The cycle of fear and hostile interactions among communal contestants creates a 'war culture': communal boundaries become petrified and prospects for cooperative interaction become poor. It is their *complex intractability* and multi-layeredness that makes these conflicts such a 'severe challenge to those concerned with peace-building' (1990: 17).

Azar's model of protracted social conflict aims to overcome conventional dichotomies by showing the continuities and connections between the internal and the external, the latent and the overt, and between war and peace. If we compare Azar's model to the other analytical approaches discussed so far, we see that it more extensively draws on insights from a variety of disciplines and research traditions. It for instance relies on anthropological and historical understandings of identity group formation, on the biology and psychology of human needs development, on political science accounts of state power and governance, and on political economy and international relations theories of global development and strategic linkages. In addition, it makes references to the importance of the use of language, framing, discourse and cultures of war. It also importantly shows the dynamics of interaction between different levels: from the individual and the communal up to the state and the international. By making a distinction between 'preconditions' and 'actions and strategies' Azar evokes the image of the 'situated agent': individuals do make choices, but in doing so they are always restricted or enabled by structures (colonial histories, models of development, regime type). Although the 'all inclusive' PSC model seems truly multidisciplinary this is not entirely true. If we take a close look, we see that also Azar's model is built on a set of fundamental underlying assumptions. In particular, his conceptualization of the relationship between the individual and group mobilization for conflict can be traced back to what will here be explained as the basic human needs approach.

Human needs approach: humans want to belong, not compete

Azar shows his indebtedness to the human needs approach when he states that 'collective recognition of individual grievances ... naturally leads to collective protest' (1990: 12). If people are deprived of satisfaction of their basic needs on the basis of their communal identity collective action is likely to occur. Azar carefully points out how collective protests do not burst out automatically: the step to collective action, and ultimately conflict, depends on a range of facilitating, contingent factors. Nevertheless, it is the individual's needs for communal identity, access and security that forms the core of his model of PSC. This leads us back to the discussion on the nature of identity and its relationship to conflict. The basic assumption underlying the human needs approach is that identity, and in particular communal identity, is an innate human characteristic. Contrary to the Hobbesian notion of humanity as in constant competition, human needs approaches support the view of human beings as social, as somehow 'programmed' to enter into social relationships (for a more elaborate explanation and critique, see: Jabri 1996: 119–41). Put more simply, human beings want to *belong*, not to *compete*. This is what Mary Clark, in support of the human needs approach, argues: 'Biologically, we are obligatory social animals, wholly dependent on a supportive social structure, and it is in the absence of such a support system that destructive, "inhuman" behaviour occurs' (Clark 1990: 39). In essence, human needs approaches trace the source of violent behaviour in the individual need for identity. They aim to support these claims by seeking evidence from biology, such as the pathological states that result from long periods of isolation in children, arguing that violation of the basic need for identity results in psychological stress for the individual, conflict within the community and ultimately violent conflicts between communities. Since Maslow's initial formulation of a 'hierarchy of needs' (1954), theories of human needs have appeared in a great number of guises.[1] Ted Gurr, for instance, drew heavily on various human needs theories to develop the founding proposition of his research in the late 1960s: that relative deprivation can lead to collective violence. John Burton applied the human needs approach to explain conflicts as complex as those in Northern Ireland, Cyprus and Israel–Palestine. He argued that individuals will seek to satisfy their basic need for identity, irrespective of context or degrees of coercion. What most human needs approaches have in common is that grievances over the deprivation of needs are directly extrapolated from the individual to the group. By implication, they argue that political behaviour and political beliefs have their basis in a set of basic needs. In her analysis of the human needs approach Vivienne Jabri points out two important underlying assumptions. First, the image that emerges is of 'the individual driven by the desire to satisfy his or her basic needs and of a community or collectivity which is the mere sum of its constitutive parts'. And second, 'the ability of leaders to mobilise support for violent conflict is explained not so much in terms of the ability of leaderships to control and manipulate the communication of issues to their masses, but in terms of the individual constituent's decision to support such action based on her or his need for identity' (Jabri 1996: 123). Individuals 'naturally' mobilize collectively once their identity is recognized as violated. The engagement in collective action is thus understood as *affective*: frustrations over basic needs deprivation provoke emotional, collective outbursts. It is this stress on *collective resentments* that sets human needs approaches apart from other approaches to collective action.

So far I have used the term collective action in a matter-of-fact kind of way. Not only is it about time to define, but also to situate the concept within the wider research tradition on collective action. This will lead us away from the discussion on identity and needs to the specific jargon of contentious politics. We will return to the role of collective grievances with the work of Ted Gurr.

Contentious collective action

Collective action research is related to the social scientific work on social movements that emerged in the 1960s. Two broad paradigms of social movement theory can be discerned. First, the resource mobilization approach, which emerged particularly in the US and is attentive to questions of individual motivation and strategies of action, based on a clear rational choice approach (e.g. Olson 1965). Second, the 'new social movements approach', which was developed by European and Latin American scholars, and emphasized the structural foundations of collective action as well as the collective identities they expressed. In Marxian tradition, authors wrote of the fundamental cleavages of capitalist society as creating a mobilization potential, but also of the role of mobilizing vehicles (a vanguard, leaders, organizations) that can recruit and unite people and prevent dispersion, and the cultural foundations necessary to build broad consensus (see: Tarrow 1994). Over the past decades, however, the boundaries between the hard-core rational choice and more structuralist approaches blurred. The field is marked by a great diversity of research perspectives drawing on both quantitative and qualitative research methods. Roughly, collective action research is interested in explaining the *how* of joint actions: in examining the mechanisms and processes that lead to collective action. How do individuals (get) mobilize(d) for collective purposes and actions? How are movements built, and what makes people join in? How can we explain the move from passive bystander to active participant? How do individuals get involved in, or turn away from, collective action? For the study of violent conflict the sub field of collective action theory, in particular contentious collective action – or contentious politics – is significant. *Contentious* collective action is understood as challenging existing social and political structures and practices. In the early definition of Charles Tilly from 1978 'collective action consists of people's acting together in pursuit of common interests. Collective action results from changing combinations of interests, organization, mobilization and opportunity'. He warns us that 'the most persistent problem we will face in analyzing collective action is its lack of sharp edges: people vary continuously from intensive involvement to passive compliance, interests vary from quite individual to nearly universal' (1978: 7). Sidney Tarrow further specifies the term by emphasizing contention: 'Collective action becomes contentious when it is used by people who lack regular access to institutions, act in the name of new or unaccepted claims and behave in ways that fundamentally challenge others' (1994: 2). This idea of contention as claim making, collective action and politics is also central to Tilly and Tarrow's latest work *Contentious Politics* (2007). Here they argue that although violent conflicts show special features that set them off from other forms of non-violent contentious politics, such as high stakes and the problem of sustaining armed force, they show important similarities as well. In fact, what is argued for is that civil wars, revolutions, genocides, lethal ethnic or religious conflict, and non-violent contentious performances such as demonstrations, petitions and sit-ins, are all related phenomena subject to a common set of explanatory mechanisms and processes.

Various forms of contention 'overlap, mutate into each other, and result from similar mechanisms and processes in different combinations, sequences, and initial conditions' (Tilly and Tarrow 2007: 138). The difference between the contentious politics framework and other conflict approaches can be highlighted by making a brief reference to the 'Arabic Revolutions' of early 2011. The pace and intensity with which the popular protests in Tunisia and later Egypt spawned copycat movements from Libya, Syria and dirt-poor Yemen to the prosperous island kingdom of Bahrain came as a surprise to many. The 'Arab spring' can be viewed through a variety of analytical frameworks. An anthropologist, for instance, may study the shifts in cultural imagining and the emergence of new martyrs and heroes, starting perhaps with the Tunisian fruit vendor Muhammad Bouazizi, who set himself on fire in the provincial town of Sidi Bouzid and became an icon of the revolution. A rational choice theorist will emphasize the cost-benefit calculations of the actors involved, and a human needs theorist will highlight the role of collective deprivation. By contrast, the contentious politics approach is interested in neither what participants want, need or feel nor in determining the necessary conditions for mobilization, but aims to capture the mechanisms and processes through which contentious politics operates. The ways in which people make collective claims change over time and differ between regimes. The question is why. This is where mechanisms such as brokerage, diffusion and coordinated action, and processes such as mobilization and scale shift, come into play. Mechanisms are events that produce the same immediate effects over a wide range of circumstances. Processes are much broader, as they assemble mechanisms in combinations and sequences that produce larger-scale effects than any particular mechanism causes by itself (Tilly and Tarrow 2007: 29). Tilly and Tarrow aim to identify common and recurring features of contentious politics that combine in different settings to result in different outcomes. They propose a typology of regimes (democratic, undemocratic, high capacity, low capacity) that grow different repertoires of contention. Simply put, peaceful forms of contention are more likely to occur in democratic regimes, while violent conflicts tend to develop in mainly authoritarian regimes. Together, opportunity structures and established repertoires shape the forms and degrees of contention. In mainly democratic regimes, the repertoire of contention leans toward peaceful forms of contention that intersect regularly with representative institutions and produce social movement campaigns. In authoritarian regimes the repertoire leans toward violent conflicts and tends to produce ethnic and religious conflicts, civil wars and revolutions (Tilly and Tarrow 2007: 161). There is much more to the framework, but these are the core ingredients.

Where motivational aspects are concerned, the contentious politics framework differs fundamentally from Azar's PSC analysis. The two approaches do, however, show resemblances not only in the way they address the process-level dynamics of conflict, but also in their joint emphasis on political opportunity structures (regime type) as shaping repertoires of contention. Also, PSC and contentious politics both construct their frameworks upon the systematic analysis of conflict/contention in series of case studies.

There is a growing, but also scattered, body of literature that draws on elements of collective action theory for the explanation of violent conflict. Scholars in this field highlight a number of crucial areas of enquiry to explain collective violence. Not very far removed from Tilly's original idea that collective action results from 'changing combinations of interests, organization, mobilization and opportunity', they select

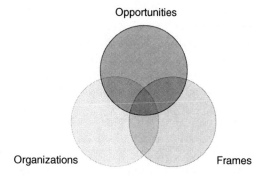

Opportunities

Organizations   Frames

Figure 4.2 Collective action: opportunities, organizations and frames

'opportunities', 'organizational structures' and 'framing' as vital building blocks (see figure 4.2). The basic argument is that to gain insight into the power dynamics of civil war one needs to examine the precise *opportunities* (material, ideological) that potential entrepreneurs of violence can seize on to get mobilization going; as well as the formal and informal *organizations* that help to sustain fights (from short-term riots to protracted insurgencies or civil wars), and the *frames* through which violent entrepreneurs interpret, present – and market – a brewing conflict (see: King 2007).

What has become quite clear by now is that the continuing question of what causes violent conflict is partly a problem of method and data, in other words, 'a matter of how explanations are constructed or supported' (Cramer 2006: 92). The study of mobilization for violent action is divided by qualitative and quantitative analysis, between scholars who build their theories on individual (or sets of) case studies (such as the ones discussed above) and those relying on statistical analysis in their aim to pin down which factors make the occurrence of violent conflict likely. The approach of Ted Gurr clearly falls into the latter, 'large-N', category and it is to his work that we turn now.

Ted Gurr: why minorities rebel

Building on his large Minorities at Risk data base, Gurr and his team conduct quantitative tests of a series of hypotheses about the causes, or at least correlates, of minority conflict. The aim is to produce global and universal explanations about the political mobilization of minorities, which can be of help to predict and prevent such conflicts from breaking out. Gurr's data base is widely used and his work has been influential, particularly as a conflict prevention tool. Nevertheless, most of my students seem somewhat disorientated by his detailed listing of propositions about factors determining communal group action. The problem with large-N analyses such as Gurr's is that they make empirical generalizations rather than providing analytical concepts. They examine how output variables (violent conflict) co-vary with input variables (e.g. ethnic fragmentation, poverty, political instability), without saying much about the complex causal chains between the inputs and the outputs. As Kar-atzogianni (2006: 53) noticed for social movement theories in general, the problem is that scholars, in an attempt to draw up a theory to explain their empirical findings, 'pick and mix from their predecessors'. For the development of the founding propositions of his Minorities at Risk model, Gurr importantly drew on human needs approaches, and complemented these with insights from social psychology, mobilization theory and structuralism. Evidently, Gurr's choice of method and data leaves less room for a process dynamics approach. This is where Gurr's model most clearly differs from the above 'dynamics of contention' approaches, which aim to theorize the interplay between actors and structures through an emphasis on mechanisms and processes.

Apart from these noticeable distinctions, Gurr's work also shows resemblances to Azar's model of protracted social conflict. Both take the identity group as starting point for the analysis of collective action, they both emphasize the importance of 'collectively shared resentments', and both aim to draw contextual factors such as the 'character of the state' and 'external support' into their models. Gurr's main puzzle revolves around why culturally distinct groups become engaged in protest and rebellion against the state. He acknowledges how structural transformations such as the rise of the modern state system and the global capitalist economy set the larger context. It is nevertheless the specifics of each group's situation which determine *how* it acts within this larger setting. For Gurr four general factors determine the nature, intensity and persistence of a group's actions. First, the salience of ethno-cultural *identity* for members and leaders of the group. Second, the extent to which the group has *collective incentives* for political action. Third, the extent of the group's *capacities* for collective action. Fourth, the availability of *opportunities* in the group's political environment that increase its chances of attaining group objectives through political action. So, if a group scores high on all four factors, rebellion is likely to break out. Let us take the example of Kosovo in the late 1990s to discuss Gurr's model in more detail. In formulating propositions about the first factor in his model, *the salience of social identity*, Gurr drew on socio-psychology, especially the work of Donald Horowitz on ethnicity (1985) as discussed in chapter two. During the late 1990s, ethnic identity was no doubt important to people in Kosovo. The wars in other parts of Yugoslavia had just come to an end, but despite the active lobby of Kosovo's 'underground president' Rugova, the international community had decided to leave the 'Kosovo issue' out of the 1995 Dayton accords. Albanian Kosovars had high *incentives* to rebel: they experienced economic and political discrimination and collective disadvantages vis-à-vis the Serbian population, and feared for the future. The concept of incentives is derived from human needs theory and Gurr's earlier work on the motivating forces of relative deprivation (1970). The basic argument is that people who have lost ground relative to what they had in the past, or who anticipate losses, experience relative deprivation. This disposes them to support movements that defend and promote the group's status. Major incentives for collective action are group discrimination, loss of political autonomy and repression. Incentives are not merely about self-interests but are characterized by their strong emotional content. 'Members of identity groups usually resent their disadvantages and seek redress not only, or even necessarily, with self-interest in mind, but with passion, self-righteousness, and solidarity with their kindred' (Gurr 2007: 139). For most of the 1990s, Kosovar Albanians had largely supported the non-violent campaign of Rugova's Democratic League of Kosovo (DLK), and its parallel system of governance. So, despite the high scores on identity and incentives, the Kosovars did not resort to violent insurgency or rebellion. This changed during the late 1990s when both their *capacity* for collective action increased and new *opportunities* became available. Both the Albanian diaspora and US foreign policy played an important role in this.

During the first half of the 1990s, the Albanian diaspora in places such as Zürich, Berlin and New York had backed Rugova's policy of non-violent resistance and had contributed financially to its parallel system of governance. It is often claimed that Rugova's position began to be undermined when Kosovo was left off the agenda at the Dayton Peace Agreement in 1995. Another important event was the sudden availability of small arms in the region due to the disintegration of Albania after what became known as the 'pyramid schemes' in December 1996, adding to the rapid militarization of Kosovar society. It was however the widely screened Drencia massacre of February 1998 which was decisive in the rise to power of the insurgency movement the Kosovo Liberation Army (KLA). The images of the mutilated corpses of villagers on news shows all over the world caused a shift in diaspora support, away from the moderate DLK to the openly militant KLA. Importantly, this was also the time when US foreign policy turned in favour of the insurgency movement. Having earlier labelled the KLA a terrorist organization, the US by May 1998 initiated high-level contacts with them.[2] It was KLA leader Hashim Thaci and not Rugova who headed the Kosova delegation at the Rambouillet negotiations in 1999. Analysts held a number of factors responsible for the US turn, such as 'No Second Bosnia', an ever-growing willingness on the side of the US to resort to military intervention, and the need to use the KLA as ground troops. Either way, the turnabout of both the diaspora and US foreign policy importantly enhanced the KLA's mobilizing capacity and provided favourable opportunities for rebellion (Heinemann-Grüder and Paes: 2001; Hockenos 2003; Sullivan 2004).

Gurr argues that the extent of a group's *capacity for collective action* depends first of all on the salience of group identity and shared incentives. Furthermore, capacity is enhanced if the group has pre-existing organizational networks and authentic leaders who can bridge internal divisions. Rebellion is also more feasible for groups that have a territorial base. In supporting this third determining factor of minority rebellion, Gurr brings in rationality: the process by which groups organize for collective action is assumed to be fundamentally a rational one. '[M]ost communal action, including all sustained campaigns of protest and rebellion, is shaped by strategic assessments and tactical decisions of the leaders and activists of politically mobilized groups' (2007: 144). Here the 'pick and mix' nature of his approach becomes apparent: collective action is understood as both emotional (passion and solidarity with the group) *and* rational (strategic and tactical). What emerges is an image of 'emotional masses' and 'strategizing elites'. The interplay between the two factors, however, is left aside. We will return to this later. Gurr's final proposition deals with the availability of *opportunity* in the group's political environment. He distinguishes 'durable' opportunity factors such as the character of the state as shaping the way in which groups organize and as affecting their long-term choices about strategies. 'Transient' factors are the changes in the structure of a group's political environment such as shifts in government policy, turnover of elites, the rise of new political allies, but also foreign military support, and regional spill-over and 'contagion'. Underlying Gurr's fourth proposition is the work of, for instance, Sidney Tarrow (1994, 1998) and his argument that 'changes in the political opportunity structure create incentives for collective action' (1994: 4). Simply put, environmental, contextual factors 'shape' human action. Gurr hence draws on insights from social psychology, human needs, mobilization theory and structure-based approaches to explain minority rebellion (see table 4.1).

Table 4.1 Gurr's model of minority rebellion

Factors	Theoretical frames and traditions
Group identity	Social psychology
Incentives	Human needs approach
Capacity	Mobilization theory
Opportunity	Structure-based approach

Explaining versus understanding

Research projects such as Gurr's Minorities at Risk, which work from a quantitative, large-N approach first and foremost aim to *explain*, not necessarily *understand*, violent conflict. The objective is to explain political action 'by any kind of identity group' (Gurr 2007: 137). So, although Gurr often uses the catchy title *Why* Do Men Rebel, he in fact does not really address this question. That is, not from the vantage point of those performing the rebellion. Rather, his research sheds light on when, generally speaking, men *are most likely to* rebel. Where Gurr argues people are most likely to rebel in case of high identity, incentives, capacity and opportunity, his colleagues in the quantitative approach come up with different, although overlapping, propositions and factors. Oberschall, for instance, works with the rubrics *discontent, mobilizing capacity* and *political opportunity* (2004); Fearon and Laitin (2003) argue that factors explaining which countries are at risk of civil war are not their ethnic or religious characteristics but rather the conditions that favour insurgency. These include *poverty* – which marks financially and bureaucratically weak states and also favours rebel recruitment – *political instability, rough terrain* and *large populations*. As we will see in chapter five, Collier and Hoeffler (2001) argue that rebellion is better explained by 'greed' than 'grievance', and that the main determinant of greed is the availability of finance and recruits for rebels. They proxy these with measures of *primary commodity exports*, the proportion of *young men* in a society and the endowment of *education*. The 'large-N' quantitative approach to civil war and violent action makes up an influential part of the field of Conflict Studies – often coined Civil War Studies – particularly in the US. It would take us too far to discuss the many internal debates about hypotheses, propositions and proxies, and to review the various sets of factors that are distinguished as explaining rebellion. This will lead us into a too technical, and unreadable, discussion. Rather, it suffices here to conclude that no matter how diverse the outcomes, quantitative research approaches depart from a joint epistemological stance: through a careful testing of a series of hypotheses it is possible to produce general explanations of group actions, in this case collective violent action. Human action is thus seen as *predictable*: the search for general explanatory propositions implies that, by and large, human action is determined. Put simply, the approach wants to know 'how most people will react most of the time'. So, if a group scores high on Gurr's four factors, or Collier and Hoefler's three proxies, be it the Kosovar Albanians in Former Yugoslavia, the Somalis in Kenya, or the Tuareg in Mali, they all are likely to resort to collective violent action. Ultimately, human action is seen as caused by a combination of particular principles or laws. As we discussed earlier, here we see the divide between *explaining* and *understanding*. Theorists differ fundamentally on whether they see human action as essentially determined and hence predictable, or whether they emphasize human creativity and social meaning and interpretation as more important. Thus, although scholars arguing from the 'understanding stance' do not deny the existence of important reg-ularities in behaviour, they emphasize instead the *creative* way in which people inter-pret meaning during the course of interaction. Our entire social world and experience of society are, they argue, things that we build up as we go along, not things that are objectively real. Consequently, one should not develop concrete propositions that impose a misleading character of fixed meaning and structure on this process (Wallace and Wolf 1999: 1–15). From this perspective, social identifications such as for instance 'ethno-cultural identity' cannot be pinned down as fixed properties, but are understood as fluid and thus as changing over the course of a conflict or even within the context of a single event. In addition, ethnicity means different things to different individuals, and country-level indications of 'salience of identity' are impossible to establish. The large-N approaches and their explanatory epistemologies are ill equipped to capture fluidity, specificity and complexity.

Underlying the explaining/understanding divide is an argument of what constitutes theory in the social sciences and humanities. Whereas theory in the large-N approaches is seen as a set of careful propositions meant to link cause and consequence, the 'understanding' position calls for a view on theory building as *sense making*: grounded in the goal of integrating the self-conscious perspectives of participants themselves (King 2004). Clearly, the different perspectives on theory building rely on different research methodologies: whereas the former work with statistical analysis of a large number of violent conflicts, the latter depend upon in-depth case-study research of individual cases. As Cramer (2006: 92) points out, the usual critique of qualitative analysis is that in-depth case studies are overly descriptive and are not able to confirm any general theoretical constancy. The more detailed they are the less useful they are for the rest of the world. On the other hand, quantitative studies, by stripping wars of their specific contexts, lose their connections to reality.

Despite this rather rigid epistemological divide, scholars have attempted to bridge the gap between explaining and understanding. For instance, by building the notion of sense-making into their (largely explanatory) models, often through a stress on the importance of 'framing' (Gurr 2007; Oberschall 2004). Gurr, for instance, acknowl-edges the shortcomings of his model when he states that the 'ways in which identity, incentives, and capacity are translated into communal actions depends on political and cultural context in ways that are difficult to summarize in general principles' (2007: 144). Others, such as Horowitz (2001) and Kalyvas (2006) and Kalyvas and Kocher (2007b), show how the use of multiple methods – drawing on large-N data as well as participant interviews and archival work – can produce a far more complex picture not only of the interests and intentions of violent actors but also of the social meanings with which their acts are invested. Before turning to the core questions of the book, I will briefly discuss these more hybrid approaches here.

Micropolitics of social violence

In a review article of 'ethnic conflict' research, Charles King indicates a clear trend toward a 'micropolitical turn' in the study of social violence (2004). The goal of this research is to theorize the connection between identities and interests and the relation-ship between leaderships and masses. Rather than merely reducing social action to individual grievances or calculation, it aims to understand how violence results from the joint actions of local and supra-local actors, and looks at how forms of collective violence might, from the vantage point of those engaged, be seen as legitimate, as making sense. Among the characteristics of the new research programme is a stress on *disaggregation* and *framing*, that is, on studying violence at analytical levels far below the nation-state level and an attentiveness to the ways violent episodes are framed.

Disaggregation

By taking a disaggregated approach to the study of violent conflict, authors such as Horowitz (2001), Beissinger (2002), Varshney (2002), Wood (2003) and Kalyvas (2006) provide added nuance to our understanding of the variation in violence during what is often lumped together as one single 'ethnic conflict' or 'civil war'. They show, for the cases of the former Soviet Union, India, El Salvador and the Greek civil war, how violence does not occur uniformly across time and space, it comes to different cities, villages and neighbourhoods at different times and in a variety of forms. For the case of India, for instance, Varshney wants to understand why despite high levels of structural similarity, some cities have high incidences of Hindu–Muslim rioting, while others seem generally immune. Others ask similar questions pertaining to the puzzling variation in violence during conflict. How are victims and enemies selected, how do local actors build alliances, how do personal rivalries play out? Doing this kind of research demands an extreme sensitivity to micro-level social interactions, but also to the complex ways in which local actors manipulate political organizations, and the 'privatization of political violence'. What most of these disaggregated research projects have in common is that they unify various methods: large-N data analysis to identify broad patterns and develop hypotheses; but also archival work, in-depth interviewing and anthropological fieldwork to uncover fine-tuned evidence. Research outcomes, of course, differ, but they generally show how country-based factors explaining violent conflict (as discussed in this chapter) seem to be a poor explanation for the variability of violence across both space and time. They also show the importance of the *reflexive power of mobilization*: both organizers and average participants in rebellion act within a particular knowledge environment. Their decisions are influenced by their assessment of what has failed or succeeded in other circumstances. As King explains, 'any single protest is thus a wave in a much larger period of "tidal politics"' (2004: 441). This appreciation of how actors themselves understand their environment also sheds light on why structurally disadvantaged groups (those who score low on all 'rebellion factors') mobilize for collective violent action: because of the mere knowledge that others have successfully done it before them. Examples of this are the wave of revolutions and anti-government uprisings that swept the Arab world in 2011 and the anti-Communist revolutions in Eastern Europe of 1989, which began in Poland and continued in Hungary, East Germany, Bulgaria, Czechoslovakia and Romania. Micro-political analyses of collective violence during conflict highlight what King calls the 'power of contingency': event-specific processes often turn out to be critical to the course of a conflict. An example of this is the earlier mentioned case of city-level variation in the incidence of Hindu–Muslim inter-communal rioting. Based on his own data-set derived from a systematic coding of riots reported in the *Times of India* between 1950 and 1995, Varshney found out that low-violence cities have strong associational ties between Hindu and Muslim communities. The origins of these differences in associational life, in turn, can be traced back to the period of the all-India national movement of the 1920s to 1940s. In these decades, elites in different cities opted for different reactions to the politics of mass mobilization of these days. Varshney indicates how they created different 'master narratives' about the nature of intercommunal relations. In cities where the master narrative became one of caste, Hindu and Muslim elites jointly cooperated across the traditional communal divide, forming solid bicommunal organizations, such as unions and business alliances, and stood against low-caste Hindus. In others, where the master narrative became one of communal identity, both groups turned inwards. In the latter, inter-communal differences were politicized, and the salience of ethnic lines as political dividers discouraged the formation of associational bonds. In the post-independence days, these differences in associational life made the difference between relative peace and deadly ethnic riots (see: King 2004).

Insights such as these help to nuance and understand violent conflict not as a binary struggle between unitary groups or blocks A and B, but rather as sets of violent episodes, which are clustered both spatially and temporally. Under the heading of one conflict label (A and B are at war) many different, and at times unrelated, violent episodes occur. Large-N approaches working from the aggregate level of the state, tend to treat the cluster themselves ('the war in Congo', or 'the Rwandan genocide') as the only serviceable dependent variable. The variety of violent episodes and their sources and dynamics are lumped together under one label and individual cases of violence are automatically processed as part and parcel of that larger conflict. At the end of 2006, the dominant view on violence in Iraq was that of 'sectarian violence' between Shia and Sunni communities. Underscoring the view that civil wars are typically aggregations of multiple highly fragmented conflicts, Kalyvas and Kocher (2007a), conversely, show how Iraq was the site of at least five conflicts. Besides anti-American insurgency in the Sunni heartland, there was sectarian strife between Shia and Sunni militias in and around Baghdad, but also conflict between Arabs and Kurds in the north, factional strife among rival Shiite militias in the south, and clashes among criminal mafias, contraband gangs and rogue party militias. An important question, often obscured by debates on dichotomies, is how the emergence of one conflict affects the intensity of the other, and vice-versa.

Framing

Another characteristic of the micropolitical approach is the attentiveness to the way violent conflict is framed. This emphasis on framing allows us to return to a question that neither the human needs approach nor Gurr's quantitative approach has tackled satisfactorily: that of the interplay between leaderships and groups. So far, the image that has emerged is of violent conflict resulting from a combination of group grievances and leadership strategizing. As we have seen, the capacity of leaders to mobilize support for violent action stems directly from their ability to give voice to the collective needs (Azar) and grievances (Gurr) of 'their' groups/masses, and has less to do with their ability to control or manipulate communication. As Gurr states: 'People get the leaders they are prepared to follow. Leaders can strengthen existing group ties and provide a greater awareness of shared interests, but they *cannot create them*' (2007: 143, my emphasis). Frame analysis questions this rather straightforward relation between groups and leaderships, and that of 'conflict agendas' as simply there, waiting to be uncovered and 'recognized'. Rather, conflict is understood as socially and discursively constructed. The rhetorical battle for control over what the conflict is about, and the way in which violence is coded and described, is seen as at least as important as the outcomes of specific violent struggles themselves. In an attempt to highlight the inter-active nature of meaning construction, and show how both leaderships and groups are involved in this, Sidney Tarrow (1994, 1998) introduced the concept of collective action frames.

In the early 1990s, Snow and Benford adopted Erving Goffman's (1974) concept of 'framing' to the field of social movements theory and argued that there is a special category of cognitive understandings that relate to how social movements construct meaning. In their definition a frame is an 'interpretive schemata that simplifies and condenses the "world out there" by selectively punctuating and encoding objects, situations, events, experiences, and sequences of actions within one's present or past environment' (1992: 137). They argue that social movements are deeply involved in the work of 'naming' grievances, connecting them to other grievances and constructing larger frames of meaning that will resonate with a population's cultural predispositions and communicate a uniform message to power holders and others (1992: 136). A couple of years later, Tarrow reformulated this idea into the notion of *collective action frames*. In his words, collective actions frames 'redefine social conditions as unjust and intolerable with the intention of mobilizing potential participants, which is achieved by making appeals to perceptions of justice and emotionality in the minds of individuals' (Tarrow 1998: 111). As he points out, this kind of 'framing work' (a term coined by Snow) is by no means easy. It is no simple matter to 'convince timid people that the indignities of everyday life are not written in the stars and can be attributed to some agent, and that they can change their condition by taking action collectively' (1994: 122–3). Although frames can be important mobilizing resources, it is not the case that organizers/leaderships can 'construct them out of whole cloth'. Tarrow emphasizes the interactive complexity of meaning construction by arguing that:

> organizers relate their goals to the predispositions of their target public. They are thus in a certain sense *consumers* of existing cultural meanings as well as producers of new ones. ... But movement entrepreneurs do not simply adapt frames of meaning from traditional cultural symbols either – if they did, they would be nothing more than reflections of their societies and could not change them. They orient their movement's frames towards action, and fashion them at the intersection between a target population's culture and their own values and goals.
>
> (1994: 123)

This process of the re-appropriation of meaning, which Snow and his collaborators call 'frame alignment' is not always uncontested. The coding of events is a highly con-flictive process, with different voices competing for cultural supremacy. For the study of violent conflict, the micro-level analysis of 'event making' has produced interesting results. Horowitz showed in his micro analysis of a large number of ethnic conflicts (1985) and riots (2001) how the 'ethnic' quality of ethnic violence is not intrinsic to the act itself: it emerges through after-the-fact interpretative claims. So, a violent incident (a family feud, a barroom brawl, a land dispute) turns 'ethnic' if the putative ethnic difference is coded – by those who have the power to define – as integral to the vio-lence. Such definitional supremacy is not always established: think of for instance the intense episodes of car burnings in the suburbs of a number of French cities, particularly Paris, in the autumn of 2005. A cacophony of frames was attached to the violence: ranging from 'the intifada of the suburbs', 'immigrant revolt', 'the uprising of the underclass' to 'youth boredom' and 'ethnic conflict' and the 'jihad against Europe'. Often 'frames of violence' are contested: creating a 'meta-conflict', that is, a conflict over the nature of the conflict (Horowitz 2001). This coding struggle may itself generate future violence. As we will discuss more elaborately in chapter six when we turn to discourse analysis, it is important to study the way in which violent incidents are framed, for violence is often accompanied by social struggles to define its meaning. Paul Brass in his study *Riots and Pogroms* (1996) is perhaps most explicit when stating that in fact causes do not really matter in understanding violence, it is the framing of the events and the meanings attached to it which in the end explain the dynamics of violent conflict:

> Violence ... can occur anywhere and can be organized or random, premeditated or spontaneous, directed at specific persons, or property or not. While these aspects of violence must be identified insofar as possible in our descriptions of particular events, we need also to examine the discourses of violence, the ways in which participants and observers – local and external, media, politicians and authorities, journalists and academics – seek to explain incidents of violence.
>
> (Brass 1996: 2)

In a slightly similar way, Stanley Tambiah in his work on rioting in South Asia emphasizes how violent action can become routinized, even ritualized, up to the point that putative 'root causes' become illusory (1996). Framing thus can be used in a variety of ways: as a component of the study of how and why people mobilize for collective violent action (next to 'mobilizing structures' and 'political opportunity'); but also as part of an 'ethnography of event making' through the systematic examination of the variety of meanings attached to violent episodes (see for examples of this: Brass 1997; Malkki 1995). Increasingly, the role of the Internet and in particular social media as 'framing space' is included in this analysis. Debate between cyber-utopians and cyber-realists on the Internet as makers or breakers of popular revolutions will certainly be part of conflict research agendas of the next decade (see: Morozov 2011; Wu 2010). Finally, one can apply frame analysis to the ways in which academics and policy makers label war and violent conflict. 'Framing is never divorced from the context in which it occurs, whether the "coder" is in the middle of a civil war or in the middle of a political science department' (King 2004: 453). For just as people in and at war are engaged in processes of 'sense making', so are the so called 'outsiders': policy makers, donor NGOs, journalists and diplomats, and academics. It is questionable whether anyone is capable of developing an understanding of violence that is separate from prevailing ideological and social scientific paradigms and interpretative frames in which they are so often placed. In the following chapter we will come back to this issue of prevailing 'frames of violence' in the field of Conflict Studies.

Conclusions

The compartmentalization of the field of Conflict Studies as Azar sketched it in 1990 has certainly partly been overcome. Most studies acknowledge the importance of internal and external dimensions of conflict, and at least seem to recognize the transformative capacity of violence. The tendency to cut up violent conflict into specific sub-categories has remained, however, as have, largely, the disciplinary distinctions.

In particular, there is an intellectual wall between research on ethnic conflict, with its theoretical positions on constructivism, primordialism and instrumentalism (see chapter one) and the above theorizing on group mobilization and collective violence. Furthermore, there are profound differences in method and data, and the ways in which explanations and understandings of violent conflict are constructed and supported. Dichotomies such as structure/agency, affection/calculation, or needs/ interests still stand. Nevertheless, new exciting research projects and theoretical frameworks have been developed over the past decades, such as Tilly and Tarrow's contentious politics, and the above discussed 'micro-political turn'.

The analytical frames discussed in this chapter aim to combine insights from a variety of disciplinary traditions, ranging from social psychology to international relations and certainly can be classified as multi-causal. Nevertheless, when we return to the work of the two 'conflict classics', Azar and Gurr, we see that the motivational aspects of collective action 'weigh more' than other components. For the development of the founding proposition of their multi-causal models both authors are informed by *human needs theory*, that is, they both emphasize how collective need deprivation can lead to violence. Where Azar emphasizes how protracted social conflict results from a complex causal chain involving both structures and actors, Gurr's agenda is to determine the necessary and sufficient conditions for mobilization. Epistemologically, Gurr, and Azar to a certain extent, fit into the research tradition of *collective action research*, with its emphasis on extracting and comparing categorized features of a large number of cases, and its aim to produce general explanations of group actions. Let us see how they would answer the three questions of this book.

What makes a group?

Both Azar and Gurr see the identity group as crucial in explaining violent conflict. With their explicit focus on 'communal contents', they were among the first scholars in the field who argued that it was the identity group – ethnic, religious, cultural and other – and not the nation-state that was at the core of most contemporary conflicts. Both take a constructivist approach to group formation: groups are historical and social constructs; the salience of communal identity varies widely among and within groups and is subject to change over time. Nevertheless, the group as such is seen as of great importance to human beings: people have a basic need for communal identity. This is most explicitly voiced by Azar, who, in line with human needs theory argues that individuals strive to fulfil their basic needs through the formation of identity groups. So, 'what makes a group' is the individual need for communal identity. Both approaches focus not so much on processes of group formation as sources of conflict but rather on external factors (incentives, capacities, regime type and international linkages) that may mobilize already existing groups for collective violent action. Whereas in chapter one we discussed approaches which stressed how 'groups are made' in the event of war, here the group is thus taken as prior. Collective grievances over need deprivation, and collective fear of marginalization are seen as importantly holding groups together. For both Azar and Gurr the unit of analysis is thus the group, whereas for others such as Horowitz (2001) or Beissinger (2002) the unit is the event (the deadly ethnic riot, the violent episode).

How and why does a group resort to violence?

Let us discuss once more the connection between identity and conflict. What is required for individuals to act collectively? Authors drawing on human needs approaches assume that the relation between collective action and the development formation of a collective consciousness among individuals who share the same resentment is rather natural: people have a need to belong and hence will act in solidarity with their kindred. It is this reasoning which underlies the approaches of both Azar and Gurr. So, to answer the 'why' part of the question: it is their joint grievances that motivate groups to resort to collective violence. Clearly, the explanatory power of the approaches does not stop there. Both identify a set of ('how') factors and conditions as prerequisites for collective action, such as the role of organizations and leaders and (political) opportunity. Whether or not short-term episodes of collective violence (riots, lynching) evolve into sustained violent conflict (insurgencies and civil wars) is seen to depend upon the political, external environment and on the strategic and organizational skills of elites and leaderships. Although Gurr explicitly coins this strategizing as 'rational' it is important to not mistake this for utility maximization (see chapter five). Gurr's Minority at Risk project shows methodological similarities to many large-N analyses informed by collective action theory; it is, however, not based, as some of them are, on rational *choice* theory. Rather, the stress is on how a vanguard of leaders aims to defend and promote the group's status through strategic and tactical action, not on the cost-benefit calculation guiding individual behaviour. As we will see in the next chapter, Azar's and Gurr's view on the individual's *affective* engagement in collective action differs from the rational choice emphasis on the individual as primarily driven by *calculation*.

How and why do they (not) stop?

The most simple – and certainly the most simplistic – way to approach the question of conflict termination is to take the factors explaining war, and stop them from operating. This is indeed the approach taken by a number of authors. If capacity is high, target the sources of income of the warring parties and make war unprofitable. If opportunities for rebellion or state repression are high, try to 'lower the opportunity costs of peace' through for instance raising the attractiveness of negotiation. When it comes to framing, external mediators could try to shift the wording of the conflict (e.g. by convincing actors to talk about 'autonomy', not 'sovereignty'). Clearly, most conflict factors are rather robust, and changing them is not easy. As both Azar and Gurr have highlighted, the complex intractability of many contemporary conflicts makes termination, let alone resolution, extremely difficult. Their approaches, however, most certainly include directions for resolution. Both authors place (the deprivation of) *needs* and not (the pursuit of) *interests* at the centre of their analytical frame. This emphasis on needs is explicit, and refers to a view of conflict transformation embedded in the human needs approach. The challenge of conflict resolution, according to the human needs approach, is to distinguish the needs underlying what actors frame as interests. For there is an important difference between the two. As Burton (1990) argued, interests are primarily about material 'goods' and can be traded, bargained and negotiated. Needs, being non-material, cannot be traded or satisfied by power bargaining. However, crucially, non-material needs are not scarce resources (as land or oil might be) and are not necessarily in short supply. In theory, therefore, conflicts stemming from unsa-tisfied needs can be resolved. As soon as parties recognize that both their needs (for identity, security) are not necessarily zero-sum, but can be satisfied at the same time, this opens a space for resolution. For instance, a conflict over territory such as in the case of Kosovo, Tamil Eelam or Jerusalem, may seem intractable: all parties have an interest in claiming the land as their own. However, if we move beyond the swollen words of politicians and leaders, and translate the conflict into the underlying basic needs of people for a secure and normal life, important steps towards resolution can be taken (see: Miall et al. 1999: 39–64). Holsti (1991) refines the human needs strategy for conflict resolution by distinguishing *values* underlying a conflict, the specific *issues* which define a conflict situation, and the *stakes* involved. Jabri (1996), takes the example of the Israel–Palestine conflict to illustrate Holsti's trilateral distinction. The Israel–Palestine conflict may be broken down into a number of *issues* which are salient to the actors involved: territorial boundaries, the nature of Palestine autonomy, the Jewish settlements, economic rights, the future of the Palestinian diaspora, the treat-ment of political prisoners and the maintenance of law and order. The *values* under-lying these issues include: national identity, political self-determination and the right to security. The *stakes* for the leaders of both sides can be defined as the maintenance of unity, legitimacy and support from their respective constituencies, and their allies in the external world. Not so far removed from Burton's observation on the difference between a focus on interests or needs, Jabri notices how the success or failure of a process of conflict resolution 'may be determined by whether it begins with addressing the underlying values, the specific issues, or the stakes involved' (1996: 20).

Although Azar acknowledges the potential for conflict resolution through a needs perspective, he also shows his structuralist face when arguing by the end of his book that to reduce people's collective grievances over basic material needs, structural solutions are required:

> Reducing overt conflict requires reduction in levels of underdevelopment. Groups which seek to satisfy their identity and security through conflict are in effect seek-ing change in the structure of society. Conflict resolution can only truly occur and last if satisfactory amelioration of underdevelopment occurs as well.

He concludes by stating that the study of protracted conflict shows us that 'peace is development in the broadest sense of the term' (Azar 1990: 155).

Many of the strengths and weaknesses of the reviewed approaches have already been discussed throughout the chapter and do not need to be listed here. They show up again as soon as we enter the question of ontology and epistemology, that is, when we try and fit Azar's and Gurr's models in the Hollis matrix. Ontologically, the human needs approach ultimately argues from the individual perspective, as human action is primarily explained by the individual's 'internal computer' to adhere to the group and act collectively in case group needs are in danger. This would make a case for placing both Azar's and Gurr's models in the (left) lower box. However, no matter how much the approaches under discussion build their founding propositions on the human needs approach, they also importantly complicate matters, and emphasize how individuals mobilize for collective violent action due to external factors, both relational and structural. Epistemologically, it is equally difficult 'to box' the approaches. Yes, both models first and foremost aim to explain human action from without, extracting and comparing categorized features of a large number of cases, and aim to produce general explanations of group actions. On the other hand, they also include sense-making components, such as frames and discourses, into their approach. This 'un-boxability' is both a strength and a weakness. The classic multi-causal approaches under review in this chapter are able to identify many valuable dimensions of conflict and produce helpful conflict maps. What remains under-theorized, however, is how these various elements interact. Yes, violent conflict results from the way society is organized and who participates in it, but how should we think through the relation between individuality and society on a more abstract level? Here again, we seem to run into the limits of multidisciplinary 'pick and mix' models: the approaches under review either work from a singular point of departure (human needs) or engage in a form of theoretical stacking, leaving questions on interplay and synthesis to others.

Table D

Ontology/Epistemology	Explaining (positivist)	Understanding (interpretative)
Structuralism		
Individualism	Human needs approach	

Further reading

Azar, Edward (1990) *The Management of Protracted Social Conflict: Theory and Cases*, Hampshire: Dartmouth, pp. 5–17.
Gurr, Ted Robert (2007) 'Minorities, Nationalists and Islamists: Managing Communal Conflict in the Twenty-First Century' in Chester A. Crocker et al. (eds.) *Leashing the Dogs of War: Conflict Management in a Divided World*, Washington, D.C.: United States Institute of Peace Press, pp. 131–60.
King, Charles (2004) 'The Micropolitics of Social Violence', *World Politics* 25: 431–55.
Tilly, Charles and Sidney Tarrow (2007) *Contentious Politics*, Boulder: Paradigm.

Recommended documentaries

The Brooklyn Connection: How to Build a Guerrilla Army (Klaartje Quirijns, 2005).
The Making of the Revolution (Katarina Rejger and Eric van den Broek, 2001)
Bringing Down a Dictator (Steve York, PBS series, 2002).

5 Rational choice theory

The costs and benefits of war

As students of violence we prioritize and connect certain aspects of violent conflict, and disregard others. Undeniably, our analysis is selective and influenced by ideological and scientific paradigms and interpretative frames. No matter how systematic, our analysis is always shaped by our 'knowledge environment' as well as our personal and political positions and preferences. Academic thinking is about the ability to articulate and situate one's own theoretical position and to critically review the dialogue between ideas and evidence. It is also about the responsibility to critically think through the political consequences of the knowledge one produces. Evidently, the way in which we frame violent conflict has implications outside academia. *Framing* also always involves *claiming*. By framing one not only 'simplifies and condenses the "world out there" by selectively encoding objects, situations, events, experiences, and sequences of actions within one's present or past environment' as Snow and Benford (1992: 137) argue, but one also puts moral claims on, for instance, the (il)legitimacy of violent conflict. One of the core arguments of this book is that the selection of an interpretative frame is not merely an isolated academic act, it is also political.

> The selection of a form and level of explanation for contemporary violent conflict is a serious political act in the sense that representations have political implications. The way in which violent incidents and conflicts are coded and categorized will play – intentionally, or not – a role in casting blame and responsibility.
>
> (Brass 1996: 4)

Taking this idea of the politics of portrayal as point of departure I aim to do two things in this chapter. First and foremost, the chapter reviews the rational choice approach to violent conflict. It will do so by highlighting the work of Paul Collier and his 'greed theory of conflict'. This theory starts from the proposition that people will conduct civil war if the perceived benefits outweigh the costs of rebellion. We will look into critiques of the greed model and discuss approaches which aim to 'rescue' the study of economic interests in war from Collier's narrow model. Wars are very often not about winning, but serve complex economic and political functions. Consequently, we will discuss the idea of rationality and look into 'thin' and 'thick' theories of rationality. The second aim of this chapter, or rather its underlying agenda, is to contextualize Collier's greed theory politically. This is where the discussion on the politics of portrayal comes back in. Why is it that despite the fact that in academia 'greed theory' is largely dismissed as flawed (even to a certain extent by Collier himself) donor policy makers continue to hold the approach in such high regard?[1] This chapter tentatively concludes that, together with 'good governance', the 'greed theory of conflict' offered policy-makers in the aid and development industry a way out of the 'crisis of neoliberalism'. By the early 2000s, institutions such as the World Bank were struggling with the disappointing results of two decades of neoliberal restructuring programmes in the developing world. The greed theory offered a way to counter mounting criticism by casting blame and responsibility on local (greedy) actors and holding at bay more complicated discussions on the connections between free market reforms and local violent conflicts. The idea of the 'evil local' as the source of war fits the paradigm shift of post 9/11, the War on Terror and the securitization of development, and underlying this, the liberal peace approach. In sum, this chapter is about rational choice theory and the impact of the greed–grievance controversy on donor policy-based thinking on conflict. It uses the rise of the greed theory to illustrate the importance of studying 'conflict theory in context'.

Rational choice

Although the academic field of Conflict Studies includes many different schools of thought, which have operated in isolation, competition and cooperation, alternatively the one or the other gained more – or less – recognition among policy makers. In the 1970s, structuralism and human needs theory was *en vogue*. In the 1990s, theories of identity and conflict gained prominence, in particular those related to 'ethnic conflict'. And since the turn of the century the trend is to explain violent conflict in terms of greed and calculation. This shift to individual calculation and opportunity, with a strong emphasis on material profitability (loot) is part of an influential paradigm in Conflict Studies stemming from neo-classical economic theories. We have made repeated references to rationality and rational choice throughout the book; it is about time we outline the theory.

Basically, rational choice theories of conflict start from the proposition that individuals will conduct civil war if the perceived benefits outweigh the costs of rebellion. Subsequently, war will be sustained as long as it is profitable. The idea is that people are rational agents, and have *choice*, also in settings of war. Violence is thus seen as a product of individual rational action, not collective resentment. Underlying this perspective are a number of axioms and assumptions. First of all, the individual decision-maker is regarded as the primary unit of analysis. This is called methodological individualism: the individual is the starting point for all social action, and therefore, explanation. Second, in formal (or thin) rational choice theory, the individual is seen as an objective utility maximizer. We continuously set goals and preferences, and calculate the probability of achieving each of these goals, by weighing costs and benefits and the utility of each outcome. In the end, we choose that which has the highest expected utility, hence the term rational *choice*. In some cases the choice is to go to war, that is, to take the risk of dying, or having to kill in combat. Underlying the idea of utility maximizing is neo-classic economic theory and its view of the human being as *homo economicus*. 'Economic man' is the rational human being, who acts out of self-interest and the desire for wealth that economists use when deriving, explaining and verifying their theories and models. The idea is that all social action can in the end be explained as responses to signals from often imperfect markets. As Wallace and Wolf put it: 'there is a prize for everything and everything has its prize' (1999: 294).

Rational action approaches underlie the realist school in the field of International Relations, referring to the grand design of states engaged in power politics, but also guide game theoretic approaches to ethnic violence such as Fearon's (1994) model of credible commitments and the work of Lake and Rothchild (1997) on inter-group and intra-group strategic dilemmas that produce ethnic violence. Deep down, rational action approaches find their roots in the work of Machiavelli and Hobbes and the underlying idea of the human being as driven by an instinct for self-preservation and a will to dominate. They also draw on eighteenth-century economists such as Adam Smith and his work on the unintended beneficial effects of the individual's profit maximizing tendency. It is beyond the scope of this chapter to discuss the theoretical foundations of rational action (for an excellent overview, see: Jabri 1996: chapter 2). Our focus is on the sub-field of rational choice theories of violent conflict.

One of the advocates of the utility maximization theory of violent conflict is Bruce Bueno de Mesquita. In *The War Trap* (1981) he argues that war is likely to emerge if actors (assumed to be unitary) on both sides expect it to be profitable. In summarizing his theory, he writes: 'The broadest and seemingly obvious generalization that emerges from the theory is the expectation that wars (or other conflicts) will be initiated only when the initiator believes that war will yield positive expected utility' (1981: 127). Within this line of thought, the origins of the decision-maker's 'beliefs' are not subject to inquiry: they are accepted as given. We will return to this later. Stripped of nuance, Bueno de Mesquita's theory holds that actors (and these can be individuals, groups or states) are unitary objective utility maximizers whose actions are consistent and goal-directed. More than two decades after *The War Trap*, Paul Collier and colleagues produced an influential World Bank report named *Breaking the Conflict Trap* (World Bank 2003). The report contains very much the same message as the book it refers to: it is utility maximization that drives wars, in this case, civil wars and rebellions. Much of the report's policy recommendations are based on Collier's earlier work with Hoefler (2001) on what has become known as the 'greed theory of war', and which marked the beginning of the proliferation of neo-classical economic theories of violent conflict.

Paul Collier's theory of greed

In his quest to find the 'true motivation for rebellion', Collier takes an explanatory epistemological stance. That is, he studies social action from without and infers motivation from patterns of observed behaviour. In this view, interpretation, meaning or sense-making are merely seen as distortions. Rebel movements, for instance, have a tendency to embed their actions in 'narratives of grievance', for this is simply more acceptable, and hence profitable. To discover the truth, in the words of Collier, is not to study what people say, but what they do. The argumentation that leads him to conclude that 'the true cause of much civil war is not the loud discourse of grievance but the silent force of greed' is based first and foremost on the construction of a dichotomy. Collier breaks down the motivation for civil war into two distinct extremes. On the one hand, 'rebellions may arise because rebels aspire to wealth by capturing resources extra-legally': this type of motivation is labelled *greed*. On the other, 'rebels aspire to rid the nation, or the group of people with which they identify, of an unjust regime': in this case the rebellion is *grievance*-based (2000: 91). Now, how do we know whether a violent conflict is driven by greed or grievance? For a good explanation of Collier's work I need to spend a few words on proxies. Building an empirical model of civil war with the tools of neo-classical economic analysis and based on rational choice assumptions implies – as is the case in all quantitative statistical large-N analyses – having to *quantify* possible causal factors, such as greed or grievance. Since it is not possible to quantify greed or grievance directly, scholars need to define the kind of evidence that would indicate whether the one or the other is at play. In more technical terms, scholars have to define quantifiable proxies, that is, 'indirect measures to stand in for the actual theoretical postulate'. Subsequently, data can be gathered on these quantifiable variables across the sample and findings can be produced. We will return to the use of proxy variables later. Collier builds his model of greed versus grievance with three proxies for greed, and four for grievance, tested against available data for a large sample of countries. Greed is reflected in the following variables: the share of *primary commodity exports* in gross domestic product (GDP); the *proportion of young males* in the total population; and average years of *schooling*. Simply put, where there is a large proportion of young men in a society, where these men have few income-earning opportunities (expressed in years of education) and where there is plenty of opportunity for economic gain by looting primary commodities, a country is much more at risk of conflict then one with opposite characteristics. Consequently, Collier contrasts his greed factors with those that proxy grievance. First, Collier measures the tendency to *ethnic grievances or religious hatreds* by the extent to which a society is factionalized by ethnicity and by religion. Second, grievances focused on *economic inequality* are measured by land ownership. Third, grievances over a *lack of political rights* are measured by levels of repression and autocracy. Finally, grievances on *government economic incompetence* are expressed in the proxy variable of the growth rate in the five years prior to the outbreak of civil war. Collier puts the above hypotheses to the test and concludes that the results overwhelmingly point to the importance of greed agendas as opposed to grievance. Indeed, he concludes that the grievance factors are so unimportant or perverse that they cannot be anything but 'seriously wrong' (2000: 96). This is, in a nutshell, the empirical part of the model.

Collier's choice of proxies has been heavily criticized, and there is a long and ongoing debate about this in the sub-field of quantitative conflict analysis (Ron 2005; Fearon 2005; Humphreys 2005). Fundamental criticism is expressed by Cramer (2002, 2006), who states that: 'The use of empirical surrogates for theoretical hunches is patchwork through and through. Thus, it is not clear that the proxy is capturing the thing it is meant to stand for in the abstract model' (2006: 131). He argues, as have many others, that Collier's proxies to measure greed might just as well be used to measure grievance. For example, a lack of education might block the way to gainful employment and therefore reveal a low opportunity cost for conflict: but it might just as well be a source of social anger and grievance. The same could be said for the share of primary commodities in GDP, as a high dependence on such exports often characterizes a country's general economic underdevelopment. Many others have critiqued Collier's representation of greed versus grievance as a misleading opposition, and stressed how the two motivations for civil war are in fact highly interrelated (Ballentine and Sherman 2003; Murshed and Tadjoeddin 2007). Empirically, critiques pertain to a general lack of reliable data, as well as to how the focus on aggregate country-levels hides the variation in violence (in line with the micropolitical turn in chapter four). It is, however, not the intention of this chapter to extensively review this discussion; others have done this very well before us (see: Cramer 2002, 2006; Goodhand 2003;

Fearon and Laitin 2003; Humphreys 2005). We focus here not so much on the methodology of Collier's work but on the theory that is used to support his findings.

Violent conflict as market

Rational choice theories of violent conflict revolve around the question of 'why do people follow' – one that continues to pop up in this book. Why would people want to join an insurgency or a rebel movement? Or, in rational choice language: 'why would they want to risk joining?' As Kalyvas and Kocher (2007b) point out, it is indeed the joining (or 'following') that needs to be explained and not so much the 'first movers', that is, the political entrepreneurs with strong motivations, who are willing to assume high risks:

> The world does not lack Che Guevaras ready to launch insurgencies. What it does lack, however, is a mass of followers willing to take the necessary risks: it is the success of entrepreneurs in recruiting followers that results in insurgencies and that calls for investigation.
>
> (2007b: 182)

Collier's explanation of why it is greed and not grievance that drives civil war is derived from the idea of the individual as utility maximizer. For the rational, utility maximizing actor the costs of taking part in a grievance-based rebellion simply outweigh the benefits. This is explained by means of Mancur Olson's 'collective action problem' (1965). The collective action problem is still canonically applied to the analysis of political groups and group action, including those engaged in civil war. Simply put, groups struggling for certain public goods (e.g. the overthrow of a dictator, freedom of speech) need to overcome three collective action problems: free riding, coordination and time-consistency. Collective action problems are seen as particularly large for rebel movements. In Gould's words (1995: 204) 'While activists, might have little trouble persuading a casual acquaintance to sign a petition, they would have great difficulty convincing such a person to risk injury, death, or imprisonment'. Rational, well-informed individuals may well feel very strongly about an injustice, but they will be unwilling to put their lives on the line for a cause unless it is likely to benefit them. No matter how badly oppressed a group is, or how sharp their hatred for a rival group, the three-fold problem of free-riding, coordination and time-consistency will foil any rebellion attempted on the basis of grievance alone. Only by appealing to individual greed can these collective action problems be overcome. Collier explains the three collective action problems as follows.

Enjoyment of a public good (such as equality, stability, cleaner air, defence) cannot be exclusive to an individual, it is always collective. So, if I am suffering under a repressive government's rule, I may very well want to join a movement that aims to overthrow this government. However, it is most likely that the fall of the regime does not depend on whether I personally join the rebellion. Hence, it is more profitable for me to have others fight, while I benefit from the justice that their rebellion achieves. This standard free-rider problem, according to Collier, will often be enough to prevent the possibility of grievance-motivated rebellions. The second problem that plagues grievance-based rebellions is that of coordination. Rebellions have to start somewhere.

The problem is that individuals would rather join large rebellions that stand a chance of military victory than small ones. Again, the costs and risks of punishment faced by individuals in a small rebel group are calculated to be high, without much prospect of achieving justice any time soon. And then there is the third, time-consistency problem: rebels have to bear the cost of fighting *before* they can enjoy the benefit of achieving justice. For the utility maximizer this is calculated as too uncertain an investment. In stark contrast, Collier argues, the above three collective action problems can be overcome by 'the logic of greed'. By engaging in violence and looting, greed-motivated rebels can benefit instantly from war. There is no free-rider problem because the benefits of the rebellion can be confined to those who take part in it. If one can benefit from looting, it can also pay to be part of a small rebellion group. The time-inconsistency problem is also overcome: for rebels do not have to patiently await the rewards of justice, or equality, or whatever public good they were fighting for, but can instantly gain individually.

The underlying view here is that of violent conflicts as markets: where individuals make *investments* in violence, and reap private *returns*. The market of grievance-based conflict shows important 'imperfections': investments but no returns, costs without benefits, risks without compensations. Hence, although real enough, grievances cannot 'produce sufficient violence to clear the market for conflict'. Greed motivations very easily can. According to Cramer, Collier's way of thinking is representative of a tremendously influential trend in the social sciences – what some have called 'economic imperialism', in which a certain brand of economic theory colonizes other social sciences, including the study of civil war. The idea is that it might be possible to explain 'virtually everything that otherwise is inarticulately garbled in the efforts of historians, sociologists, political theorists' as – not partial, but complete – responses to signals from often imperfect markets (Cramer 2006: 125).

Critiques

At a fundamental level, scholars simply reject the assumptions underlying rational choice theory. Tarrow, for instance – and this was long before Collier's research – argued that social movements simply do not fit Olson's collective action approach. He points out that Olson (1965) modelled his theory on the study of interest groups, in particular economic associations. It is misleading to transplant these very specific findings onto the study of other social formations, such as social movements. For when it comes to the more complex phenomenon of social movements 'people join for a wide spectrum of reasons: personal advantage, group solidarity, principle, desire to belong etc.' (Tarrow 1994: 15). Others have added to this critique by highlighting the implicit assumptions underlying the idea of greed-motivated conflict. Cramer, for instance, playing the devil's advocate, argues that in fact Collier's model evokes an image of the poor as somehow holding a 'comparative advantage' in violence. For if indeed wars result from utility maximization, poverty is an obvious circumstance that might tip the balance in favour of conflict. It is not that Collier argues that poor people are in any way inherently more prone to violence. However, his work implies that for the poor the 'opportunity cost' of violence is relatively low: there is little else on offer for them anyway. For Cramer, there is an interesting – and rather crude – assumption in this idea, but one that is often not made explicit:

Given that war often involves not only killing and maiming but being killed or maimed, one thing rather possibly forgone in war is life. Thus it must be assumed that poverty is so gruelling that the opportunity cost of being killed is very low. The poor engage in war because life is cheap.

(2006: 126)

Not only is there a substantial body of scholarly literature contradicting the link between poverty and rebellion by pointing out that guerrillas and insurgents often do not fit the suggested profile of being poor and ill-educated (for a good review of the connections between poverty and conflict see: Goodhand 2003), what is also contested is the rather crude image emerging from rational choice theories of civil war of people as perfectly capable of calculated, self-interested brutishness and violence for the purpose of 'acquiring wealth'. Rational choice theory might be useful in analysing inter-state conflict and decision-making processes of governments weighing the pros and cons of military action in their war rooms ['Gentlemen, you cannot fight in here, this is the war room!'] – as is done in realism. Transplanting a realist analytical frame onto the level of the individual, however, is problematic. The idea that violence is an unambiguous, individual 'cost' that people are ready to bear in order to attain certain individual 'ends' is flawed. As Nicholson argues: 'People's attitudes to the use of violence are ambiguous, ambivalent and complex, and one cannot treat violence simply as an unambiguous cost' (1992: 104–5). There is a rich body of literature on the anthropology of violence supporting this claim (see for example: Bourke 1999; Scheper-Hughes and Bourgois 2004).

Closer to home, Kalyvas and Kocher (2007b) contest Collier's use of the free-rider problem. They give a detailed account of why the free-rider problem cannot be unambiguously applied to the study of insurgent mobilization. Through an analysis of anecdotal evidence on the use of violence from a number of harsh counterinsurgency operations (the Phoenix Program in Vietnam and regional data from the Greek Civil War) Kalyvas and Kocher show how the standard approach to benefits versus costs underlying classic collective action theories fails to understand the nature of a major subset of violent conflict. For in many situations, it turns out to be actually less risky for an individual to be *inside* the rebellion than outside. That is, the chances of getting killed by indiscriminate violence (everyone is a target) as a non-combatant turn out to be larger than those of being killed as an insurgent by targeted violence. These findings underscore Nordstrom's remark that 'the least dangerous place to be in most contemporary wars is in the military' (1992: 271). The standard collective action paradigm thus tends to overestimate the risks to rebel fighters and underestimate the risks faced by non-combatants. These findings have important implications for our understanding of and theorizing about insurgency and recruitment, and the social dynamics of civil war.

Of course, it is exactly the greed theory's simplicity that is appealing for many people. In particular, the 'hard science' language of measuring might have its attractions to some. More widely, the approach gained recognition for putting the economy, and the role of resources (in this case resource abundance rather than scarcity) back on the research agenda, a component seriously absent in for instance the model of Ted Gurr. In response, scholars working on war economies have urged that we should 'rescue the study of economic agendas in war' from Collier's thin utility maximization theory. Keen (2008: 15), for instance, supports the idea that 'wars very often are not about winning'. Rather than conceptualizing war as a contest or a collapse, he suggests investigating war and disaster as alternative systems of profit, power and protection. For Keen, 'events, however horrible and catastrophic, are actually *produced*, they are made to happen by a diverse and complicated set of actors who may well be achieving their objectives in the midst of what looks like failure and breakdown' (2008: 15). Contrary to Collier, Keen applies his framework to all parties involved, including donor agencies, multinationals and NGOs – and not exclusively to insurgents, warlords and rebels. In addition, he has a very different, what we will explain below as a 'broad', understanding of 'rationality'.

Rationality

What do we do when we act rationally? The classic, thin, version of rational choice theory begins with a single, ideally rational individual, who has three components: fully ordered preferences, complete information and a perfect internal computer. According to this view an individual acts rationally 'in as much as he chooses the action which he correctly calculates to be most instrumental in satisfying his preferences' (Hollis 1994: 116). Obviously, this is an abstract and ideal-typical position. As Hollis explains, none of us ever has a complete and consistent set of preferences, we have nothing close to complete information and we are not blessed with perfect internal computers. Particularly in settings of conflict, the individual's potential to make rational choices is distorted by stress, misinformation and psychological processes such as 'group think' and over-confidence. Where classic rationalist approaches assume predictable decision-making having precise calculations of costs, benefits and probabilities, the 'cognitive rationality' approach takes into account the complexities of conflict settings. While the first version of rational choice theory is characterized by calculative precision, the latter seeks to uncover the input of cognitive processes in the distortion of such precision. Both, however, put emphasis on human action (including violent action) as generated by individual utility maximization, with any information – distorted or not – influencing the cost-benefit calculation as made by the agent (see Jabri 1996: 55–9). So, the ideal-type case of a simple and potent notion of instrumental rationality would argue that: 'We act rationally, when we know what we want, have a shrewd idea how likely each course of action is to satisfy us at what cost, and choose the action which is thus the most effective means to our ends' (Hollis 1994: 118). In Collier's model, 'benefits' are understood quite literally, and quantifiably, as material resources: diamonds, gold, coltan, timber or overall loot. Generally, rational choice theory is applied in a broader sense with costs and benefits meaning many different things: for example money, health, stability, time, even happiness.

In the thin version of rationality, the origins of our preferences are accepted as a given: they are not subject to investigation. It does not matter why or what people prefer. Individuals are rational if and only if their choices maximize their expected utility accordingly. As pointed out by Elster (1989) the focus of investigation is thus on *how* an actor best achieves his goals, irrespective of the origins or merit of these goals. 'To explain human behaviour, rational choice theory must, in any given case, proceed in two steps. The first step is to determine what a rational person would do in the circumstances. The second step is to ascertain whether this is what the person actually did' (1989: 30). Hence, rational choice theory does not aim to uncover *why* that actor held the goal preferences he or she did, nor does it question the beliefs underlying his or her choice of action. In simple terms, the individual is seen as a free-floating and self-contained unit, who is steered by his or her 'utility maximizing' internal computer. In Collier's terms: in contexts where other options to make a living are low, actors are likely to make the rational choice of engaging in violent rebellion if there are good prospects for instant material rewards.

Conversely, the 'broad theory of rationality' does aim to examine the genesis of beliefs and preferences, by incorporating within its framework both psychological and operational processes within a more broadly conceived decision-making model. Jabri (1996) applies this idea to the realm of violent conflict and explains how within the broad theory of rationality, the actor or party to a conflict becomes a 'situated entity'. She points out that war is a result of decision-making paths which, far from suggesting rationality as defined by strict criteria of consistency, point to the view that 'rationality is *bounded* by institutional roles and established norms' (1996: 63, my emphasis). This directs our attention to the relation between rational action and roles, and the study of role theory. Role theorists argue that any theory of action must incorporate the notion of role if it is to provide an understanding of human behaviour. Martin Hollis (Hollis and Lukes 1982; Hollis 1996, 1998), one of the foremost theorists of role theory, defines role as 'a set of normative expectations attached to a social position' (1994: 180). As in the famous line from Shakespeare's *As You Like It*: 'all the world's a stage, and all the men and women merely players' – each individual plays a variety of roles throughout his or her life (e.g. parent, bureaucrat, street sweeper, minister, soldier). The role played by individuals influences definitions of grievances, perceptions of the enemy, preferences of outcomes, as well as calculations of the distribution of advantage. To understand a particular action, therefore, requires that we 'situate the party within its identifiable social and institutional position'. It also requires that we know or understand the normative expectations associated with each of these positions (Jabri 1996: 66). That is, we have to gain insight into how people's actions have subjective meaning. So, instead of studying human action as motivated solely by utilities, we see it as the outcome of a more complex, and scripted set of norms, rules and roles. Hence, the researcher requires inside knowledge of the normative expectations and meanings associated with each role and whether they are likely to be fulfilled. It is not difficult to see that by studying action in this way, we move from an explanatory (action is explained from without) to an interpretative (action is explained from within) epistemology.

In the broad understanding of rationality, the actor is still seen as a purposeful agent capable of rational decision-making. However, his or her evaluations and perceptions of the costs and benefits associated with particular options are influenced by the normative expectations associated with his or her role. As Jabri states: 'there is an interplay between personal and bureaucratic preferences' (1996: 68). For Hollis (1994: 248–60), there is a fundamental difference between these two notions of rational reconstruction. One reconstructs action as instrumentally rational choice by a self-contained individual unit, with any normative or expressive elements fed in as influences on the pay-offs as perceived by the agent. So, although structural background conditions are seen as certainly shaping the context of choice, ultimately people's actions – including violence – are explained as motivated only by utility. People act upon their internal computer in largely predictable ways. The other notion reconstructs action as 'intelligent obedience' to the rules of the game being played, in a sense of 'game' which makes players no longer self-contained. The individual is here understood as 'situated', with room for reflexive self-direction and moral and normative engagement, motivated not exclusively by utility but by social meanings. The actor is firmly placed within an institutional context where action results from the interplay between his or her preferences and all that constitutes his or her role(s). The balance between institutional framework and individual intentions differs from role to role and from individual to individual (Jabri 1996: 70). Only by taking these specificities into account can we study human action in a meaningful way.

Since we have already discussed the two different epistemological views (explaining versus understanding) of rational action, we might as well bring in ontology (individualism versus structuralism). Juxtaposing the individualist analysis of role occupancy against its structuralist opponent may help us to get a fuller picture of the 'purposeful agent' living in Hollis' lower right box.

Structuralist views on role occupancy argue that actors are fully obedient rule followers. As Hollis explains, roles are performed by incumbents – the parents, bureaucrats, street sweepers, ministers, soldiers who form the social fabric. On a structuralist analysis, these incumbents do just what their positions require of them, being driven 'top down' by the demands of the role. Roles are maintained by institutions and their individual incumbents are highly replaceable. The image that emerges is of actors as puppets on invisible strings. That is, your role defines your action. Or: 'where you stand depends on where you sit'. Institutions and organizations are presented as the source of action. Importantly, power thus resides in institutions and individuals exercise power only in so far as they represent powerful institutions. Perhaps this is why it is so fascinating to see individuals such as Milosevic and Karadzic stand before the Yugoslavia Tribunal in The Hague: once extremely powerful, but taken out of their institutional roles, they seem infinitely small, insignificant and strangely human, too. In contrast, the individualist retort to structuralism is that individuals are *not* puppets. The individualist view of role occupancy argues that actors have room for manoeuvre, even when the pressure to conform is great, as is for instance the case in the military. People can both refuse to enforce, as well as obey, certain role-related regulations. Individualist analyses argue that institutions are nothing but sets of rules and practices. Their power depends on whether individuals are willing to accept them, or on individuals forcing other individuals to comply with them. Even though continuity is more usual than revolutionary change, both can be explained only by looking at the beliefs and desires of individuals. As Hollis explains the individualist position on social change:

> Gradual change is common enough and is most readily explained as a sum of small individual choices tending in the same direction. For institutional or revolutionary changes we can look to concerted action, mass or elite, to account for what single individuals cannot do alone.
>
> (1994: 110)

In sum, the individual role occupant 'remains an active decision-maker potentially capable of nonconformity even where the cost is censure or even loss of life' (Jabri 1996: 70). The individualist view proposes looking at the individual not as a free-floating and self-contained utility maximizer, nor as slavishly obedient to his or her institutional roles, but as a purposive agent, who is both enabled and constrained by institutional roles and normative expectations. This is illustrated by table 5.1.

Table 5.1 Three views of the individual

	Puppet on a string *Homo sociologicus*
Utility maximizer *Homo economicus*	Purposive agent

What can we learn from this discussion for the analysis of violent conflict? What the above analysis offers is a view of rationality not merely as goal-seeking, that is, to explain an action intentionally is to point to a future state it was intended to achieve, as is implied in rational choice theory. Rather, it emphasizes how rational action is also importantly rule-governed. It thus offers a thick understanding of the choice of war, not simply as the outcome of a cost-benefit evaluation of options, but as well as resulting from role expectations, and what March and Olsen call the 'logic of appropriateness'. As Hollis argues, 'whereas for homo economicus to be rational is to calculate, for homo sociologicus to be rational is to follow a rule' (1994: 151). Again, the above discussion highlights the distinction between individuality and society, and agency and structure. Do actors make individual rational choices to engage in war, or are they merely acting 'appropriately'? As Jabri frames the question: 'Can individuals stand alone as rational autonomous beings, or are they constituted by the group or polity which surrounds them?' (1996: 41). The notion of 'thick rationality' takes insights from both individualism and structuralism, and hints at the mutually constitutive relationship between individuality and society. In chapter six we will build on this idea and the place of war within it. In the remainder of this chapter, however, we once more turn to the core assumption underlying Collier's economic approach to rational choice, and try and account for its popularity.

The power of words

Although the 'greed theory of war' certainly stirred up a lot of debate within academia on rationality and violence, its most important impact has been political. Obviously, Collier's position as director of Development Research at the World Bank was important for the staging of a rational choice theory of war. But its success in the world of policy-making is also related to the ways it provided the 'right' answer for a pressing problem at the right time.

By the turn of the century, policy-makers in international financial institutions such as the World Bank and many aid and development agencies were struggling with the disappointing results of the neoliberal restructuring policies of the 1980s and 1990s. In spite of the rhetoric about curing sick economies, 'neoliberalized' regions (particularly the former Soviet Union and large parts of Africa) were plagued by high levels of unemployment, poverty, growing income disparities, political turmoil and violence, as well as a sudden rise of the parallel economy, black marketeers and criminal networks. All this seemed to suggest that the neoliberal project could not live up to its expectations. Mounting criticism, also from within the main institutions themselves (e.g. by Stiglitz 2002) put pressure on the advocates of the free market. In reaction, two explanatory models became popular: 'good governance' and 'greed theory'. As we discussed in chapter three, advocates of the good governance idea claimed that it was not the neoliberal model that was to blame for the political turmoil and lack of economic progress, but rather the immature, corrupt and inefficient state administrations of developing countries and transition economies. Global neoliberalism could only successfully proceed in a 'sound' governance environment. From the early 1990s onwards, the call for *less* state was gradually substituted by a call for a *better* state. The good governance recipe claimed to promote free market democracy, which protects human and civil rights, combined with a competent, non-corrupt and accountable public administration (World Bank 1997). The great attractiveness of the good governance argument is that it hides disagreement by disregarding the trade-offs between the various goals of development (such as, for instance, free trade and pro-poor growth), making complex issues seem manageable and providing a practical answer to the disappointing results of the neoliberal restructuring programmes.

What the good governance theory did for the economy, the greed theory does for war: it places blame and responsibility at the level of the local actor. Where advocates of the good governance recipe argue that it is 'bad leadership, not neoliberalism' that causes stagnation, the greed theory holds that it is 'greed, not grievance' that causes violent conflict. It is not difficult to see the attractiveness of such an idea, not only for politicians and policy-makers, but also for the media industry hunting for 'footage'. Instead of understanding the new forms of violence as manifestations of systemic failures and mechanisms, it was the faces of local actors that became the flash point for policy discourses and media imagery.

Like the 'good governance' idea, the 'greed theory' of war was a product of the World Bank. The publication of the report *Breaking the Conflict Trap* in 2003 marked the proliferation of the greed theory of war, as a neoclassical economic theory of violent conflict. Clearly, by that time neoliberalism had long established itself as a hegemonic political project. Nevertheless, it was particularly after the crisis of structural adjustment programs (SAPs) that the approach was adopted by government agencies and the aid industry. Since that time, the aid industry has increasingly – and often unconsciously – embraced a neoliberal understanding of war, where actors in war are seen as utility maximizers going for their own individual, optimal benefits. Let us look for a moment at the exact wording of its most influential policy document.

The 2003 World Bank report *Breaking the Conflict Trap* opens with a metaphor. 'The damage from a [civil] war ripples out in three rings' it says on page one. The 'inner ring' is the damage inflicted upon civilians in the country at war. The second 'ring of suffering' affects neighbouring countries. The outer ring of suffering is global. 'Civil war creates territory outside the control of any recognized government, and this territory is used as a safe haven for international terrorists such as Al Qaeda and for the production and transportation of drugs'. The report stresses how the global mortality caused by hard drugs and international terrorism is a significant toll, and that the wider social costs are immense. For example, the World Bank estimates that 'the September 11 attacks alone may have increased global poverty by 10 million people' (World Bank 2003: 3). By using the metaphor of the three rings the report brings home a clear message: 'civil wars matter, they have an impact on global security, too'. At first sight, the use of the 'ring metaphor' is understandable: the authors aim to attract the attention of policy-makers in donor countries by making the west (as 'victims of terrorist attacks, consumers of drugs') part of the problem. Only this will make governments move and spend development money on conflict resolution and post-conflict reconstruction. However, the ring is more telling. It also shows how civil wars are framed, and, particularly, where the *causes* of contemporary wars are located. To stay with the metaphor – who is making the waves? What is causing these three 'rings of suffering' to ripple out? The report is clear about that: wars are caused by local actors acting rationally. The underlying causes are the economic conditions which trigger *homo economicus* to wage a war. Not because of ancient hatreds or a desire for vengeance, but because 'war is profitable'. In order to stop these 'rings of suffering' a number of policy recommendations are made. These are largely geared at isolating the rational actor rebel and depend heavily on the classic neoliberal recipe. The report distinguishes two phases: conflict and post-conflict, each demanding a different set of 'interventions'. In *current* conflict countries, the World Bank suggests that 'curbing the finances of rebel organisations' – by blocking them from the market and by stopping diasporas from funding them – will 'restrict their capacity to fight a war'. The other 'policy options' are 'military intervention' and the 'supporting of peace negotiations'. In *post conflict* countries, 'military peace forces, economic growth, development assistance and the support and investment of diaspora and DDR (disarmament, demobilisation and reintegration of fighters)' are presented as 'successful strategies'. Local markets should be made 'as competitive as possible': this will 'end war-time monopolistic trading' as 'competition will reduce profits to normal levels and reduce attraction for wartime traders'. Aid should also focus on the diversification of local economies. This position has become known as the 'liberal peace approach'.

The selection of metaphors and words is neither contingent, nor innocent. The word 'greed' has a strong normative connotation. Greed is 'an excessive desire to acquire more than one needs or desires'. The image that the greed theory provokes is that of actors in civil war as immoral, bad and unrestrained and as bringers of global misery. Greed is simply an immoral human desire that needs to be restrained, not explained. Just in the same way that terrorists 'need to be eliminated, not understood'. Hence, policy recommendations for conflict resolution are equally simple: target the rebel actors and allow the market to create a context in which war is no longer profitable. Grievances, by contrast, complicate things. Grievances might very well be justified, and can not be seen in isolation from the larger context that causes these grievances, implying that contexts (economic, political, social) should be addressed when resolving conflict. This results in much more complex discussions on poverty, inequality and politics, inevitably leading into discussions on the interconnectedness between violence in poor countries and actions taken in and by rich countries. Cramer names the most well-known examples as follows:

> the consequences of US (and other rich country) policies in nurturing Mujahideen groups in Afghanistan and Saddam Hussein's regime in Iraq; the barely controllable consequences of international arms trade and its regulation; the economic policies naively fostered on poor countries; and the political policies of shoring up militaristic, elite-controlled governments in some countries while propounding a liberal rhetoric of good governance globally.
>
> (2006: 282)

Ultimately, the differences in framing violent conflict and the choice of words thus plays an important role in casting blame and responsibility. Whereas 'greed' explanations point to the local bad actors as the source of suffering, 'grievance' explanations – identified by Collier as 'seriously wrong' – would refer to the global interconnectedness of violence. In sum, the neoclassical individualist economic explanation of violent conflict has been influential in its coding of contemporary political violence in poor countries, particular Africa, as greedy. Critics of the greed theory claim that its impact is not merely analytical, but suits the dominant neoliberal project and liberal peace approach. Just as in the 1990s most conflicts driven by struggles for power were framed in ethnic terms, in the era of the War on Terror it is local 'entrepreneurs of violence' who are identified as at the source of contemporary conflict and global suffering (World Bank 2003: 4). The idea of 'local evils as source of violence' has become an influential explanatory model of contemporary violence and war in poor countries (above all in policy-making circles) and is accused by its critics of providing a justification for continued surveillance and engagement.

Conclusions

The rational choice approach to violent conflict is a mono-causal approach, allowing for straightforward policy answers to our three book questions. The answer to what makes a group is 'the individual'. Only if individuals perceive the benefits of group membership as outweighing the cost of participation will they be interested in collective action. Clearly, the group is not considered an appropriate unit of analysis. Action is generated not by social or institutional dynamics but by individual calculation. It is the individual utility maximizer who is the starting point for all collective action, and thus explanation. As we have outlined in the first section of this chapter, rational choice theory starts from the proposition that individuals will conduct violent conflict if the perceived benefits outweigh the costs of war. In line with this, wars will be sustained as long as they are profitable. Here rational choice theory shows its close links to neoclassical economics. The image that emerges is of violent conflicts as 'markets', and individuals as 'investors' who are only interested in joining a rebellion if the returns are immediate and profitable. Rational choice theories of violent conflict, however, include more than mere cost-benefit calculations. This becomes clear in the way rational choice scholars of civil war think about our third question on conflict resolution and peace.

Underlying rational choice theories is a liberal peace approach. This idea finds its origins in the work of scholars like Kant, Montesquieu and Adam Smith, who were – all in their specific times and places – engaged in projects of liberating the individual from the reign of various forms of military regime, royalty and feudal aristocracy. One of the fundamental views emerging from the classic formulations of liberalism is that war is an aberration. According to this view, the natural condition of society is peace. War, by implication, is a distortion of this natural, rational order. As Cramer (2006) explains the argument in the language of today: there were basically two main sources of distortion: political and economic. Politically, war was fought in the narrow interest of ruling elites, who managed to sustain the misunderstandings on which wars were built. Economically, the general lack of free trade interfered with the individual's natural tendency to pursue his or her self-interest and so, indirectly, promote the good of society. This idea, coming from Adam Smith, is central to the principles of neoclassical economics that emerged in the second half of the nineteenth century. It is based on Smith's famous dictum from the *Wealth of Nations* (1776) which holds that the individual, 'by pursuing his own interest ... frequently promotes that of the society more effectually than when he really intends to promote it. I have never known much good done by those who affected to trade for the public good.' Another important element of the liberal peace approach is that the impact of war on the economy is always and exclusively negative. The proposed solutions to war, not surprisingly, were to democratize and to encourage free trade. Although highly simplified here, this recipe continues to form the base of today's liberal peace approach. As we can see in for instance the World Bank report, civil war is understood as a distortion, an abnormality. Violent conflict breaks out when somehow countries go off track, and end up in unlucky conjunctures of demography, geography and policy. When this occurs, individuals grab the opportunity to engage in greedy and perverse practices, further distorting the balance of society, provoking war and 'rings of suffering'. Only by filtering out these rogue elements and (re)installing free trade and liberal democracy can countries be put back on the rails of sound development. It is here that the irony of the use of the word 'greed' becomes apparent. From a neoclassical economy perspective, it is precisely this individual and natural 'greed tendency' that promotes the public good. Or to agree with Gordon Gekko, the broker in Oliver Stone's movie *Wall Street*, who became a symbol in popular culture of the unfettered rule of global capitalism: 'greed – for lack of a better word – *is good.*' Apparently, in neoclassical economics greed is good, but greedy rebels are not.

The main critique of the liberal peace interpretation is that analysts fail to make a distinction between liberal peace as a utopian project to realize global peace and stability and liberal peace as a political project to sustain power. Undoubtedly, it is argued, the liberal peace tradition, as an oppositional idea, has a noble history. However, as Cramer puts it: 'It has lost its innocence' (2006: 282). In his book *Civil War is not a Stupid Thing* (2006) Cramer, arguing from a political economic approach to war, sums up a range of reasons why this view on violent conflict is unsuitable for use as a guide to understanding and responding to contemporary violence and war. First of all, a weakness of the liberal peace approach is that it is a-historic. The historical record of capitalist expansion shows that it does not rest, initially at least, on free trade. Modern capitalist democracies all have histories of strong state intervention and protectionist economic policies. 'While protectionism is often wasteful and stultifying, protectionist policy has been a keystone in the economic development of Britain, the United States, Germany, Japan, South Korea, China and other countries' (Cramer 2006: 281). In addition, when it comes to the relation between war and development, history shows that the two are not mutually exclusive. Modern societies have not dismissed violence, or outgrown it, and modern liberal democratic, capitalist societies clearly have foundations in brutality. 'War, and non-war violence, have often provided an enabling environment for the accumulation of wealth, social organisation and institutional and technical change that feed development'. Often, in many ways, development has been an unintended consequence of war (2006: 281). Second, he takes issue with the idea that free trade growth ends violence. Again, when studied in context, the abstract idea that free market growth is efficient and uncomplicated shows serious shortcomings. For one, in many countries rapid growth has not diminished violence. Often, growth and diversification have been compatible with continued institutional mess, extreme income inequalities and widespread violence. And whereas liberal economists often point to the example of post WWII Europe as evidence for how growth brings peace, Cramer argues that this has less to do with free trade and more with the effectiveness and expansion of the state, and the development of mechanisms to exercise 'voice' and for renegotiating the terms of accumulation and distribution.

What complicates the liberal versus political economy discussion – in fact any discussion on the causes of violent conflict – is that often fundamental differences of opinion, that is, differences in ontological and epistemological stance, are not differentiated from debates on the differences in the gathering and interpretation of evidence. Much of the discussion consists of confronting the other with falsifying evidence (e.g. 'it was not free trade, but the strong state that brought peace to post WWII Europe'). As this chapter highlights, the gap between various accounts of contemporary violent conflict partly stems from fundamental differences in the way explanations are constructed and supported. While picking one's way through the competing explanations of war and violence it is therefore helpful to lay bare the basic assumptions upon which a theoretical approach is built, and think through one's own position. In this respect, the idea of the utility maximizing individual as key unit of analysis and the methodological quest for statistical event regularities can be contrasted with a view of the individual as purposive agent and a stress on historic specificity and complexity.

This chapter began and ended with rational choice theory and its view of the individual as guided by his or her internal computer (Hollis' lower left box), and made brief visits to the structuralist *homo sociologicus* as puppet on a string (upper right) down to the self-reflexive embedded agent (lower right). In the next and final chapter, we will continue this discussion on individuality and society from a critical discourse analysis of violent conflict.

Table E

Ontology/Epistemology	Explaining (positivist)	Understanding (interpretative)
Structuralism		
Individualism	Rational choice theory	

Further reading

Ballentine, Karen and Jake Sherman (2003) *The Political Economy of Armed Conflict: Beyond Greed and Grievance*, Boulder: Lynne Rienner Publishers.

Collier, Paul (2000) 'Doing Well out of War: An Economic Perspective' in Mats Berdal and David M. Malone (eds) *Greed and Grievance: Economic Agendas in Civil Wars*, Boulder: Lynne Rienner Publishers, pp. 91–112.

——(2007) *The Bottom Billion: Why The Poorest Countries Are Failing And What Can Be Done About It*, Oxford and New York: Oxford University Press.

Cramer, C. (2002) '*Homo Economicus* Goes to War: Methodological Individualism, Rational Choice and the Political Economy of War', *World Development* 30 (11) 1845–64.

6 Telling each other apart
A discursive approach to violent conflict

In his book *LTI: the Language of the Third Reich* the philologist Victor Klemperer describes the slow and steady transformation of the everyday use of language in Nazi Germany. He shows how Hitler's nazism took hold on the lives of people not so much through Nazi propaganda – the many explicit speeches, articles, posters, flags and pamphlets – but through their mechanical and unconscious adoption of single words.

> nazism permeated the flesh and blood of the masses through single words, idioms, and sentence structures which were imposed on them in a million repetitions and taken on board mechanically and unconsciously.

He argues that:

> language does not simply write and think for me, it also directs my feelings, it directs my entire being the more unquestioningly and unconsciously I surrender myself to it. ... Words can be like doses of arsenic: they are swallowed unnoticed, appear to have no effect, and then after some time the toxic reaction sets in after all. ... The Third Reich only made up a very small number of the words of its language, perhaps, or most probably, none at all ... But it changes the value of words and the frequency of their occurrence, it makes general that which used to be the preserve of individuals or a small group, it confiscates for the party that which was previously common good, and it saturates words and groups of words and sentence structures with its poison, it subjugates language to its horrible system and turns it into its most powerful, public and most secretive means of advertisement.

> (2000 [1947]: 30–1, translation JD)

Klemperer's aim is to 'expose the poison of the language of the Third Reich and warn against it'. It is precisely this aim of exposing the 'power of words' in the build-up, waging and legitimization of war that is at the core of what is now known as the critical discursive approach to violent conflict. Half a century after Klemperer's *LTI*, Philip Gourevitch in his account of the Rwandan genocide phrases the power of discourse succinctly by stating that: 'Power consists in the ability to make others inhabit your story of their reality' (1998: 48). This chapter is about these 'stories of reality'.

War as social phenomenon

By drawing on critical discourse analysis and structurationism, the approach presented in this chapter aims to overcome simplistic dichotomies of elite/mass, greed/grievance, identity/economy or agency/structure. The chapter begins by looking at critiques of both agency and structure-based theories, and then explains and builds on Giddens' duality of structure, by bringing in social practices and discursive and institutional continuities. It explains how the discursive approach understands war and violent conflict as social phenomena, and how discourse analysis aims to understand specific cases of violent conflict by looking at the social process of discourse formation. It emphasizes the relation between discourse formation and power, and the institutionalization of discourse in, and prior to war and violent conflict.

Originating in the writings of Nietzsche and Wittgenstein, and central to the work of Gramsci, Foucault and Lacan and more recent authors such as Habermas, Laclau and Mouffe, the discursive approach includes a vast variety of schools and sub-schools. Over the past decades discourse analysis has evolved as a prominent terrain of study in both the Humanities and Social Sciences (in particular sociolinguistics, anthropology and political science). In Conflict Studies, the view that 'discourses matter' is widely held. Throughout this book brief references were made to the role of discourse in violence and conflict. We talked about the 'production of meaning' (in constructivism), 'belief structures' (when discussing social identity theory), Gramsci's notion of 'cultural hegemony' and Tarrow's 'collective action frames'. In each case, people are understood as 'doing things with words' – as in Austin's paradigmatic work *How To Do Things With Words* (1962). However, the study of words in these approaches is often a side dish. Approaches placing the role of discourses at the core of their theories of violence and conflict focus on – at least – six overlapping lines of research. First, the politics of naming and coding of violence and conflict (Bhatia 2005; Peteet 2005; Der Derian 2005; Brass 1996, 1997; Ferrari 2007). Second, the examination of the processes of the legitimization of violence (Apter 1997; Schröder and Schmidt 2001). Third, the reconstruction of subjectivities, memory and narratives of survival (Norris and Jones 2005; Jackson 2002). Fourth, the examination of discourses of the body in violent conflict (Appadurai 1998; Norris 2000; Feldman 1994). Fifth, the role of discourse in policy-making and conflict resolution (Duffield 2007; Dexter 2007). The final approach focuses on 'conflict as constructed discourse' and examines the power relations embedded in discursive repertoires and the ways they construct meaning and identity (Jabri 1996; Brass 1996). It is this final approach, with Vivienne Jabri's *Discourses on Violence* (1996) as the most important text, which forms the backbone of this chapter. Jabri argues that both agency-based and structure-based theories of conflict are inadequate to fully understand war. They have failed to show how war is a recursive human social activity: it repeats itself and reproduces itself through human actions. War is normal: it is not an aberration. It is not a breakdown of social structures led by deviant leaders. War is a social institution that is reproduced through discourses, which confer legitimacy on it. For Jabri (1996: 1):

> War as a social phenomenon involves individuals, communities and states and any attempt to uncover its genesis must incorporate the discursive and institutional continuities which render violent conflict a legitimate and widely accepted mode of human conduct.

But let us start with a concrete example.

Beyond elite/mass

As a first step in outlining the discursive approach to violent conflict we go back to the discussion of ethnicity of the first chapter. There we discussed Barth's constructivist approach to the making of ethnic groups. Barth argued that we should stop concentrating on the 'cultural stuff' that ethnic groups may share and focus instead on the boundaries that separate ethnic groups. The 'cultural stuff' very often shows as much overlap with neighbouring groups as it shows variety within its boundaries. What makes ethnic identity 'ethnic', therefore, is to be sought in the social processes of maintaining boundaries that people recognize as ethnic. Barth's constructivist approach to ethnicity has become mainstream, and many scholars since have written about the process of boundary drawing and maintenance. Somewhat simplified, this research on boundaries is divided into scholars who emphasize the key role of elites and leaderships in drawing, protecting and maintaining ethnic boundaries, and those who highlight bottom-up processes of social group dynamics, often informed by ideas on culturalism or the individual's inherent need for the group. There are also voices aiming to bridge this gap by incorporating both the 'elite' and 'mass' view into their approach. Typically, the discursive approach to the process of group boundary drawing would argue for going beyond the elite–mass controversy and focusing on the way social boundaries are constructed by narratives. In more abstract terms, the discursive approach focuses on the 'narrative reconstruction of reality'. As Sayyid and Zac (1998: 261) explain:

> The discursive approach focuses on the way in which communities construct their limits; their relationship to that which they are not or what threatens them; and the narratives which produce the founding past of a community, its identity, and its projections of the future.

So, the discursive approach places the story at the core of the analysis. It aims to give an explicit and systematic description of discourses within their specific historical and power context. It focuses on the dialectical formation and contestation of 'collective narratives'; on the 'shared stories' people tell about themselves and their situation, about who they are and who they are not. From this perspective conflict is a time at which the language of the everyday becomes 'a discourse of exclusionist protection against a constructed enemy, who is deserving of any violence perpetrated against it' (Jabri 1996: 134). This focus on 'stories' is not as straightforward as it may seem. How 'to do' discourse analysis? Where do we begin? First we will turn to Jabri's aim to unite structuralist and agency-based approaches by means of Giddens' theory of structuration.

Beyond structure/agency

It will come as no surprise that an approach focused on narratives and stories, and thus on the construction of meaning, works from an interpretive epistemology: human action is studied from within. The aim is to examine the ways in which people understand violence and war, and act upon this. The idea that social action is driven by predictable, mechanistic psychological laws (social identity theory), natural, given preferences (human needs approach), or utility maximization (rational choice theory) is a priori dismissed. This automatically pushes the discussion to the right column of the

Hollis matrix. Here the two opposing positions are that of individualism versus structuralism, with each placing either agency or structure as ontologically prior entities. Individualist, agency-based approaches emphasize how human beings and their organizations are 'purposeful actors whose actions help reproduce or transform the society in which they live'. Conversely, structure-based theories understand society as 'made up of social relationships, which structure the interaction between these purposeful actors' (Wendt 1987: 346 in Jabri 1996: 76) This is what we referred to earlier as the chicken-and-egg discussion. Does the structure of the social system determine the actions of individuals, or vice versa? The discursive approach rejects both individualist and structuralist theories of violent conflict. In line with much of the critique discussed throughout this book, Jabri rejects the individualist approach to violent conflict as mono-causal, and as too objective regarding human rationality. It fails to examine the origins of people's desires and beliefs and does not explain how social structures condition actors to choose war. On the other hand, structuralist approaches are seen as too static. They leave out a theory of individual action, and fail to explain how inherent contradictions eventually transform into actual violence. The view of individuals as merely rule followers is rejected: individuals can always create new rules and redefine roles. In sum, there are problems with both approaches. For Jabri, the portrayal of agency and structure as standing in a radical, and insoluble chicken-or-egg conflict with one another is misleading. She aims to show how they are in fact not oppositional, but complementary (1996: 76):

> The problem is to bridge the assumed ontological gap between individualist orientations and those which perceive social structures as determining behaviour. Social theory is often presented in terms of this opposition or dualism where 'like Carthage and Rome, it is the war of the whale and the elephant'. The problem is to see both agency and structure as implicated in the production and reproduction of social systems.

It is as short-sighted to look only at structural constraints as it is to concentrate only on the individual as the source of initiative. Both are necessary. To think through this synthesis Jabri suggests that we turn to the work of Giddens and his idea of the duality of structure.

The duality of structure

In *The Constitution of Society: Outline of the Theory of Structuration* (1984) the sociologist Anthony Giddens outlines his idea of the duality of structure. In the book Giddens accuses social theorists of being 'imperialist': they tend to claim all the ground for their own favoured concepts. Where structuralism sees only the constraining qualities of structures at work, agency-based approaches only have eyes for the individual actor. Instead, he argues, the basic domain of study of the social sciences is neither the experience of the individual actor, nor the existence of any form of societal totality, but social processes ordered across time and space. For Giddens, it is important to recognize that social theory must reconceptualize its subject matter as a duality: the duality of structure. He argues for seeing structure and agency not as ontologically prior, but as mutually constitutive entities. He thus sees structure and agency as each constituting the other, and as each complementing the other. The one cannot exist without the other. Individuals can act purposively, but they are not completely free to do so. We are all 'children of our time'. We are born into social structures that are both enabling and constraining to us. These social structures do not exist independently of us: we make them, and are made by them. Structures and agents thus stand in a dialectical relationship to one another. We could picture this as an interactive closed loop running between agency and structure:

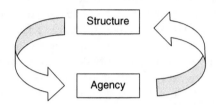

Figure 6.1 Structure and agency as mutually constitutive entities

Let us take the structure of language as an example. We use language as a *medium* to express ourselves. However, by talking we also *reproduce* language as structure. This is the duality of structure: structure's two-sided existence as both a *medium* and *outcome* of social practices. So, individuals recreate through their actions the structures that in turn constrain those actions (we cannot speak outside our language). Giddens focuses on how social life is formed in the course of the most normal routine activities. He argues that 'the structural properties of social systems exist only in so far as forms of social conduct are reproduced chronologically across time and space' (1984: xxi). This emphasis on social practices' continuation from day to day or year to year (time) and in different places (space) runs through all Giddens' writings (see: Wallace and Wolf 1999: 180–8). Importantly, however, this is by no means a mechanistic repetitive process in which we simply reproduce what came before. For Giddens, there is also the creative aspect of human action: we have agency and hence have the capacity to modify structures. As in the language example: by talking we, intentionally or not, alter the – grammatical – structure of language. This is what structuration theory is about: it is agents who bring structure into being, and it is structure which produces the possibility of agency. So, in Giddens' view human beings are reflexive 'knowledgeable agents' in that they exhibit a familiarity with the rules of social life. In historical processes, under the influence of repeated action, structures change. The main point here is thus to not see agency and structure as oppositional, but as mutually constitutive. Now how can we use this insight for the study of violent conflict and war? The next step is to bring in discourses and institutions.

Discursive and institutional continuities

We are born into societies which are organized along certain rules of social life. In abstract terms, these rules of social life are what Giddens names structures. Giddens (1979: 64) defines structures as 'rules and resources recursively implicated in the reproduction of social systems'. Structures are thus 'rules that are articulated in social interaction and tell people how to "do" social life, and the resources on which people can call to achieve their objectives' (Wallace and Wolf 1999: 181). Giddens is interested in studying how social systems are produced and reproduced in interaction. Often, we are not aware of the rules of social life we live by. Sometimes the rules that tell us 'how to do' social life are so deeply embedded in time and space that we have come to see them as natural and self-evident. Of course, at times we can feel highly constrained by the formal and informal rules of life. Most people, however, simply engage in their daily routines without much thought: they go to work or school, plan their wedding party, pay taxes, salute the flag and celebrate national holidays. The rules of social life become manifest and visible – and hence researchable – to us in discourses and institutions: in stories about signification (what value things have, what is their meaning) and legitimation (what is considered 'normal' and 'acceptable' and not), and in the tangible products of the institutionalization of these values and norms: the school, the city hall, the shopping mall, the funeral home, the court, the prison and yes, the army and the body-bag. Giddens thus speaks of structures of signification and legitimation. As explained by Jabri (1996: 83):

> Structures of signification imply shared symbolic orders and modes of discourse which enable as well as constrain everyday interaction and situate or position actors in time and space ... Structures of legitimation define a second element of the rules of social life, namely norms and the sanctions which accompany their application in social interaction. Normative expectations refer to those codes of conduct, some enshrined in law, and others more informal, which legitimate some actions while censoring others. Dominant norms are central in the definition and constitution of society and can be subject to conflict at different times in the historical process.

It is through these symbolic orders and codes of conduct that power is exercised. Power is a key component of all social systems, and as we have seen in Giddens' definition of structure: some agents can draw on more resources than others in seeking to achieve desired outcomes. Giddens distinguishes 'allocative' and 'authoritative' resources. The first refers to control over material facilities, the latter to control over the activities of human beings. Apart from structures of signification and legitimation, Giddens thus defines a third structure of *domination*. The asymmetrical distribution of power results in certain agents simply having more 'power to define'. Jabri (1996: 96) ties the three structures together in arguing that 'structures of *signification* are mobilized to *legitimate* the *sectional interests* of hegemonic groups' (my emphasis).

Although using very different words, this is precisely what Gourevitch argues in his study on Rwanda: 'power consists in the ability to make others inhabit your story of their reality' (1998: 48). So, power is constituted through the use of language (discourse), and is supported by symbolic and material resources. This sounds rather abstract, but the power of words should not be underestimated. The struggle over words is a power struggle. A struggle about meaning. As is so painfully and meticulously documented by Klemperer in the context of Nazi Germany, the power of media and governments is based for a large part on their capacity to control the language in which people discuss societal problems. As Foucault shows, this kind of power is not exclusively repressive, it is also positive (constructive). People need to make sense of the overwhelming complexity of life and hence embrace and (re)construct symbolic orders, modes of discourse and codes of conduct. Power is seen not as exclusively held top-down and wielded over people. Instead, power is constituted and transformed at all levels of society. But how does all this fit into the discussion of agency and structure, and, ultimately, the study of war? We have seen how the rather abstract notion of

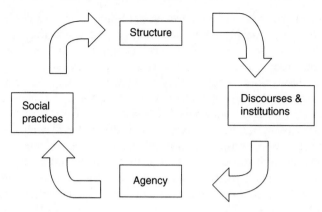

Figure 6.2 Discourses and practices

'structure' becomes manifest in discourses and institutions (the formal and informal 'rules of life') and in the way people (re)produce these rules through social practices. Social practices can be defined as 'relatively stabilized forms of social activity' such as for example classroom teaching, medical consultations, family meals and television news, but also military combat (Fairclough 2003: 205). The somewhat abstract closed loop running from structure to agency can thus be made more concrete by bringing in discursive and institutional continuities on one side and social practices on the other.

Let us look at the connection between these items by means of an example. In many societies the dominant norm and normality is for a man and a woman to form a household unit. This idea is manifested in discourses of religion and biology and institutionalized in the legal institution of marriage. People engage in the social practice of marriage and reproduce the structure. Powerful agents such as the church and the state manage to sustain structures of signification and legitimation in favour of male–female marriage. However, in the 1960s somewhere in western Europe, a counter-narrative on the normality of homosexuality gained ground, and decades later this narrative became institutionalized in the legal construct of gay marriage. In turn, a number of people engaged in the social practice of gay marriage, contesting and transforming dominant discourses on normality and appropriateness (hence, the rules of social life). The social system transformed through interaction. Stripped of nuance, this is the structurationist approach. An extremely important question, that we come to later, is of course why this counter-narrative managed to gain ground in this specific time and space, and why, for instance, in other parts of the world gay marriage is completely out of the question. What are the connections between structural transformations and the rise of (counter-)discourses? For instance, what is the link between the rise of free market capitalism and the concomitant 'individualization' of society? In fact, here the question pops up again of where the 'seeds of change' are located: in the structure of the system, or in the agency of actors? Does the theory of structurationism really solve this problem? Let us first move to war.

The Big Red One: war as institutional form

In the final scene of the movie *The Big Red One* (1980), a film about how four American privates and their legendary 'Sergeant' (Lee Marvin) try to survive WWII, we see the Sergeant sitting in a forest, at night, having just buried a small boy he had befriended after liberating a concentration camp. Out of the fog a German soldier approaches, the Sergeant turns, and stabs him. Soon after, his squad arrives on the scene informing him, excitedly, that the war has ended: 'The war has been over for four hours.' They quickly pack their things to go back to their headquarters. But as the others leave, one of the privates checks the body of the German and calls out: 'Hey, sarge, the dead Kraut, he's still warm!' When it turns out the German is still alive, the men come running back and proceed to give him First Aid treatment. The German seems to recover and opens his eyes. The Sergeant then lifts him on his shoulders, mumbling 'Live, you son of a bitch. ... You're gonna live if I have to blow your brains out.'

Some think *The Big Red One* is the ultimate film about the absurdity of war, others see it as one among many war movies on male-bonding, masculinity and glory. The point I like to emphasize here is that what the film shows, intentionally or not, is that apart from horrific and tough, war is normal. To us, the audience, the shift in the soldiers' code-of-conduct, from killing the enemy to giving him First Aid, is not in the least surprising. We all know that these are the rules of the game. Actions that are considered taboo in peacetime are glorified in times of war. And vice versa. Discourse theorists argue that it is not aggressive instinct, identity competition, or collective need deprivation, utility maximization or exploitation that makes these soldiers kill. No, it is the simple and straightforward routines of warfare that steer their actions. Underlying their routines is the idea of war as an accepted and institutionalized form of human conduct. It is against this background of 'war as institution' that discourse theorists argue we can understand violent action, not just in cases of 'regular' inter-state warfare, but also in situations of 'irregular' war and conflict. In this debate, Jabri's focus is on how deeply embedded discourses centred around concepts such as militarism, statehood, nationalism and masculinity have conditioned us, through time and across space, to see war as normality. War repeats and reproduces itself through discourses which render it acceptable and necessary, and through social institutions (armies, Ministries of Defence, war cabinets) which serve as war-making machinery. For Jabri (1996: 4):

> War and violent conflict are social phenomena emerging through, and constitutive of, social practices which have, through time and across space, rendered war an institutional form that is largely seen as an inevitable and at times acceptable form of human conduct.

The idea of war as routine and social phenomenon can help to explain why both decision-makers and audiences can shift relatively easily into what Richardson (1948) named a 'war mood'. This is the sudden and widespread support for war that takes hold of entire populations. How can audiences be mobilized so quickly? For Jabri, the war mood can arise because the language of war draws upon deeply embedded discourses of moral legitimacy and superiority. The language of war contains two classic dualisms. First, the dualism between 'self' and 'other' (or: us/them), where the self is associated with courage and civilization while the other is represented as barbaric and diabolical. The second dualism is that between 'conformity' and 'dissent'. Individuals and groups refusing to participate in the war effort are seen as traitors to their community and therefore deserving of censure, punishment or even banishment (Jabri 1996:

108). War as a social continuity hence draws upon discursive repertoires framed around exclusion and inclusion, be it at the level of the nation, the community or the group. This context, of discursive and institutional continuities, is central to Jabri's view of the role of the individual and the constitution of identity. For identity is assumed to be the link between the individual and mass mobilization for conflict. 'A central aspect of the mobilisation of support for armed conflict is identity with the group, community, or state whose representatives decide on the use of force as a means of handling conflict' (1996: 121). The categorization of 'self' and 'other' is not merely a product of cognition and the need for social identity differentiation, as for instance claimed by social identity theorists, but derives from discursive and institutional continuities which are reproduced through everyday acts of stereotyping and categorizing. Individuals are born into discursive and institutional continuities which define and bind societies. They form their identities on the basis of these continuities. As societies are containers of a plurality of discourses and discursive sites, this implies that identity is always a point of active selection and contestation. Active selection, however, is not the same as free selection: our freedom to construct our identities is limited by dominant norms, and symbolic orders. Ultimately, it is through structures of domination and control that discourses of identity emerge. For Jabri, social identity is constituted through deeply engrained institutional and discursive continuities which situate the self within bounded communities, the definition of which is based on modalities of inclusion and exclusion. Social identity, therefore, is 'a product of all that which is located in the realm of society, as context of communication, power relations, contestations, and dominant discursive and institutional practices' (1996: 134).

There is a tension between Jabri's analysis of power, identity and discourse, and her goal to advocate 'counter-discourses' of peace. Staying rather close to the abstract level of Giddens' theory of structurationism, Jabri argues that since structure and agency are mutually constitutive, actors can act to change the war structure in which they operate. Since we have agency, we can emancipate ourselves (and 'de-identify') from dominant rules of social life and create new discourses of peace, which in turn could serve to institutionalize a context of peace as social continuity. These discourses of peace, established in the public arena, reject exclusionary discourses of us/them dichotomies in favour of a tolerance of diversity and recognize difference as a formative component of subjectivity (1996: 185). Put simply, as long as enough people participate in the discourse of peace, it will become an alternative structure that can legitimize decisions for peace. In her discussion of peace discourse, however, Jabri seems determined to overlook – if only for a moment – that which she explains so eloquently in her book: that is, how discourses are produced in contexts of power asymmetry and how hegemonic groups can mobilize structures of signification to legitimate their sectional interests. This seems to imply that a 'hegemony of peace' – and again, whose peace are we talking about? – needs to be not only socially meaningful but also politically functional.

So far, we have discussed the discursive approach to violent conflict on the abstract level of war as an institutional form: of war as institutional and discursive continuity. In the second part of this chapter we will see how discourse analysis can also be used to study down-to-earth and concrete cases of violent conflict: this is the study of war as constructed discourse. We hence move from a focus on war as social continuity to war as manifestation. Clearly, these latent and manifest levels in war are highly intertwined.

War as constructed discourse

In a documentary named *We are All Neighbours* (1993, Granada TV), the anthropologist Tone Bringa shows how relationships between neighbours and friends change in a small village near Sarajevo in the early 1990s, in the run-up to war. The distant shelling, the constant rumours and the stories of refugees slowly begin to affect relationships within the village. People turn inwards, away from each other. They stop visiting old friends for a cup of coffee. Slowly, ethnic boundaries become salient. 'People change their faces' – as one woman describes it – 'It happened to me in a day.'

As we have seen in the introductory chapter, conflict is defined as a situation in which two or more entities or 'parties' perceive that they possess mutually incompatible goals. It is in the study of this perception that discourse analysis becomes useful.

Discourse theory aims to study the formation of discourses in and on war. It aims to give an explicit and systematic description of the ways in which people form discourse communities, and how collective narratives on the origins of war, the enemy, victims and perpetrators are formed and sustained. An important underlying principle is that discourse formation is seen as a social process. Powerful groups (elites, specialists, intellectuals, leaders) may try – for a variety of reasons – to convince their audiences that a certain incompatibility of goals is threatening them, and try to turn this into a dominant discourse. This can, however, not be established top-down. Discourse formation has a dynamics of its own, where coding, interpretation and meaning are the outcome of a complex dynamics of interaction between a wide variety of actors: the so-called 'crafters' of discourse.

Now, for the sake of clarity: what is a discourse? There are many definitions of discourse, but they all share the idea that discourses are stories about social reality. These stories are stated in relational terms, and give a representation of what is considered the 'social truth'. The shortest definition of discourse states that 'discourse is action'. Discourses are not just words or descriptions, they actually do things. These two notions of 'discourse as relational' and 'discourse as action' underlie the definition of discourses given by Jabri (1996: 94–95):

> Discourses are social relations represented in texts where the language contained within these texts is used to construct meaning and representation ... The underlying assumption of discourse analysis is that social texts do not merely *reflect* or *mirror* objects, events and categories pre-existing in the social and natural world. Rather, they actively *construct* a version of those things. They do not describe things, *they do things*. And being active they have social and political implications.

What is implied here is that although classifications such as 'terrorism', 'ethnic identity' or 'race' are the product of our imagination, this does not make them imaginary. Since people perceive certain classifications as real, they act upon them as real, and therefore they have very real consequences. This is the power of discourse. In the BBC documentary *Racism: a History* (2007) by Tim Robinson, one of the commentators explains the very real everyday practice of the mythology of race through sketching a scene of a black man in New York City trying to hail a cab.

> Black man: Excuse me, cab, I know you think I am a black man, and that race exists. But I am a fiction! I am a figment of your imagination! I am a social construct! There is no biological base or empirical verification for my differential. I am simply another human being possessing a different magnitude of melanin.
> Cab: I still ain't picking you up, 'cause you're trying to go to Harlem, brother. That's race.

Another example of the social and political implication of the use of text is the case of the 'listing' of the Liberation Tigers of Tamil Eelam (LTTE) as a terrorist organization by the Council of the European Union in May 2006. As can be deduced from the Council's statement, by putting the LTTE on their terrorist list, they hoped to push the organization (back) to the negotiation table. The formal categorizing of persons, groups or entities on the list allows the EU to take specific restrictive measures such as a ban on the provision of funds, financial assets and economic resources, as well as police and judicial measures. The Council argued that the decision to list the Tigers was invoked by 'the actions of that organisation'. At the same time, the EU recognized that the LTTE could not be held solely responsible for the upsurge in violence. The Government of Sri Lanka was also urged to clamp down on all acts of violence and stop the culture of impunity. However, it was the LTTE, and not the Government of Sri Lanka that was given the terrorist label. What was striking about this case is that the EU did not accuse the LTTE of changing tactics: violence intensified, but remained largely the same. Although it is impossible to track the precise rationale behind the 'terrorist labelling' of the LTTE, it seems the EU expected that the use of this label would effectively cut off the organization's economic resources. This then would leave the Tigers powerless and hence willing to renegotiate peace. Although the EU measures certainly had an effect on the LTTE fund-raising capacity, the 'terrorist' label, however, above all offered the incoming Rajapakse Government a justification to start a full-fledge war against the LTTE. For terrorists, in the post 9/11 meaning of the term, are people 'without moral conscience', with whom you 'do not negotiate' and who 'need to be smoked out of their holes'. In the discursive context of the 'war on terror', labelling an organization as terrorist in order to push it to the negotiation table is, at best, paradoxical.

As Michael Bhatia (2005: 7) points out, the pronouncement of the 'war on terror' has forced many to 'verbally negotiate and assert who they are, who they are allied with, and who they are against':

> This is the new dominant framework in which both governments and non-state armed movements present their acts. Indeed, a transnational element has again been transplanted onto a series of pre-existing local disputes, as occurred during the Cold War. From Uzbekistan to Colombia, from the Philippines to Algeria, the conflict over 'names' and 'naming' is becoming furious.

The underlying assumption is that, in contradiction to the old childhood axiom of 'sticks and bones', in armed conflict 'names and images' do matter and are seen to 'hurt' (Bhatia 2005: 6). Or as Foucault argued, discourse can be conceived as 'a violence which we do to things' (1984: 127). Discourse is a tool for governments and organizations and a battleground and contested space in war and conflict.

In studying 'text in context' discourse theorists do not focus on words alone. Schröder and Schmidt (2001) describe how violence becomes sanctioned as the legitimate course of action through the imagining of violent scenarios. These 'violent imaginaries' include *narratives, performances* and *images*. Narratives keep violence alive in stories, either by glorifying one's own group or derogating the enemy. Performances are public rituals in which antagonistic relationships are staged and enacted, here the many formal and informal 'war ceremonies' come to mind, such as memorial days and parades. Discourses can also be inscribed in the cultural landscape as images on walls, bodies, buildings, flags and banners. Murals, graffiti, but also clothing are all important sources of discursive expression (Peteet 1996, 2005). In our highly media-tized world, an image is indeed 'worth a thousand words' and the role of visual displays of antagonisms in the (new) media is highly influential in staging a message before an audience.

Discourse analysis hence is about the 'politics of portrayal', examining how names and images are made, assigned and disputed, and how this battle at times translates into political and judicial measures and instruments (such as 'terrorist listing'). Discourse analysts are interested not only in the contested 'naming' of parties in war and the 'portrayal' of episodes of violence but also importantly aim to gain insight in the functions of discourse. Discursive representations are seen to fulfil at least two functions: (1) to recruit supporters by propagating a concrete us/them divide, and (2) to legitimize violent action.

Discursive constructions of the other

We have seen how identities are constructed representations of the 'self' in relation to 'the other', and also how a key aspect of the mobilization of support for armed conflict is identity with the group, community or state whose representatives decide on the use of force against the 'other'. The role and function of constructing 'the Enemy' has been thoroughly examined in both international relations theory and other areas of the social sciences. Discourses on othering and belonging are integral to war, up to the point that '"we" are intrinsic to an understanding of what "we" fear' (Campbell 1998: 73). The methods used and discourses developed to separate us and them vary over time: from the colonizer/colonized, East/West to distinctions between freedom/terror, and metropolitan/borderlands. As Bhatia argues, different words assume dominance at different times, with the word choice selected according to the power assigned at different levels (local, national, international). Some groups or governments aim to frame their local struggle in terms of a larger international conflict system, in order to receive diplomatic, financial or even military support. As occurred earlier during the Cold War, and as evident in the example of the Rajapakse response to the LTTE, certain actors rapidly adapted to the 9/11 US terrorist rhetoric to describe their own local enemies. 'It is decidedly in the interest of some quasi-authoritarian governments to over-emphasize the militant Islamist character of their opposition, in the hope of US assistance or a *carte blanche* for repression, as may be the case in Uzbekistan, Egypt and Algeria' (Bhatia 2005: 13). Others play to more local histories of rebellion and revolution, drawing on a glorious and heroic past as a way to attain the support of the population.

An example of how a local victory is framed in terms of a larger international conflict system is the thousand rupee note issued by the Central Bank of Sri Lanka portraying the victory over the Tamil Tigers of May 2009. The note, which depicts the hoisting of the national flag by members of the security forces, strongly resembles the well-known image of US marines hoisting the US flag on mount Iwo Jima during WWII, photographed by Joe Rosenthal.

In the large majority of cases, the (ethno)nation – the most commonplace of identity – is the location of discursive practices of othering and belonging. Jabri (1996: 134) argues how a *discourse of origins* is at the heart of conflict as constructed discourse:

> The conflicts of our post Cold War era centre around a discourse of origins, where the traditions and territorial claims of forebears are relived and in whose name contemporary and future wars are legitimated. The categories of origins exemplified in constructs such as Israeli, Palestinian, Arab, Muslim, Serb, Turkish, Kurdish, Christian, Hutu, Tutsi, Catholic, Protestant, hark back to a distant past in order to mobilize a bounded, exclusionist present. This is a process of selections and definition, where a dominant identity emerges from a plethora of other possibilities. It seeks to negate and deny difference, to obliterate dissent, in the name of a mythical unified entity, an effective fighting force.

One of the main challenges of discourse theory is to understand how, but also importantly, *why* it is that such reified notions of the self and other emerge in certain times and places. How, for instance, can we account for the rise of right-wing, anti-Islam political parties in western Europe and Scandinavia in the early 2010s? Evidently, in the post 9/11 era politicians, particularly new ones, find it opportune to play on discursive representations of the 'Evil Muslim' to recruit voters and political support, but why are these images so radically embraced by the larger public? Often, discourse theorists emphasize how the xenophobic turn in Europe is the product of ethnic entrepreneurs and media regimes of representation, greatly enhanced by the Madrid and London bombings, and the influx of 'non-western' immigrants. Another way to look at the rise of xenophobia is not to focus exclusively on the instrumental functionality of discursive strategies of othering, but also on the *societal processes* which condition whether and to what degree people are receptive or resistant to such discourses. This way of thinking – with roots in Durkheim's writings of anomie and Simmel's stranger – has proliferated in the work of authors such as Arjun Appadurai (2006) on the fear of small numbers and Zygmunt Bauman (2006) on the role of the stranger in postmodern society, but also in the earlier writings on ethnic violence of anthropologists such as Malkki (1995), Nordstrom (1997) and Tambiah (1996). In most of these works, authors aim to lay bare the relation between social uncertainty and forces of globalization. Appadurai, for instance, explains that 'given the growing multiplicity, contingency, and apparent fungibility of the identities available to persons in the contemporary world, there is a growing sense of radical social uncertainty about people, situations, events, norms and even cosmologies' (Appadurai 1998: 906). The most apparent form of uncertainty, effectively exploited by the new populism, is that of the 'Muslim other' framed in terms of *invasion* (numbers) and *hidden agendas*: how many of 'them' are among 'us' and 'who are they *really*'? In an interview on a Danish news show, days after his party had won five seats in the mid 2009 elections for the European Parliament, becoming the second largest party in The Netherlands, the leader of the anti-Islam 'Freedom Party', quite explicitly played upon these two forms of uncertainty:

The amount, the influx of mass immigration from Islamic countries and also the demographic changes are enormous. The more they come, the stronger it becomes, the less freedom we will get ... Like I said, an enormous amount of [Muslim] people, 50 million people, are living in Europe today. And I assure you, that even though the majority of the people in our society today are non-violent, they are not terrorists or criminals, that the sooner the numbers are increasing, if a society will have say, 20, 30, 40 percent Muslims, an entire society will change. It will cost us our freedom. ... In the Netherlands there was a survey that one out of three Muslim youths want to install Sharia. In the United Kingdom there was a survey that 30 to 40 percent of the Muslim students there want to get rid of democracy, want to install the Caliphate, the Sharia. You see the same numbers in Sweden, even in your own country, Denmark. You see that it is still a minority. But the huge amount of Muslims really want a different society, than the democratic societies that we have today. And as soon as they become stronger, they will, I am sure, change their tune and it will be too late to fight back.

These are powerful and classic recipes for fear. The image of the other, whose true evil face will only be revealed when it is too late. Muslims as body snatchers, innocent-looking perhaps, until the horrid moment they collectively 'change their tune' and take over, is a significant metaphor which easily taps into popular cultural repertoires of outsider invasion. Others point at neoliberal reform – now a generation or more in the making – to explain the public's receptiveness to exclusionist discourses. Greenhouse, for instance, argues that neoliberalism has 'restructured the most prominent public relationships that constitute *belonging*: politics, markets, work and self-identity' (2010: 2). Similarly, Demmers and Mehendale (2010) argue for the need to identify and grapple with the complexities of the relation between xenophobia and the political project of neoliberalism. The rise of xenophobia is seen to be part of a larger process of a mostly market-controlled reclaiming of symbolic forms of collectiveness in an increasingly atomized society. Where the neoliberal project has, largely unnoticed, abolished the collective standards and solidarities of the post WWII era, the faces of immigrants have served as ideal, identifiable flash points for new repertoires of belonging and othering. Although the neoliberal project may be technically agnostic on matters of culture and race, it is well served by the permanent construction of an enemy (either within or without) who can satisfy the consumer-citizen's need for inclusion and belonging. Discourses of exclusion are most powerful when they are both socially meaningful and politically functional.

What these approaches share is their aim to put 'text in context' and to study the connections between social, cultural, political and economic transformations in the organization of society and the rise of certain group antagonisms. As explained by van Dijk: 'Discourse analytical approaches systematically describe the various structures and strategies of text and talk, and relate these to the social and political context' (1993: 35). In particular Critical Discourse Analysis (CDA) is concerned with how discourse figures within processes of change. In his book *Analysing Discourse* Norman Fairclough (2003) shows how discourse is a crucial aspect of social transformation. He also, importantly, makes a case for detailed analysis. 'Without detailed analysis one cannot really *show* that language is doing the work one may theoretically ascribe to it' (2003: 204). Fairclough provides a set of analytical tools and concepts necessary to make us 'discourse literate' (such as genres, styles and clauses). Although it is beyond the scope of this book to elaborate on discourse analysis in a technical sense, we will briefly discuss Fairclough's helpful distinction between enactment and inculcation.

Enactment and inculcation

Fairclough points out how discourse figures in ways of (inter)*acting* and ways of *being* and hence is important in understanding both practices and identities. For Fairclough (2003: 207) discourses include 'representations of how things are and have been, as well as imaginaries – representations of how things might or could or should be'. These imaginaries may be *enacted* as actual practices. Imagined activities, subjects or social relations can become real activities, subjects and social relations. Such enactments include what Faiclough calls 'materialisations of discourse'. Economic discourses, for example, become materialized in the instruments of economic production, including the 'hardware' (plant, machinery, offices) and the 'software' (management systems, training). Such enactments are also in part themselves discursive. He illustrates the idea of discursive enactment as follows (2003: 208):

> Consider, for example, new management discourses which imagine management systems based upon 'teamwork', relatively non-hierarchical, networked, ways of managing organisations. They become enacted discursively as new genres, for instance genres for team meetings. Such specifically discursive enactments are embedded within their enactment as new ways of acting and interacting in pro- duction processes, and possibly material enactments in new spaces (e.g. seminar rooms) for team activities.

Closer to our field of study, Duffield describes how the policy discourse on the secur- itization of aid (see chapter 3) has a clear 'spatial dimension' and becomes materialized in what he names the 'fortified aid compound' in for instance South Sudan, where increasingly, the aid industry is 'bunkering itself'. Such compounds typically have strengthened double gates and inner and outer walls or fences with razor-wire, and movement in and around these visibly defensive and guarded structures is hedged with security protocols. The irony of the situation, Duffield states, is 'that for ordinary Southerners, after decades of war and dislocation, these militarised buildings are the first material expressions of peace' (2010a: 455–6). In a critical discussion of the 'politics of aid' Keen (2008) takes a discursive look at the functionality of 'camps' (relief, aid, refugee camps) as the favoured solution among humanitarian agencies to refugees' problems. The materialization of humanitarian aid in camps serves important functions for aid agencies: camps can be easily organized and monitored, any improvements in the refugees' health status can be readily measured and reported and visiting journalists can come to publicize the good work of the agency (Harrell-Bond 1986: in Keen 2008).

Discourses are not only enacted in practices and materialized in tangible products, they also may come to be *inculcated* as new identities, as new ways of being. This process of inculcation is closely related to what Klemperer aimed to express when writing how: 'Language does not simply write and think for me, it also directs my feelings, it directs my entire being the more unquestionably and unconsciously I sur- render myself to it (2000 [1947]: 30). Fairclough explains how inculcation is a matter of people coming to 'own' discourses, 'to position themselves inside them, to act and think and talk and see themselves in terms of new discourses' (2003: 208). Inculcation is a complex process, and less easy to pin down than enactment. An important step towards inculcation is *rhetorical deployment*: people may use certain discourses for certain purposes while at the same time self-consciously keeping a distance from them. 'One of the mysteries of the dialectics of discourse is the process in which what begins as self-conscious rhetorical deployment becomes "ownership" – how people become unconsciously positioned within a discourse' (2003: 208). Inculcation also has its material aspects: 'discourses are dialectically inculcated not only in styles, ways of using language, they are also materialised in bodies, postures, gestures, ways of moving, and so forth' (2003: 208).

For an illustration of the step from rhetorical deployment of a 'war discourse' to war as a 'way of being' we once more turn to Slavenka Drakulic's analysis of the war in Former Yugoslavia. In an essay named 'High-Heeled Shoes' she tells of the visit of her friend Drazena, who has fled Sarajevo, and who now carries the yellow certificate which states that she is a refugee from Bosnia and Herzegovina. With razor-sharp honesty, Drakulic analyses her unease with Drazena's bodily presence. She feels, for instance, it is inappropriate for her friend to continue to wear make-up and high-heels. This is not what a refugee should look like (1993: 142–3):

> The moment I thought Drazena ought not wear make-up or patent high-heeled shoes was the very moment when I myself pushed her into the group 'refugee', because it was easier for me. But the fact that she didn't fit the cliché, that she was disappointing me by trying to keep her face together with her make-up and her life together with a pair of shoes, made me aware of my own collaboration with this war.

This is when Drakulic realizes that she 'is the war'. How it has crept into her unconscious cruelty towards her friend, and changed emotions, relationships and values. 'So we all get used to it', she writes. 'I understand now that nothing but this "otherness" killed Jews, and it began with naming them, by reducing them to the other. Then everything became possible.' (1993: 144). She is careful to point out that she is not trying to equate the cruelty of othering to the cruelty of cold-blooded murder. 'All I am saying is that it exists, this complicity: that out of opportunism and fear we all are becoming collaborators or accomplices in the perpetuation of war' (1993: 145).

Fairclough emphasizes that there is nothing inevitable about the dialectic of discourses as he describes them. Discourses may become enacted, but never fully inculcated. What his analysis highlights is how ways of (inter)acting and ways of being are represented in discourses, which may in turn contribute to the production of new imaginaries, which may in turn be enacted and inculcated. This is not say, however, that discourses are random and flexible. Fairclough, drawing on structurationism, emphasizes that we have to consider the *conditions* of possibility for, and the constraints upon, the dialectics of discourse in particular cases. One thus has to take into account the circumstances which condition whether and to what degree people are receptive of or resistant to certain discourses. Concretely, this can be done by asking the question whether the social order in a sense 'needs' a certain problem (e.g. an 'evil invader', an 'ethnic other'), and whether 'those who benefit most from the way social life is now organized have an interest in the problem not being solved' (2003: 210). This brings us to the second function of discursive representation: the legitimization of action.

The legitimization of violence

It is not hard to see how discourse plays an important role in the legitimization of action. The struggle over the representation of war and violence involves a struggle over the legitimacy of violent acts. In his book *The Legitimation of Violence*, David Apter succinctly argues that 'people do not commit political violence without discourse, they need to talk themselves into it' (1997: 2). Discourse analysis can thus be helpful in understanding the onset of war, and the step to violence in conflict. As we have seen above, discourses include 'representations of how things are and have been, as well as imaginaries – representations of how things might or could or should be' (Fairclough 2003: 207). For violence to start, it first has to become imaginable. A crucial stage in the run up to war is hence its 'dress-rehearsal' in the form of Klemperer's 'million repetitions' of 'single words, idioms, and sentence structures' imposed on people. Anthropologists Schröder and Schmidt argue that 'violence needs to be imagined in order to be carried out' (2001: 9). In describing the processual characteristics of violent action they propose a four-stage model leading from 'conflict' to 'war'. The first stage, 'conflict', is seen as the (socio-economic) contradiction at the base of intergroup competition. However, organized violence ('war') does not automatically result from contradiction. 'Wars are made by those individuals, groups or classes that have the power successfully to represent violence as the appropriate course of action in a given situation' (2001: 5). So, for war to break out, a second and third stage, named 'confrontation' and 'legitimation' are necessary. 'Confrontation' relates to the parties involved coming to look upon the 'contradiction' as somehow *relevant*, creating an antagonistic relationship. During the third stage ('legitimation') violence is officially sanctioned as the legitimate course of action through the imagining of violent scenarios, what Schröder and Schmidt call 'violent imaginaries'. Finally, during 'war' violence is put into practice (2001: 19). It is thus in particular the third stage of 'legitimation' in which violence becomes 'possible'. For Schröder and Schmidt 'the most important code of war is its historicity' (2001: 9):

> Wars are fought from memory, and they are often fought over memory, over the power to establish one's group view of the past as the legitimate one. From this perspective violence is not only a resource for solving conflicts over material issues, but also a resource in world making, to assert one group's claim to truth and history against rival claims, with all the social and economic consequences this entails.

But by what means is the legitimacy of violence 'impressed upon those who are to march into battle and those who are to cheer them on?' (2001: 9). Violent imaginaries, 'the emphasising of the historicity of present-day confrontations' play an important role in the creation of a 'hegemonic accord' among the larger public. Through their participation in narratives, performances and inscriptions people come to accept and support the violent course of action proposed by their leaders as legitimate and justified. Violent imaginaries, although strongly related to the strategic interests of those who disseminate them, are reproduced through a complex and multifaceted dynamics of interaction. As Schröder and Schmidt highlight, there are wide variations in the degree of people's acceptance of the hegemonic message. 'They correspond with one another on a general level, but in practice each conflict party is made up of numerous subgroups pursuing their own agendas' (2001: 10). In his documentary series *Blood and Belonging: Journeys into the New Nationalism* (1993, BBC), in the episode on the Orange marches in Belfast, Michael Ignatieff shows us how the 'Loyalist' community constructs its limits, its relationship to that what it is not or what threatens it, and the narratives, performances and inscriptions through which violence against 'the Catholics' is imagined and legitimated.

Ignatieff travels to Belfast in Northern Ireland to study the meaning of the Orange marches that take place every summer between 1 and 12 July. What he finds is a discourse community, a very diverse group of people who call themselves Loyalists and who all produce a similar answer when asked what it is they are celebrating: the victory of 'King Billy' (William of Orange) at the Battle of the Boyne in 1690, and the Battle of the Somme in 1916, when 'thousands of Ulstermen gave their lives for Britain'. But whereas the July celebrations mean adventure and fun for the little boys building and protecting the huge stacks of wood that are set on fire on the evening of 12 July, with an effigy of the Pope on top, the same celebrations are seen as a yearly display of 'victory' over 'the Catholics', with teenage males staging the message 'we won' to their 'rivals' on the other side. They paint the curb stones in the colours of the Union Jack to mark off 'their territory', and enjoy the 'buzz' of being part of one of the brass bands that lead the marches. There is also the older generation of males, who enjoy status through their participation in the dignified 'Orange Order', with its sashes and flags. And then there is the role of the Church as guardian of the community, and, ultimately, the para-military Ulster Defence Force, whose images are depicted on murals, and who in many ways make this a discourse community at gun point. Whereas the little boys' July bonfires speak to an audience of neighbourhood pals ('ours is higher'), and the teenagers enjoy 'pissing off' rival gangs through ethnic marking and marching in bands, the Church, Orange Order and UDF use the July celebrations to convey a political message to 'the mainland' and to their political adversaries, in both Northern Ireland and Ireland. Where the celebration of the victory of King Billy brings the message of religious superiority (of Protestants over Catholics) the ceremonies around the Battle of the Somme emphasize how Ulstermen have made great sacrifices for the British nation and how they are loyal to the Crown. Clearly, there is a very contemporary and political message contained within these celebrations of the past.

In showing the multiple meanings and functionalities of violent imaginaries the documentary is a wonderful illustration of what Schröder and Schmidt call 'the dialectic nature of violence', and the complex relation between violent imaginaries and violent practices. Violence and its many symbolic displays is not merely a strategy of bargaining for power, it is also a 'form of symbolic action that conveys cultural meanings, most importantly ideas of legitimacy' (2001: 8). Schröder and Schmidt base their understanding of legitimacy on Weber's (1972) classic definition, which states that a social order is accepted as valid either due to its historicity, its emotional value or to instrumental reasoning. The legitimization of violence through the re-enactment of narratives, performances and inscriptions can be based upon all of these three aspects: it recreates the past, it appeals to strong feelings of inclusion, based on the experience of either suffering or superiority, and it is a direct route to the assertion of power, established by the other two mechanisms (2001: 8). As the example of Belfast shows, the symbolic meaning of prior wars or violent confrontations is reinterpreted and adapted to the present, and is generating symbolic value to be employed in the future.

Violence is thus communicative and expressive: it has a performative quality. 'Violence without an audience will still leave people dead, but is socially meaningless. Violent acts are efficient because of their staging of power and legitimacy, probably even more so than due to their physical results' (2001: 6).

So far, we have discussed approaches which emphasize how discourses are helpful in preparing audiences for violence and war, and hence how discourse theory helps us to understand the step to (the normalization of) actual violence. An author who would very much agree with the above quotation from Schröder and Schmidt, but who adds a slightly different tack on the role of discourses on violence, is Paul Brass (1996). Where Schröder and Schmidt (2001) and also Apter (1997) emphasize the stage *prior* to the violence, Brass has looked at the dynamics of after-the-act interpretations of violence as of key importance. He suggests focusing on the interpretative processes in the *aftermath* of violent practices. The core idea underlying this approach is to not simply identify the multiple contexts in which violence occurs 'because it can occur anywhere and can be organized or random, premeditated or spontaneous, directed at specific persons, groups, or property, or not' (1996: 2). Brass acknowledges that these aspects of violence must be identified insofar as possible. However, he claims that we also need to examine the discourses on violence, and the ways in which participants and observers seek to explain incidents of violence. In his work Brass aims to go beyond analysing the violent struggle to investigate as well the struggle to *interpret* the violence. That is, 'the attempts to govern a society or a country through gaining not a monopoly on the legitimate use of violence, but *to gain control over the interpretation of violence*' (1996: 45, my emphasis). For Brass, the contest for gaining control over the interpretation of violence is 'at least as important, and probably more important' than the outcome of specific struggles themselves (1996: 45):

> The struggle over the meaning of violence may or may not lead to a consensus or a hegemonic interpretation. It will certainly not lead to the 'truth' but at most to a 'regime of truth' which will give us a pre-established context into which we can place future acts of a similar type into the same context and for the reinterpretation of previous acts of violence in history.

This analysis of the struggle over meaning is not different from the study of violent imaginaries: both approaches focus on how and why certain acts of violence are selected from a plethora of other possibilities and how they are turned into symbolic markers of power and belonging, which, in turn, legitimize future acts of violence.

What Brass' analysis brings to the fore, is how over the past centuries the power to define and interpret local instances of violence, to place them in specific contexts of local knowledge, has been removed from the local societies in which they occur. From colonial racism, to the Cold War ideological stand-off, and the War on Terror, different systems of 'knowledge' have all produced 'authorities' who define and interpret local incidents of violence, but also, and importantly, act upon these interpretations. We have seen many examples of this throughout the book. Brass argues that the very tendency to place particular kinds of violence (e.g, hooliganism, rape, land grabbing, car burning) into a particular frame often involves misplacement, which in turn may contribute to the distribution and persistence of those events in space and time (1996: 2). The portrayal of a bar room brawl as an 'ethnic clash', car-burnings in French suburbs as a 'new intifada', and sexual violence in the Democratic Republic of the Congo as 'an instrument of war' are all examples of how violent acts are increasingly framed in terms that are removed from – but certainly feed into – the local settings in which they occur. It is this global–local dialectics of framing, in which a variety of actors fight a discursive battle over image, the justification of violence, blame and accountability, which is at the core of a discursive approach to violent conflict.

Conclusions

The discursive approach to violent conflict examines the ways in which people engage in discursive practices that render violence against 'the other' legitimate and inevitable. The approach looks at stories, both as narratives and images, but also as *enacted* in practices, *materialized* in tangible products and *inculcated* in forms of being. It studies the narrative reconstructions of reality and analyses how these stories have come about. That is, it addresses the circumstances that condition whether and to what degree people are receptive or resistant to certain discourses. Concretely, it examines how and why stories are reinforced, ritualized, resisted and policed, and, ultimately, institutionalized and turned into 'truth' and tradition.

The three book questions have been answered more or less explicitly throughout this chapter, still, it may be useful to summarize them here. The answer to the first question ('what makes a group?') is given by Sayyid and Zac (1998): group boundaries are constructed discursively. Groups are collectively constructed representations of the 'self' in relation to the 'other'. Individuals and groups thus discursively construct their limits. As is explained above, although identity formation is always a point of active selection and contestation, it is not the same as free selection: it is through deeply engrained institutional and discursive continuities that people situate the self and the other in certain categories of belonging. The large majority of contemporary conflicts revolve around a discourse of origins, where us and them divides are formulated along reified, mythical and unified notions of culture, ethnicity and religion.

The second question, 'how and why does a group resort to violence?', can be answered in two ways: from the more abstract understanding of 'war as institutional form', and from a concrete analysis of 'war as constructed discourse'. From the abstract perspective, perhaps the most simple answer would be that groups resort to violence, or support those who march into battle in the name of the group, because this is largely deemed 'just' and appropriate, or at least inevitable. Here we can refer back to Jabri's argument that war and violent conflict are social phenomena emerging through, and constitutive of, social practices which have, through time and across space, rendered war an institutional form that is largely seen as an inevitable and at times acceptable form of human conduct (1996: 4). This notion, of war as normality, particularly applies to the more classic cases of what is often called 'regular warfare'. Here, the privates in *The Big Red One* come to mind, and the heavily scripted routines of violence that characterize inter-state war. However, the idea of 'war as normality' also importantly underlies cases of irregular war, more often referred to as violent conflict. This type of conflict revolves around much less institutionalized organizations and group formations. The analysis of these concrete cases of violent conflict from a discursive approach requires a fine-tuned examination of the formation and function of specific 'violent imaginaries'. Two processes are of particular importance at this stage. First, the discursive construction of the 'enemy-other'. Second, the way in which violence against the other is sanctioned as the legitimate course of action through the imagining of violent scenarios. Combined, exclusionist group identities and violent imaginaries importantly normalize, and legitimize, violent practices against 'the other'. However, the cruelty of othering is not the same as the cruelty of killing. As critics of discourse theory retort, explaining the ways through which violence is legitimized and normalized is not the same as accounting for its actual outbreak. Discourse theory cannot help us highlight the how and why of the concrete violent act itself. At least, not in the way rational choice theory, human needs theory, social identity theory or collective action theory can, through a respective focus on utility maximization, frustration, anger or the combination of opportunity, framing and organizational structures. Rather, discourse theory examines how and why the violent act – if and when it occurs – is interpreted and represented, how it is glorified or criminalized, and how it is placed in a larger narrative of us and them, good and bad, victim and perpetrator, past and future. And, importantly, how this process of 'sense making' may help to legitimize certain acts of violence and punish others (by categorizing these as criminal or terrorist), how it can institutionalize identity boundaries (by producing identity cards, passports and fences), and enforce laws and regulations (dealing with resettlement, detention, deportation) that were previously rendered illegal. Perhaps the best way to answer the second question from an applied discursive approach is that inter-group, or 'cross-party' violence is likely to occur – for whatever personal or political motive – if it is interpreted and represented as legitimate within a dominant discourse. As both Klemperer and Drakulic, and here again Jabri, emphasize: war is the time at which the language of the everyday becomes a discourse of exclusionist protection against a constructed enemy, which is deserving of any violence perpetrated against it. War both repeats and reproduces itself through discursive practices of naming and othering, which convey legitimacy to it.

So, 'how and why do they (not) stop?' What we failed to emphasize in the above is how discourse figures within contexts of power asymmetry, and how we need to examine the conditions of possibility for, and the constraints upon, the dialectics of discourses in certain cases. In brief, some actors have greater 'powers to define' than others, allowing for hegemonic groups to mobilize structures of signification to legitimate their sectional interests (as in Gramsci's notion of 'cultural hegemony', discussed in chapter three). Again, the question of how and why violence is perpetuated or ended can be answered at two levels. At an abstract level, discourse theorists highlight how 'the institution of war' reproduces itself through deeply embedded discourses centred around statehood, nationalism, property, militarism and masculinity, and how we are conditioned to see war as normality. Hence, as long as this remains the case, we will see the perpetuation of war as a social phenomenon. As a possible alternative, Jabri proposes the idea of a 'discourse of peace', in which exclusionary us/them dichotomies are rejected in favour of a tolerance of diversity and the recognition of difference as a formative component of subjectivity. Agents can act to change the institution of war through their participation in a counter-discourse of peace. In turn, these discourses on peace could serve to institutionalize a context of peace as social continuity. In theory, and ideally, this would help to end war and violent conflict.

In concrete settings of war and violent conflict, discourse theorists may argue that parties will continue to resort to the use of violence as long as this is seen as a legitimate act by the larger public, and as long as they 'can talk themselves into it'. This may be because strict codes of warfare discipline fighters into obedience, but also because actors, at times unconsciously, strongly identify with the concrete discourse of war.

Violent conflict may end, or transform, if dominant discourses begin to crumble, and doubt creeps in. As we have seen, discourses are rarely fully hegemonic: there is always some room for counter-discourses. The ways in which the Serbian youth movement Otpor! engaged in discursive practices of resistance against the Milosevic regime, mainly through ways of symbolic inversion, satire and ridicule, and the dissemination of 'non-violent imaginaries', are examples of how a dominant discourse can be 'toppled'.[1] The *delegitimation* of violence is a crucial stage in the transformation of conflict, and is strongly connected to transformations in the underlying political and material structures of domination.

A final word on ontology and epistemology. Epistemologically, discourse theory is firmly rooted in the 'understanding' side of the Hollis matrix and takes an interpretative stance. The approach is fundamentally concerned with the ways in which people make sense of violence and act upon this is in specific historical contexts and structured relations of political and material inequality. Ontologically, discourse theory – that is, the strand of discourse theory discussed in this chapter – departs from Giddens' theory of structurationism, and hence aims to synthesize structure and agency. In Hollis' matrix, this approach could be depicted as sitting on the fence separating structuralism and individualism. Or, perhaps a better metaphor: the approach does away with the fence and emphasizes how structures and agents stand in a dialectical relationship to each other: they are seen as mutually constitutive entities. This is not a new thought. Although this final chapter – *finally* – theorized the connection between individuality and society, we have touched upon the topic of human beings as 'role follower' and 'purposive agent' in earlier chapters. Discourse theory in this sense is not presenting us with anything new. What it does provide is an entry point by which we can – through the systematic analysis of discourses on violence – study war as a social phenomenon. Through a focus on discursive and institutional continuities and social practices the dialectics between the abstract 'structure' and 'agency' becomes researchable. However, the approach is also critiqued for its too crude representation of the agency–structure dichotomy, and its claim that agency and structure are not ontologically prior entities. Here opponents accuse structurationism of stating the bleeding obvious. For it is not that agency-based theory claims that there is no social context, or that structuralists see no human beings at work: they do. What is proposed by the structure–agency stand off, however, is that what *primarily* moves people is yes, either structures (as in rules or games) or individual properties. Ontologically, by 'sitting on the fence' structurationist theory blurs the conceptual distinction between 'agency' and 'structure'. It is exactly through this (yes, abstract, conceptual) distinction that scholars aim to create clarity and order in the messy complexity of the study of social life. One of the main premises of a structurationist theory of conflict is that violence is the result of 'human decisions made within the context of structured social relations' (Jabri 1996: 4). The questions remains, whether we choose to emphasize the individual's capacity to make a decision, or the structures that tell him or her how to do social life, as the starting point of our analysis.

Table F

Ontology/Epistemology	**Explaining (positivist)**	**Understanding (interpretative)**
Structuralism		The discursive approach
Individualism		

Further reading

Fairclough, Norman (2003) *Analysing Discourse*, London and New York: Routledge.
Jabri, Vivienne (1996) *Discourses on Violence: Conflict Analysis Reconsidered*, Manchester and New York: Manchester University Press.
Schröder, Ingo W. and Bettina Schmidt (2001) 'Introduction: Violent Imaginaries and Violent Practices' in B. Schmidt and I. Schröder (eds) *Anthropology of Violence and Conflict*, London and New York: Routledge, pp. 1–24.

Recommended documentaries

Episode 'Northern Ireland' in *Blood and Belong: Journeys into the New Nationalism* (Michael Ignatieff, BBC, 1993).
The Making of the Revolution (Katarina Rejger and Eric van den Broek, 2001).
Bringing Down a Dictator (Steve York, PBS series, 2002).

Conclusions

We live in an interconnected and complex world, in which violence and its various forms of social realization are subject to a cacophony of interpretations. After each new act of 'breaking news' violence, editorial writers, media pundits, newscasters and experts desperately try and make sense of what happened. At times, a specific classification of the violence 'clings' and becomes hegemonic. But quite often, a dizzying diversity of readings prevails, which are so contradictory that they confuse the larger public into a state of indifference. In the summer of 2011, the UK went through a series of intense urban riots. Four consecutive nights of looting and arson left five people dead and more than 2000 suspects arrested. What distinguished these violent acts from other forms of 'street violence' taking place simultaneously, in Syria and Yemen, was – among other things – the lack of any kind of programme. Those engaged in the violence demanded nothing. The 'wordlessness' of the riots gave ample room for speculation. Conservative politicians where quick to label the violence as 'pure criminality'. They stuck to the mantra that there is no justification for such vandalism and all necessary means should be used to restore order, punish those who participated and step up police surveillance. The reaction from leftist liberals was no less predictable: they framed the violent outbursts as a way for people to express their grievances and dissatisfaction. The deprivation and marginalization of second- and third-generation immigrants and their complete lack of economic prospects and constant police harassment, the liberals claimed, is what caused the riots. Others pointed at the key role of social media, gang rivalry or the 'morphology of violence', that is, how a local violent incident can mutate into other forms of violence. Social theorists referred to the riots as acts of 'defective consumers', as a manifestation of a consumerist desire violently enacted when unable to realize itself the proper way: by shopping (Bauman 2011); or highlighted how the UK has become a *securitocracy* (Gilroy 2011).

In many ways, the complementary and contradictory readings of the 'London riots' reflect the heterogeneity of explanatory frames in the field of Conflict Studies. It is not hard to see how notions on rational violence, human needs, collective action, structural violence, discourse and cultural hegemony are underlying the above interpretations. Certainly, conflict theory is 'out there'. But how do these bodies of abstract knowledge about social life relate to one another? To draw the book together, we shall return to the question of multidisciplinarity and the related discussion of theoretical affinities and tensions. But first, a word of caution. What the book shows us, I think, is that theoretical divides are inevitable. Theories depart from a variety of positions and it seems naive to think we can reconcile them and merge them into one grand theory of violent conflict. The opposite position, however, of rejecting any form of engagement outside one's theoretical 'box' at best lacks creativity. At worst, it may result in dogmatism. So, those interested in inter-disciplinary research would need to look beyond their boxes. The question is how to combine elements from different theoretical traditions, and what limits to set. My own position in this discussion, is that the 'understanding' column of the Hollis matrix leaves room to try to combine ontological individualism and structuralism, but that the epistemological stances of explaining and understanding do not combine as readily. Certainly, not everybody will agree with this, and the discussion that follows here should be treated critically.

The majority of theoretical traditions reviewed in this book reject a strictly singular approach, and almost all aim to draw on a variety of elements in explaining or understanding violent action. Here we should distinguish between what Hollis calls theories that are engaged in *adding* and those that seek *blending*. The former set of theories typically argues that violent conflicts are multi-causal and multi-levelled, and result from how a certain society is organized (e.g. state-form, economy, political culture) and who participates in it: here structures and individuals are treated as independent factors. Distinctive theories, however, do single out a specific (set of) component(s) as integral, rather than incidental, to the outbreak of violence. Social identity theorists, for instance, acknowledge how elite machinations and economic inequality can *add to* group hostility. However, these additional factors may exacerbate group conflict, *but do not cause it*. Similarly, elite theories of conflict may recognize social psychological processes of group closure and bonding as important elements, but only in so far as that they can be put to use by predatory elites. So, what happens in the 'adding' version of theory-building is that particular traditions incorporate elements of other theories but without changing their ontological and epistemological positions. They remain seated in their boxes, one might say. Although perhaps not radically adventurous, such a position can produce interesting results. Reading through this book, it is not hard to imagine how approaches can profit from this kind of bricolage. Of course, combining has its problems, too. It is one thing to say various elements play a role in conflict, it is yet another to produce abstract knowledge on how these elements interact.

I encourage the formulation of composite theoretical frameworks for analysing violent conflict if supported by coherent ontological and epistemological positions. Initially, this concluding chapter's goal was to outline how aspects of theories in this book can be combined. How, for instance, the idea of 'beliefs systems' in social identity theory can profit from discourse analytical notions of enactment and inculcation. But I soon realized that this would result in an awfully dense and detailed text, and worse, it would translate into theoretical spoon feeding. I argue that one should piece together a coherent framework for oneself. Authors such as Edward Azar, Christopher Cramer, Vivienne Jabri, Stathis Kalyvas, Charles King, Donald Horowitz, Hugh Miall and Andreas Wimmer have done a lot to inspire in this direction.

The other approach to theory-building (blending) is perhaps more exiting, but also trickier. The question here is one not of incorporating, but of synthesizing: of actually merging approaches. We have touched upon aspects of this discussion in the book, but certainly not comprehensively. Let us take Hollis by the hand and walk through, if only briefly, the four quadrants of the matrix.[1] We may begin in what is perhaps the least plausible of positions, located in the upper left quadrant. Here rules the idea that social structures are external and prior to human action and determine them fully. We have seen little evidence in the book to support this position and it is hard to imagine how this idea relates to the other boxes. So, we take a step down to the lower left quadrant, where we find our self-contained actor: the maker of all action, and possibly, structure, too. The usual view here is of individual actors as self-contained and the source of action, as independent. The problem, however, is that if indeed these individuals act upon their internal computers (as in thin rational choice theory) or psychological laws (as in the theory of optimal distinctiveness), they do seem 'oddly mechanical' (Hollis 1994: 248). Can they really stand alone as autonomous beings, and, in a way, be the victim of their preferences? Is not their independence at least threatened by external accounts of how their preferences are determined, and what governs their perception of value? That is, are they not also constituted by the group or polity that surrounds them? But if that is the case, if actors are merely computers plugged into a system, we are back up studying systems in the structuralist box. We can also decide to stay in the bottom left box but refuse to accept the mechanical view of the individuals living there. Do they not, after all, make creative interpretations of their own situation, do they not reflect upon their own performances and fashion their preferences? If we think so, we are carried to the quadrant next door, where actions have subjective meaning. This is where our purposive agent lives, whose actions are not limited by given preferences, but result from an intelligent playing of the sets of meaning rules that surround him or her. But then again, if we think about meaning we realize that meaning is constructed collectively, and that actors are merely part of an inter-subjective social order. These are the sets of meaning rules, or social structures, that tell us how to do social life and hence account for social action. So, up we are again, but now on the understanding side of structuralism. Not dizzy yet? Let us then finish by asking the question whether these sets of meaning rules, these forms of life, which perhaps mean nothing beyond themselves, can be really self-sustaining. Surely, they do not exist in a natural vacuum, but in some way are affected by 'material scarcities, natural conditions, and the physical state of technology' (Hollis 1994: 249)? This then will bring us back to the upper left box, and prepare us for another round.

Some scholars will be thrilled by the idea of building an all-inclusive social theory where 'structure is the medium in which action reproduces structure and where the dialectical interplay evolves in a dynamic synthesis' (Hollis 1994: 249). And surely, it is important to think through the interplay between the various positions. My own reckoning is to acknowledge the linkages between the various positions but not try to undo them by means of a dizzying merry-go-round type of grand theory building. As we discussed in chapter six, research needs a proper ontological and epistemological grounding, where the analyst may indeed try to draw on a variety of traditions, but critically and knowledgeably. There are limits to interdisciplinarity, and certainly to multidisciplinarity. X is not B, and Z is incompatible with A, we simply have to work with, and learn from, our heterogeneous research community.

What to do with theory

Where there are limits to multidisciplinarity in research, the opposite is true for education. A multidisciplinary training and exposure to a variety of theoretical approaches will equip conflict analysts with the capacity to think through violent conflict at different levels, and through a variety of lenses and vocabularies. All this has to do with literacy, with 'becoming theoretically literate' that is to say, in the field. By *theoretical literacy* I mean the ability to recognize, define, deploy, critique and construct abstract knowledge about social life, in particular about the aspect of social life that is defined as violent conflict. Just as a trained musician is able to recognize chords, distinguish baroque from classical periods and play different styles of music and an architect knows about functionalist and postmodern approaches, so a good conflict analyst is versed and literate in a diversity of theoretical languages. This literacy is crucial for a number of reasons. First, it helps one to *recognize the templates* and paradigms underlying explanations of violent conflict in a variety of texts, be it media reports, policy documents or academic research. If one knows how and where to 'place' a text, the second step, of assessing the text, is significantly simplified, for the strong and weak points of its underlying assumptions are well known to us, and can be drawn upon in the way we formulate our evaluation. This kind of literacy is helpful in many settings: in writing a book review, evaluating policy or acting as a discussant in an academic seminar, but also when debating a certain conflict case, or merely when viewing the news, or discussing politics. Second, theoretical literacy will guide one in grasping the complexities of violent conflict, that is, in *making analyses*. We have seen how different theoretical approaches require appropriate methodologies and research designs. These form an important recourse in the unravelling of the complex dynamics of interactive processes that make war. Theory thus helps us to interpret and explain text, talk and practice. Evidently, in making an analysis of violent conflict we do not have to re-invent the wheel, we can draw on the body of abstract knowledge that others have produced, and, ideally, we can work towards an accumulation of knowledge. By applying a particular approach to new evidence (e.g. a different case-study) new insights are produced that may lead to an overall improvement of the theory. By contrast, if a theoretical approach fails to receive evidence-based support it may gradually lose appeal, as was the case with primordialist views on ethnic war. But there is more than application and refinement of earlier knowledge alone. Third, theoretical literacy allows for a *critical assessment* of the production of knowledge. Here, one looks at how knowledge is put to use, particularly outside academia. This third form of literacy builds on the abilities of 'recognizing' and 'making analyses' in addressing frame politics: why are certain explanatory frames of war selected; what are the implications of such a selection in terms of casting blame and responsibility; how is this politically functional; and also, what is the role of the conflict analyst in all of this? Fourth, theoretical literacy will help you to argue your own position, and to *construct social theory*. For this is what academic training comes down to in the end: finding your own position. As argued by Ragin (1994) academic thinking and theorizing comes out of a huge, on-going conversation among social scientists and other social thinkers. This conversation is an ever-changing pool of ideas and vocabularies, a resource to draw on and to replenish with new thinking. Theoretical literacy is thus different from fluency: the end goal is not to have you 'speak' the language of constructivist instrumentalism, social identity theory or critical discourse analysis without a flaw. Rather, it is about using these ideas and vocabularies, acknowledging their underlying affinities and tensions, and finding your own voice.

In an area as fraught with human suffering as the study of violent conflict, we should be both critical and responsible in using that voice.

Notes

Introduction: conflict analysis in context

1 Often Richard Holbrooke's memoires on the Dayton Peace Agreement are given as a source here. Although Holbrooke (1998) does describe how the 'ancient hatreds' idea was expressed by many officials and politicians over the course of the war, Clinton's 'change of heart' after receiving the book for Christmas is not explicitly mentioned.
2 Sambanis (2004) acknowledges how distinctions are blurry at times. He identifies such cases as 'ambiguous' in his data set.
3 With thanks to Judith Large's course on Peace, Conflict and the Global Economy, European Peace University, Stadtschlaining, Austria, November 2002.
4 Here Hollis builds on the work of Wittgenstein.

1 Identity, boundaries and violence

1 This apparent contradiction has led some scholars to argue in favour of dismissing the concept entirely. Apart from the double-sidedness of the term Brubaker and Cooper (2000) see another deficit. Their problem with 'identity' is that although semantically 'identity' implies *sameness across time or persons*, most analysts continue to speak of 'identity' while at the same time repudiating this implication of 'sameness'. Dropping the term, clearly, is not an option. However problematic, people make use of, and act upon the notion of identity. They even kill and die in the name of identity. It makes up part of our social world, and hence deserves analytical attention.
2 Handelman (1977) introduced a typology of degrees of ethnic incorporation: from the very loose ethnic category, to the ethnic network, the ethnic association and, ultimately, to the tight corporate ethnic group or community. Brubaker (2004: 39) defines the group – as the highest degree of collectivity – as a 'mutually interacting, mutually recognizing, mutually oriented, effectively communicating, bounded collectivity with a sense of solidarity, corporate identity, and capacity for concerted action'.
3 The account of the priest was reported in the *National Catholic Reporter* (www.natcath.com/NRC_Online/archives/0222202/022202a.htm).
4 Weber (1968: 389) defined ethnic groups as

> those human groups that entertain a subjective belief in their common descent because of similarities of physical type or custom or both, or because of memories of colonization and migration: this belief must be important for the propagation of group formation: conversely it does not matter whether or not an objective blood relation exists ... ethnic membership does not constitute a group; it only facilitates group formation of any kind, particularly in the political sphere. On the other hand it is primarily the political community, no matter how artificially organized, that inspires the belief in common ethnicity.

5 Other important contemporary scholars in the boundary and group making approach are Michèle Lamont (2000) and Charles Tilly (2006).

6 Although Barth's boundary metaphor is widely recognized, his approach to ethnicity is also seen as over-emphasizing rules of membership and as ignoring the specific nature of ethnicity (that is, *content*), see for instance: Jenkins (1996); Roosens (1994); Cornell and Hartmann (1998), and let us not forget Barth himself (1994).

7 For a multilevel process theory of the making and unmaking of ethnic boundaries see Wimmer (2008).

8 The elite theory of ethnic war is rooted in long-existing scholarly traditions on state-making and war, see for instance the work of Georg Simmel and Lewis Coser.

9 This ethno-symbolic tradition may be located in sociological approaches which have their basis in Durkheim's notion of the 'collective conscience'. Societies contain dominant norms and institutions which are deeply embedded in the histories and memory traces of collectivities. Emile Durkheim recognized the power of such cross-generational social norms in the ability of leaders to mobilize dissimilar individuals into a seemingly unified entity transformable into a fighting force against other collectivities. The 'collective conscience' is manifest not merely in the leadership but in the 'nature of the societies they govern'. In order, therefore, to understand the ability of a leadership to mobilize entire populations, we 'must observe the common beliefs, the common sentiments which, by incarnating themselves in a person or in a family, communicate each power to it' (Jabri (1996: 123) quoting Durkheim, *The Division of Labour in Society*, New York: Free Press, 1964, p. 196).

10 This quotation is taken from Michael Ignatieff's documentary series *Blood and Belonging: Journeys into the New Nationalism* (1993, BBC).

11 According to figures of Wimmer and Min (2006) wars fought in the name of national liberation or ethnic autonomy comprise only one-fifth of the wars between the Congress of Vienna (1814) and the Treaty of Versailles (1919). From Versailles to 2001, however, the share of ethno-nationalist wars rose to 45 per cent, and since the Cold War ended it has reached 75 per cent.

12 See Pierre Bourdieu (1991), Loic Wacquant (1997) and Wimmer (2004) on ethnicity as the outcome of political and symbolic struggles over the categorical division of society.

2 On love and hate: social identity approaches to inter-group violence

1 This is why Tajfel defines social identity as 'that part of an individual's self-concept which derives from his knowledge of his membership in a social group (or groups) together with the *value* and *emotional* significance attached to that membership' (Tajfel 1981: 63, my emphasis, see also chapter one).

2 As he noted himself, Tajfel's distinction between social mobility (individual status enhancement through group crossing) and social change (collective status enhancement) shows linkages with political economist Hirschman's famous work on 'exit' and 'voice' (1970). Hirschman defines 'exit' as the situation when 'some customers stop buying the firm's products or some members leave the organization'. 'Voice' is heard when 'the firm's customers or the organization's members express their dissatisfaction directly to the management or to some other authority … or through general protests addressed to anyone who cares to listen' (1970: 4). Hirschman discusses how the black power doctrine in the US confronted American society with a shockingly new approach to upward social mobility: success not via exit from the group, but via open advocacy of the group. 'The successful individual who starts out at a low rung of the social ladder, necessarily leaves his own group as he rises; he "passes" into, or is "accepted" by, the next higher group. He takes his immediate family along, but hardly anyone else' (1970: 108–9). The civil rights movement hence spurned and castigated a 'supreme value' of the American society: success as conceived in terms of evolutionary individualism.

3 Violence and structures

1 Most scholars under review here do not qualify as 'Marxists' or 'Durkheimists'. It is because they – often implicitly – follow the general logic of Marx's or Durkheim's explanation of structure, and its relationship to violence and conflict, that they can be classified as *Marxian*

or *Durkheimian* (for a more elaborate explanation of the relation between Marxian and Durkheimian traditions and collective action see Tilly 1978: 1–51. This section is based on Tilly's interpretation).

2 'War is like a delicious piece of cake' writes the Croatian novelist Dubravka Ugresic, 'that everyone wants a piece of: politicians, criminals and speculators, profiteers and murderers, sadists and masochists, the faithful and the charitable, historians and philosophers, and journalists' (Ugresic quoted in Schmidt and Schröder 2001: 5).

3 This is where Galtung's definitions remain fuzzy: I assume that he means to say that any conflict that is based on an unrealistic (false) image should also be classified as a structural conflict.

4 Mobilization for collective violent action: multi-causal approaches

1 Maslow argues that human beings first have to fulfil a set of basic physiological and safety needs before they can reach higher levels of need satisfaction such a love, esteem and self-actualization.

2 In 1997 the KLA was included on the US State Department's list of terrorist organizations. In February 1998 it was removed again.

5 Rational choice theory: the costs and benefits of war

1 In 2005 an entire issue of the *Journal of Conflict Resolution* ('Paradigm in Distress', 49 (4)) was dedicated to demonstrating the non-robustness of the main conclusions of Collier's greed hypothesis.

6 Telling each other apart: a discursive approach to violent conflict

1 See the documentaries *The Making of the Revolution* by Katarina Rejger and Eric van den Broek (2001) and *Bringing Down a Dictator* by Steve York (PBS series, 2002).

Conclusions

1 Not surprisingly, I am indebted here to Hollis' own – and more elaborate – discussion of the linkages between the four boxes.

References

Abrams D. and M.A. Hogg (1998) 'Prospects for Research in Group Processes and Intergroup Relations', *Group Processes & Intergroup Relations* 1: 7–20.

Anderson, Benedict (1991) *Imagined Communities*, London and New York: Verso.

Appadurai, Arjun (1998) 'Dead Certainty: Ethnic Violence in the Era of Globalization', *Public Culture* 10, 2: 225–47.

——(2006) *Fear of Small Numbers*, Boulder: Duke University Press.

Apter, David E. (ed.) (1997) *The Legitimization of Violence*, New York: New York University Press.

Arendt, Hannah (1963) *Eichmann in Jerusalem: A Report on the Banality of Evil*, New York: Penguin Books.

Ashmore, Richard et al. (2001) *Social Identity, Intergroup Conflict, and Conflict Reduction*, Oxford: Oxford University Press.

Ayoob, Mohammed (2007) 'State Making, State Breaking, and State Failure' in Crocker, Chester A. et al (eds) *Leashing the Dogs of War: Conflict Management in a Divided World*, Washington, D.C.: United States Institute of Peace Press.

Azar, Edward (1990) *The Management of Protracted Social Conflict: Theory and Cases*, Hampshire: Dartmouth.

——(1991) 'The Analysis and Management of Protracted Social Conflict' in V.D. Volkan, D.A. Julius and J.V. Montville (eds), *The Psychodynamics of International Relationships*, vol. II. Lexington, MA: D.C. Heath.

Ballentine, Karen and Jake Sherman (2003) *The Political Economy of Armed Conflict: Beyond Greed and Grievance*, Boulder: Lynne Rienner Publishers.

Barth, Fredrik (1998) [1969] *Ethnic Groups and Boundaries: The Social Organisation of Cultural Difference*, Long Grove, IL: Waveland Press.

——(1994) 'Enduring and Emerging Issues in the Analysis of Ethnicity' in Hans Vermeulen and Cora Govers (eds) *The Anthropology of Ethnicity: Beyond 'Ethnic Groups and Boundaries'*, Amsterdam: Spinhuis.

Bauman, Zygmunt (2006) *Liquid Fear*, Cambridge: Polity Press.

——(2011) 'The London Riots – On Consumerism coming Home to Roost' *Social Europe Journal*, http://www.social-europe.eu/2011/08/the-london-riots-on-consumerism-coming-home-to-roost/ (retrieved 14 December 2011).

Baumann, Gerd (1999) *The Multicultural Riddle: Rethinking National, Ethnic and Religious Identities*, London and New York: Routledge.

Beissinger, Mark R. (2002) *Nationalist Mobilization and the Collapse of the Soviet State*, Cambridge: Cambridge University Press.

Berenschot, Ward (2011) 'The Spatial Distribution of Riots: Patronage and the Instigation of Communal Violence in Gujarat, India', *World Development* 34, 2: 221–30.

Berger, Peter and Thomas Luckmann (1967) *The Social Construction of Reality: A Treatise in the Sociology of Knowledge*, Harmondsworth: Penguin Books.

Bhatia, Michael (2005) 'Fighting Words: Naming Terrorists, Bandits, Rebels and Other Violent Actors', *Third World Quarterly* 26, 1: 5–22.

Bourdieu, Pierre (1990) *The Logic of Practice*, Cambridge: Polity Press.

——(1991) *Language and Symbolic Power*, Cambridge: Polity Press.

——(2004) *Firing Back: Against the Tyranny of the Market*, London: Verso.

Bourke, Joanna (1999) *An Intimate History of Killing*, London: Granta and New York: Basic Books.

Bowman, Glenn (2007) 'Constitutive Violence and Rhetorics of Identity: A Comparative Study of Nationalist Movements in the Israeli Occupied Territories and Former Yugoslavia' in A.C. G.M. Robben and Francisco Ferrándiz (eds) *Interdisciplinary Clues for Peace and Conflict Research: a View from Europe*, Bilbao: Humanitarian Net, University of Deusto.

Braedley, Susan and Meg Luxton (2010) *Neoliberalism and Everyday Life*, Montreal and Kingston: McGill-Queen's University Press.

Brass, Paul (1996) *Riots and Pogroms*, New York: New York University Press.

——(1997) *Theft of an Idol: Text in Context in the Representation of Collective Violence*, Princeton: Princeton University Press.

Brewer, Marilynn (1991) 'The Social Self: On Being the Same and Different at the Same Time', *Personality and Social Psychology Bulletin* 17: 475–82.

——(2001) 'Ingroup Identification and Intergroup Conflict: When does Ingroup Love become Outgroup Hate?' in Richard Ashmore et al. (eds) *Social Identity, Intergroup Conflict, and Conflict Reduction*, Oxford: Oxford University Press.

Brubaker, Rogers (2004) *Ethnicity without Groups*, Cambridge, MA: Harvard University Press.

Brubaker, Rogers, and David D. Laitin (1998) 'Ethnic and Nationalist Violence', *Annual Review of Sociology* 24: 423–52.

Brubaker, Rogers and Frederick Cooper (2000) 'Beyond Identity', *Theory and Society* 29: 1–47.

Bueno de Mesquita, Bruce (1981) *The War Trap*, New Haven: Yale University Press.

Burton, J.W. (1990) *Conflict: Human Needs Theory*, London and New York: Macmillan and St. Martin's Press.

Campbell, David (1998) *Writing Security: United States Foreign Policy and the Politics of Identity*, Manchester: Manchester University Press.

Castells, Manuel (1996) *The Rise of the Network Society: The Information Age: Economy, Society and Culture Vol. I*, Cambridge, MA and Oxford: Blackwell.

——(1998) *End of Millennium, The Information Age: Economy, Society and Culture Vol. III*, Cambridge, MA and Oxford: Blackwell.

Clark, Mary (1990) 'Meaningful Social Bounding as a Universal Human Need' in J. Burton (ed.) *Conflict: Human Needs Theory*, London and New York: Macmillan and St. Martin's Press.

Collier, Paul (2000) 'Doing Well out of War: An Economic Perspective' in Mats Berdal and David M. Malone (eds) *Greed and Grievance: Economic Agendas in Civil Wars*, Boulder: Lynne Rienner Publishers.

——(2007) *The Bottom Billion: Why The Poorest Countries Are Failing And What Can Be Done About It*, Oxford and New York: Oxford University Press.

Collier, Paul and Anke Hoeffler (2001) 'Greed and Grievance in Civil War' *World Bank Working Paper* No. 28126.

Condor, Susan (1982) 'Social Stereotypes and Social Identity' in D. Abrams and M.A. Hogg (eds) *Social Identity Theory: Constructive and Critical Advances*, London: Harvester Wheatsheaf.

Cornell, Stephen and Douglas Hartmann (1998) *Ethnicity and Race: Making Identities in a Changing World*, Newbury Park, CA: Pine Forge Press.

Coser, Lewis A. (1956) *The Functions of Social Conflict: Political Opportunism and Ethnic Conflict*, Glencoe, IL: Free Press.

Cox, Robert W. (1983) 'Gramsci, Hegemony, and International Relations, an Essay on Method', *Millennium: Journal of International Studies* 12 (2): 162–75.

——(1995) 'Civilizations: Encounters and Transformations', *Studies in Political Economy* 47 (Summer): 7–31.

Cramer, Christopher (2002) '*Homo Economicus* Goes to War: Methodological Individualism, Rational Choice and the Political Economy of War', *World Development* 30 (11): 1845–64.

——(2006) *Civil War is Not a Stupid Thing*, London: Hurst & Company.

Danforth, Loring (1995) *The Macedonian Conflict: Ethnic Conflict in a Transnational World*, Princeton: Princeton University Press.

Della Porta, D. and S. Tarrow (1986) 'Unwanted children: political violence and the cycle of protest in Italy', *European Journal of Political Research* 14: 607–32.

Demmers, Jolle (1999) *Friends and Bitter Enemies: Politics and Neoliberal Reform in Yucatán, Mexico*, Amsterdam: Thela Publishers.

Demmers, Jolle, Barbara Hogenboom and Alex E. Fernández Jilberto (2004) *Good Governance in the Era of Global Neoliberalism: Conflict and Depolitisation in Latin America, Eastern Europe, Asia and Africa*, London and New York: Routledge.

Demmers, Jolle and Sameer S. Mehendale (2010) 'Neoliberal Xenophobia: the Dutch Case', *Alternatives: Global, Local, Political* 35 (1): 53–70.

Deng, Francis M. (1995) *War of Visions: Conflict of Identities in the Sudan*, Washington, D.C.: The Brookings Institution.

Der Derian, James (2005) 'Imaging Terror: Logos, Pathos and Ethos', *Third World Quarterly* 26 (1): 23–37.

Dexter, Helen (2007) 'New War, Good War and the War on Terror: Explaining, Excusing and Creating Western Neo-interventionism', *Development and Change* 38 (6): 1055–71.

Dougherty, James E. and Robert L. Pfaltzgraff (1981) *Contending Theories of International Relations: A Comprehensive Survey*, New York: Harper and Row.

Douma, Piet (2003) *The Origins of Contemporary Conflict*, Clingendael Studies 18, The Hague: Clingendael.

Drakulic, Slavenka (1993) *The Balkan Express*, New York: W.W. Norton & Co.

Duffield, Mark (2002) 'Social Reconstruction and the Radicalization of Development: Aid as a Relation of Global Liberal Governance', *Development and Change* 33 (5): 1049–71.

——(2007) *Development, Security and Unending War: Governing the World of Peoples*, Cambridge: Polity.

——(2008) 'Global Civil War: The Non-Insured, International Containment and Post-Interventionary Society', *Journal of Refugee Studies* 21 (2): 145–65.

——(2010a) 'The Liberal Way of Development and the Development–Security Impasse: Exploring the Global Life-Chance Divide', *Security Dialogue* 41 (1): 53–76.

——(2010b) 'Risk-Management and the Fortified Aid Compound: Everyday Life in Post-Interventionary Society', *Journal of Intervention and State Building* 4 (4): 453–74.

Durkheim, Emile (1933) *The Division of Labor in Society*, New York: The Free Press.

Elster, J. (1989) *Nuts and Bolts for the Social Sciences*, Cambridge: Cambridge University Press.

Eriksen, Thomas Hylland (1993) *Ethnicity and Nationalism: Anthropological Perspectives*, London: Pluto Press.

Erikson, Erik H. (1966) 'The Concept of Identity in Race Relations: Notes and Queries', *Daedalus* 95: 145–201.

Fairclough, Norman (2003) *Analysing Discourse*, London and New York: Routledge.

Farmer, P. (1996) 'On Suffering and Structural Violence: a View from Below', *Daedalus* 125: 261–83.

Fearon, James D. (1994) *Ethnic War as a Commitment Problem*, paper presented at Annual Meeting of the American Political Science Association, New York.

——(2005) 'Primary Commodity Exports and Civil War' *Journal of Conflict Resolution* 49 (4): 483–507.

Fearon, James D. and David D. Laitin (2000) 'Violence and the Social Construction of Ethnic Identity' *International Organization* 54 (4): 845–77.

——(2003) 'Ethnicity, Insurgency and Civil War', *American Political Science Review* 97 (1): 75–90.

Feldman, Allen (1994) *Formations of Violence: The Narrative of the Body and Political Terror In Northern Ireland* (revised second printing), Chicago: The University of Chicago Press.

Ferguson, James and Akhil Gupta (2002) 'Spatializing States: Toward an Ethnography of Neoliberal Governmentality', *American Ethnologist* 29 (4): 981–1002.

Ferrari, Federica (2007) 'Metaphor at work in the Analysis of Political Discourse: Investigating a Preventive War Persuasion Strategy', *Discourse and Society* 18: 603–25.

Festinger, L. (1954) 'A Theory of Social Comparison Processes', *Human Relations* 7: 117–40.

Foucault, Michel (1984) 'The Order of Discourse' in M.J. Shapiro (ed.) *Language and Politics*, New York: New York University Press.

Freeman, M.A. (2001) 'Linking Self and Social Structure: A Psychological Perspective on Social Identity in Sri Lanka', *Journal of Cross-Cultural Psychology* 32: 291–308.

Freud, Sigmund (1918) 'The Taboo of Virginity', *S.E.*, 11: 191–208.

Gagnon, V.P, Jr. (1997) 'Ethnic Nationalism and International Conflict' in M. Brown et al. (eds) *Nationalism and Ethnic Conflict*, Cambridge, MA: MIT Press.

Galtung, Johan (1969) 'Violence, Peace, and Peace Research' *Journal of Peace Research* 6(3): 167–91.

——(1996) *Peace by Peaceful Means: Peace and Conflict, Development and Civilization*, London: Sage.

Geary, Patrick J. (2002) *The Myth of Nations: the Medieval Origins of Europe*, Princeton and Oxford: Princeton University Press.

Gellner, Ernest (1983) *Nations and Nationalism*, Oxford: Blackwell.

Giddens, Anthony (1984) *The Constitution of Society: Outline of the Theory of Structuration*, Berkeley and Los Angeles: University of California Press.

——(1979) *Central Problems in Social Theory*, Berkeley: University of California Press.

Gilroy, Paul (2011) 'Paul Gilroy Speaks on the Riots' Indymedia London, http://london.indymedia.org/other_medias/10049 (retrieved at 14 December 2011).

Goffman, Erving (1974) *Frame Analysis: An Essay of the Organization of Experience*, New York: Harper Colophon.

Gomes Porto, Joao (2002) 'Contemporary Conflict Analysis in Perspective' in Jeremy Lind and Kathryn Sturman (eds) *Scarcity and Surfeit: the Ecology of Africa's Conflicts*, Pretoria: Institute for Security Studies.

Goodhand, Jonathan (2003) 'Enduring Disorder and Persistent Poverty. A Review of the Linkages between War and Chronic Poverty', *World Development* 31 (3): 629–46.

Gould, Roger V. (1995) *Insurgent Identities: Class, Community and Protest in Paris from 1848 to the Comune*, Chicago: University of Chicago Press.

Gourevitch, Philip (1998) *We Wish to Inform You that Tomorrow We Will Be Killed With Our Families: Stories from Rwanda*, New York: Farrar, Straus & Giroux.

Greenhouse, Carol J. (2010) *Ethnographies of Neoliberalism*, Philadelphia: University of Pennsylvania Press.

Gurr, Ted Robert (1970) *Why Men Rebel*, Princeton: Princeton University Press.

——(2007) 'Minorities, Nationalists and Islamists: Managing Communal Conflict in the Twenty-First Century' in Chester A. Crocker et al. (eds) *Leashing the Dogs of War: Conflict Management in a Divided World*, Washington, D.C.: United States Institute of Peace Press.

Handelman, D. (1977) 'The Organization of Ethnicity', *Ethnic Groups* 1: 187–200.

Hardt, Michael and Antonio Negri (2004) *Multitude: War and Democracy in the Age of Empire*, London: Penguin Books.

Harvey, David (2003) *A Brief History of Neoliberalism*, Oxford and New York: Oxford University Press.

Harbom, Lotta and Peter Wallensteen (2005) 'Armed Conflict and its International Dimensions, 1946–2004', *Journal of Peace Research* 42 (5): 623–35.

——(2010) 'Armed Conflicts, 1946–2010', *Journal of Peace Research* 47 (4): 501–9.

Heinemann-Grüder, Andreas and Wolf-Christian Paes (2001) *Wag the Dog: The Mobilization and Demobilization of the Kosovo Liberation Army*, Bonn: Bonn International Center for Conversion.

Hirschman, Albert O. (1970) *Exit, Voice, and Loyalty: Responses to Decline in Firms, Organizations and States*, Cambridge, MA: Harvard University Press.

Hobsbawm, Eric J. (1990) *Nations and Nationalism since 1780: Programme, Myth, Reality*, Cambridge: Cambridge University Press.

Hockenos, Paul (2003) *Homeland Calling: Exile Patriotism and the Balkan Wars*, Ithaca, NY: Cornell University Press.

Hogg, M.A. (2006) 'Social Identity Theory' in P.J. Burke (ed.) *Contemporary Social Psychological Theories*, Palo Alto, CA: Stanford University Press.

Hogg, M.A. and C. McGarty (1990) 'Self-Categorization and Social Identity' in D. Abrams, and M.A. Hogg (eds) *Social Identity Theory: Constructive and Critical Advances*, London: Harvester Wheatsheaf.

Holbrook, Richard (1998) *To End a War*, New York: Random House.

Hollis, Martin (1994) *The Philosophy of Social Science: an Introduction*, Cambridge: Cambridge University Press.

——(1996) *Reason in Action: Essays in the Philosophy of Social Science*, Cambridge: Cambridge University Press.

——(1998) *The Cunning of Reason*, Cambridge: Cambridge University Press.

Hollis, Martin and Steven Lukes (1982) *Rationality and Relativism*, Oxford: Blackwell.

Holsti, K.J. (1991) *Peace and War: Armed Conflicts and International Order 1648–1989*, Cambridge: Cambridge University Press.

——(1996) *The State, War, and the State of War*, Cambridge: Cambridge University Press.

Horowitz, Donald (1985) *Ethnic Groups in Conflict*, Berkeley: University of California Press.

——(2001) *The Deadly Ethnic Riot*, Berkeley: University of California Press.

Human Security Report 2005 (2005) *War and Peace in the 21st Century*, published for the Human Security Centre, New York and Oxford: Oxford University Press.

Humphreys, M. (2005) 'Natural Resources, Conflict, and Conflict Resolution: Uncovering the Mechanisms', *Journal of Conflict Resolution* 49 (4): 508–37.

Ignatieff, Michael (1999) *The Warrior's Honor*, London: Vintage.

Jabri, Vivienne (1996) *Discourses on Violence: Conflict Analysis Reconsidered*, Manchester and New York: Manchester University Press.

Jackson, Michael (2002) *The Politics of Storytelling: Violence, Transgression and Intersubjectivity*, Copenhagen: Museum Tusculanum Press.

Jacobs, D. and R. O'Brien (1998) 'The Determinants of Deadly Force: a Structural Analysis of Political Violence', *American Journal of Sociology* 103: 837–62.

Jacoby, Tim (2008) *Understanding Conflict and Violence: Theoretical and Interdisciplinary Approaches*, London and New York: Routledge.

Jenkins, Richard (1996) *Social Identity*, London: Routledge.

Kaldor, Mary (1999) *New and Old Wars: Organized Violence in a Global Era*, Stanford, CT: Stanford University Press.

Kalyvas, Stathis N. (2003) 'The Ontology of "Political Violence": Action and Identity in Civil Wars', *Perspectives on Politics* 1 (3): 475–94.

——(2006) *The Logic of Violence in Civil War*, New York: Cambridge University Press.

Kalyvas, Stathis and Matt Kocher (2007a) 'Ethnic Cleavages and Irregular War: Iraq and Vietnam, Politics and Society', *Politics & Society* 35 (2): 183–223.

——(2007b) 'How Free is "Free Riding" in Civil Wars? Violence, Insurgency, and the Collective Action Problem', *World Politics* 59: 2: 177–216.

Kaplan, Robert (1993) *Balkan Ghosts: A Journey Through History*, New York: Vintage Books.

Karatzogianni, Athina (2006) *The Politics of Cyberconflict*, London and New York: Routledge.

Kaufmann, S.J. (2001) *Modern Hatreds: The Symbolic Politics of Ethnic War*, Ithaca, NY: Cornell University Press.

——(2006) 'Symbolic Politics or Rational Choice? Testing Theories of Extreme Ethnic Violence', *International Security* 30 (4) (Spring): 45–86.

Keen, David (1998) *The Economic Function of Violence in Civil Wars*, Adelphi Paper 320, London: International Institute of Strategic Studies.

——(2008) *Complex Emergencies*, Cambridge: Polity Press.

Kent, G. (1999) 'Structural Violence Against Children', *Nexus* 1: 27–50.

King, Charles (2004) 'The Micropolitics of Social Violence', *World Politics* 25: 431–55.

——(2007) 'Power, Social Violence and Civil Wars' in Chester A. Crocker et al. (eds) *Leashing the Dogs of War: Conflict Management in a Divided World*, Washington, D.C.: United States Institute of Peace Press.

Klemperer, Victor (2000 [1947]) *LTI. De Taal van het Derde Rijk*, Amsterdam: Atlas.

Kurspahic, Kemal (1997) *As Long As Sarajevo Exists*, Stony Creek, CT: Pamphleteer's Press.

Lake, David and Donald Rothchild (1997) 'Containing Fear: The Origins and Management of Ethnic Conflict' in M. Brown et al. (eds) *Nationalism and Ethnic Conflict*, Cambridge, MA: MIT Press.

Lamont, Michèle (2000) *The Dignity of Working Men: Morality and the Boundaries of Race, Class and Immigration*, Cambridge, MA: Harvard University Press.

Lemarchand, Réne (2009) *The Dynamics of Violence in Central Africa*, Philadelphia: University of Pennsylvania Press.

Malkki, Liisa H. (1995) *Purity and Exile: Violence, Memory and National Cosmology among Hutu Refugees in Tanzania*, Chicago: University of Chicago Press.

Mamdani, Mahmood (2009) *Saviors and Survivors: Darfur, Politics and the War on Terror*, London and New York: Verso.

March, James G. and Johan P. Olsen (2006) 'The Logic of Appropriateness' in Michael Moran, Martin Rein and Robert E. Goodin (eds) *The Oxford Handbook of Public Policy*, Oxford: Oxford University Press.

Marx, Karl (1963 [1859]) 'Preface to a Contribution to the Critique of Political Economy' in T.B. Bottomore and M. Rubel (eds), *Karl Marx: Selected Writings in Sociology and Social Philosophy*, London: Penguin Books.

Maslow, Abraham H. (1954/1970) *Motivation and Personality*, New York: Harper and Ron.

Miall, Hugh, Oliver Ramsbotham and Tom Woodhouse (1999) *Contemporary Conflict Resolution: the Prevention, Management and Transformation of Deadly Conflicts*, Cambridge: Polity Press.

Milgram, Stanley (1963) 'Behavioral Study of Obedience', *Journal of Abnormal and Social Psychology* 67 (4): 371–8.

Mitchell, C. (1981) *The Structure of International Conflict*, Basingstoke: Macmillan.

Moerman, Michael (1965) 'Ethnic Identification in a Complex Civilization: Who Are the Lue?' *American Anthropologist* 67: 1215–30.

Morozov, Evgeny (2011) *The Net Delusion: How Not To Liberate The World*, London: Allen Lane.

Mueller, John (2001) 'The Banality of Ethnic War' in M. Brown et al. (eds) *Nationalism and Ethnic Conflict*, revised edition, Cambridge, MA: MIT Press.

Murshed, Mansoob S. and Mohammad Zulfan Tadjoeddin (2007) 'Reappraising the Greed and Grievance Explanations for Violent Internal Conflict' MICROCON research Working Paper 2, September 2007.

Nicholson, Michael (1992) *Rationality and the Analysis of International Conflict*, Cambridge: Cambridge University Press.

Nordstrom, C. (1992) 'The Backyard Front' in C. Nordstrom and J. Martin (eds) *The Paths to Domination, Resistance and Terror*, Berkeley: University of California Press.

——(1997) *A Different Kind of War Story*, Philadelphia: University of Pennsylvania Press.

Norris, Margot (2000) *Writing War in the Twentieth Century*, Charlottesville: University Press of Virginia.

Norris, Margot and Rodney H. Jones (2005) *Discourse in Action: Introducing Mediated Discourse Analysis*, London and New York: Routledge.

Oberschall, Anthony (2004) 'Explaining Terrorism: The Contribution of Collective Action Theory', *Sociological Theory* 22 (1): 26–37.

Olson, Mancur (1965) *The Logic of Collective Action*, Cambridge, MA: Harvard University Press.

Peteet, Julie (1996) 'The Writing on the Walls: The Graffiti of the Intifada', *Cultural Anthropology* 11 (2): 139–59.

——(2005) 'Words as Interventions: Naming in the Palestine–Israel Conflict', *Third World Quarterly* 26 (1): 153–72.

Preti, A. (2002) 'Guatemala: Violence in Peacetime – a Critical Analysis of the Armed Conflict and the Peace Process', *Disaster* 26: 99–119.

Prunier, Gerard (2008) *Africa's World War: Congo, the Rwandan Genocide and the Making of a Continental Catastrophe*, Oxford: Oxford University Press.

Ragin, Charles (1994) *Constructing Social Research*, Thousand Oaks, CA: Pine Forge Press.

Raleigh, Clionadh, Andrew Linke, Havard Hegre and Joakim Karlsen (2010) 'Introducing ACLED: An Armed Conflict Location and Event Dataset', *Journal of Peace Research* 47 (5): 651–60.

Richani, Nazih (2002) *Systems of Violence: the Political Economy of War and Peace in Colombia*, Albany: State University of New York Press.

Richards, Paul (1996) *Fighting for the Rainforest*, London: Heinemann.

Richardson, Lewis F. (1948) 'War Moods', *Psychometrika* 13, Part I (3): 147–74.

Riches, D. (1986) 'The Phenomenon of Violence' in D. Riches (ed.) *The Anthropology of Violence*, Oxford: Blackwell.

Robinson, W. Peter (ed.), 1996 *Social Groups and Identities: Developing the Legacy of Henri Tajfel*, Oxford: Butterworth-Heinemann.

Ron, James (2005) Special issue, 'Primary Commodities and Civil War', *Journal of Conflict Resolution* 49 (4).

Roosens, Eugeen E. (1994) 'The Primordial Nature of Origins in Migrant Ethnicity' in Hans Vermeulen and Cora Govers (eds) *The Anthropology of Ethnicity: Beyond 'Ethnic Groups and Boundaries'*, Amsterdam: Spinhuis.

Sambanis, N. (2002) 'Defining and Measuring Civil War: Conceptual and Empirical Critique of the Theoretical', Yale University, Department of Political Science.

——2004) 'What is Civil War? Conceptual and Empirical Complexities of an Operational Definition', *Journal of Conflict Resolution* 48 (6): 814–58.

Sayyid, Bobby and Lilian Zac (1998) 'Political Analysis in a World without Foundations' in E. Scarborough and E. Tanenbaum (eds) *Research Strategies in the Social Sciences: A Guide to New Approaches*, Oxford: Oxford University Press.

Scheper-Hughes, Nancy and Philippe Bourgois (2004) *Violence in War and Peace: An Anthology*, Malden, MA: Blackwell.

Schröder, Ingo W. and Bettina Schmidt (2001) 'Introduction: Violent Imaginaries and Violent Practices' in B. Schmidt and I. Schröder (eds) *Anthropology of Violence and Conflict*, London and New York: Routledge.

Scott, James (1990) *Domination and the Arts of Resistance*, New Haven: Yale University Press.

Seul, Jeffrey R. (1999) '"Ours is the Way of God": Religion, Identity, and Inter-group Conflict', *Journal of Peace Research* 36 (5): 553–69.

Sherif, M., O.J. Harvey, B.J. White, W.R. Hood and C.W. Sherif (1961) *Intergroup Conflict and Cooperation: the Robbers Cave experiment*, Norman: University of Oklahoma Book Exchange.

Simmel, Georg (1955) *Conflict* (translated by Kurt H. Wolff), Glencoe, IL: Free Press.

Smaje, C. (1997) 'Not Just a Social Construct: Theorising Race and Ethnicity', *Sociology* 31 (2): 307–27.

Small, M. and J.D. Singer (1982) *Resort to Arms: International and Civil Wars, 1816–1980*, Beverly Hills, CA: Sage.

Smith, Anthony (1996) *The Ethnic Origins of Nations*, Oxford: Blackwell.

Snow, D.A. and R.D. Benford (1992) 'Master Frames and Cycles of Protest' in A.D. Morris and C.M. Mueller (eds) *Frontiers in Social Movement Theory*, New Haven: Yale University Press.

Stiglitz, Joseph E. (2002) *Globalization and its Discontents*, New York: Norton.

Storey, Andy (1999) 'Economics and Ethnic Conflict: Structural Adjustment in Rwanda', *Development Policy Review* 17: 43–63.

Sullivan, Stacy (2004) *Be Not Afraid, For You Have Sons in America: How a Brooklyn Roofer Helped Lure the U.S. into the Kosovo War*, New York: St. Martin's Press.

Sumner, William Graham (1906) *Folkways and Mores*, New York: Schocken Books.

Tajfel, Henri (1978) *Differentiation between Social Groups: Studies in the Social Psychology of Intergroup Relations*, London: Academic Press.

——(1981) *Human Groups and Social Categories*, Cambridge: Cambridge University Press.

Tajfel, Henri and John Turner (1986) 'The Social Identity Theory of Intergroup Behaviour' in S. Worchel and W. Austin (eds) *Psychology of Intergroup Relations*, Chicago: Nelson-Hall.

Tambiah, Stanley J. (1996) *Leveling Crowds: Ethnonationalist Conflicts and Collective Violence in South Asia*, Berkeley: University of California Press.

Tarrow, Sidney (1994) *Power in Movement: Social Movements, Collective Action and Politics*, Cambridge: Cambridge University Press.

——(1998) *Power in Movement: Social Movements and Contentious Politics*, 2nd edn, Cambridge: Cambridge University Press.

Tilly, Charles (ed.) (1975) *The Formation of National States in Western Europe*, Princeton: Princeton University Press.

——(1978) *From Mobilization to Revolution*, Reading: Addison-Wesley.

——(1990) *Coercion, Capital and European States, AD 990–1990*, Cambridge, MA: Basil Blackwell.

——(2006) *Identities, Boundaries, and Social Ties*, Boulder: Paradigm Press.

Tilly, Charles and Sidney Tarrow (2007) *Contentious Politics*, Boulder: Paradigm Press.

Turner, John (1975) 'Social Comparison and Social Identity: Some Prospects or Intergroup Behaviour' *European Journal for Social Psychology* 5: 5–34.

——(1996) 'Henri Tajfel: an Introduction' in W. Peter Robinson (ed.) *Social Groups and Identities: Developing the Legacy of Henri Tajfel*, Oxford: Butterworth-Heinemann.

Turner, J.C., M. Hogg, P. Oakes, S. Reicher and M. Wetherell (1987) *Rediscovering the Social Group: A Self-categorization Theory*, Oxford: Blackwell.

Van Creveld, Martin (1991) *The Transformation of War*, New York: Free Press.

Van Dijk, Teun A. (1993) 'Principles of Critical Discourse Analysis', *Discourse and Society* 4 (2): 249–83.

Varshney, Ashutosh (2002) *Ethnic Conflict and Civic Life: Hindus and Muslims in India*, 2nd edn, New Haven: Yale University Press.

Verkuyten, Michael (2005) *The Social Psychology of Ethnic Identity*, Hove and New York: Psychology Press.

——(2007) 'Social Psychology and Multiculturalism', *Social and Personality Psychology Compass* 1 (1): 280–97.

Wacquant, L. (1997) 'Towards an Analytic of Racial Domination', *Political Power and Social Theory* 11: 221–34.

——(2009) *Punishing the Poor: The Neoliberal Government of Social Insecurity*, Durham, NC and London: Duke University Press.

Wallace, Ruth A. and Alison Wolf (1999) *Contemporary Sociological Theory: Expanding the Classical Tradition*, Upper Saddle River, NJ: Prentice Hall.

Watts, Michael (2008) 'Blood Oil: Anatomy of an Oil Insurgency in the Niger Delta', *Focaal: European Journal of Anthropology* 52 (8): 18–38.

Weber, Max (1968) 'Ethnic Groups' in Guenther Roth and Claus Wittich (eds) *Max Weber, Economy and Society: An Outline of Interpretive Sociology*, New York: Bedminster Press.

——(1972/1921–22) *Wirtschaft und Gesellschaft: Grundriss der verstehenden Soziologie*, Tübingen: J.C.B. Mohr.

Wendt, Alexander (1987) 'The Agent-Structure Problem in International Relations Theory', *International Organisation* 41 (3): 335–70.

Willett, Susan (2010) 'New Barbarians at the Gate: Losing the Liberal Peace in Africa', *Review of African Political Economy* 32 (106): 569–94.

Wimmer, Andreas (2004) 'Introduction: Facing Ethnic Conflicts' in Andreas Wimmer et al. (eds) *Facing Ethnic Conflicts: Toward a New Realism*, Lanham, MD: Rowman & Littlefield.

——(2008) 'The Making and Unmaking of Ethnic Boundaries: A Multilevel Process Theory', *American Journal of Sociology* 113 (4): 970–1022.

Wimmer, Andreas and Brian Min (2006) 'From Empire to Nation-State: Explaining Wars in the Modern World, 1816–2001', *American Sociological Review* 71: 867–97.

Wood, Elisabeth (2003) *Insurgent Collective Action and Civil War in El Salvador*, New York: Oxford University Press.

Woodward, Susan L. (1995) *Balkan Tragedy: Chaos and Dissolution after the Cold War*, Washington, D.C.: Brookings Institution Press.

World Bank (1997) *World Development Report. The State in a Changing World*, Washington, DC: World Bank.

——(2003) *Breaking the Conflict Trap: Civil War and Development Policy*, Policy Research Report, Washington, D.C.: World Bank.

Wu, Tim (2010) *The Master Switch: The Rise and Fall of Information Empires*, New York: Knopf.

Zizek, Slavoj (2008) *Violence*, London: Profile Books.

Index